Danger and Opportunity

Danger 危 and Opportunity 机 form the Chinese word crisis. Ancient Chinese wisdom sees an opportunity in danger. While cultural diversity brings challenges to the workplace, how do we turn these challenges into opportunities? Drawing on their extensive experience working with multicultural and multinational organizations, Lionel Laroche and Caroline Yang provide an in-depth analysis of cross-cultural dynamics in the workplace and offer practical suggestions at both the individual and organizational levels.

The book analyzes cross-cultural challenges in six areas: the relative importance of technical and soft skills; cross-cultural communication; cross-cultural feedback; hierarchy; individualism; and risk tolerance. It then provides a solutions framework that encompasses people, systems and environment to bridge the issues that arise from cultural differences. The analysis and solutions are applied in four business contexts: managing a multicultural workforce; competing in the global talent market; collaborating with joint venture partners; and working with offshore resources.

If you work with colleagues, managers, employees and customers from diverse cultures, if you are with an organization that has a multicultural workforce and/or global operations, or if your organization collaborates with joint venture partners or off shore resources from different cultures, then *Danger and Opportunity: Bridging Cultural Diversity for Competitive Advantage* is the book for you.

Lionel Laroche is the founder of MultiCultural Business Solutions, based in Canada. He consults on the impact of cultural differences in multinational organizations. Lionel has written two books and runs regular training programs.

Caroline Yang is a partner and human resources consultant at MultiCultural Business Solutions. With over fifteen years' experience in human resources, she has authored articles on leadership, teamwork, total rewards and global human resource policies.

Danger and Opportunity

危 机

Bridging Cultural Diversity for Competitive Advantage

Lionel Laroche & Caroline Yang

Routledge
Taylor & Francis Group

NEW YORK AND LONDON

First published 2014
by Routledge
711 Third Avenue, New York, NY 10017

and by Routledge
2 Park Square, Milton Park, Abingdon, Oxon OX14 4RN

Routledge is an imprint of the Taylor & Francis Group, an informa business

Library of Congress Cataloging-in-Publication Data

Laroche, Lionel.
 Danger and opportunity : bridging cultural diversity to competitive
advantage / Lionel Laroche & Caroline Yang.
  pages cm
 Includes bibliographical references and index.
 1. Diversity in the workplace. 2. Corporate culture.
3. Management—Cross-cultural studies. 4. Organizational
behavior—Cross-cultural studies. 5. Human resources.
6. Immigration. I. Yang, Caroline. II. Title.

 HF5549.5.M5L367 2013
 658.3008—dc23
 2013022600

ISBN: 978-0-415-65806-5 (pbk)
ISBN: 978-0-203-07529-6 (ebk)

Typeset in Caslon
by Apex CoVantage, LLC

To my coauthor, for inspiring me to achieve
what I did not know I could.

Contents

Acknowledgements

This book is based on our many years of experience working with people all over the world, both as employees of global organizations and as external consultants. We want to first thank our former managers and colleagues, who have taught us so much on how organizations work as a whole and how individuals are expected to operate within organizations. In particular, Caroline wants to thank Jenny Winter, who hired Caroline and a number of other recent immigrants into her team, a true multicultural Canadian team; and Jan McIntyre, another one of Caroline's managers in the corporate world, for teaching Caroline what being a good manager means in Canada and leading by example.

Much of this book's material has been tested extensively through our work with various client organizations. We want to thank you for the opportunity to work with your organization. Your questions and comments have helped shape our thoughts and ensured that our work focuses on real-life challenges and concrete solutions. We hope you will recognize the concepts, stories and solutions and look forward to our future collaboration.

As this is a Canadian project, we cannot launch it without an extensive "pilot." We have piloted this book by asking colleagues and friends in our network to review parts of the manuscript in draft and give us feedback. Many provided extensive written or verbal feedback, which has been invaluable to our writing. In particular, we want to thank the following people for taking the time to provide comments and suggestions and for their dedication to make our workplace inclusive:

Aaron Brown	Isabel Campbell	Nancy Toth
Alain Boissier	Inge Fleet	Nina Woods
Alyson Nyiri	James Spearing	Paul Aston
Andrej Zdravkovic	Janice Aston	Philippe Bastié
Annette Montgomery	Jennifer French	Richard Pinnock
Arlene Lack	Jessica Musslewhite	Roger Lin
Astrid Donaldson	Jordan Wiess	Sante Tesolin
Brian Gray	Kari Giddings	Saylor Millitze-Lee
Danielle Boils-Boissier	Khaled Elfekhfakh	Shirley Marie Garcia
Diane Wilding	Liliane Laroche	Sue Nador
Donna Bergles	Lise Laroche	Susan Brown
Doug Archibald	Luis DeSousa	Suzanne Winterflood
Emily Wong	Luminita Tihan	Thierry Guillaumont
Francine Charette	Madelaine Currelly	Xin Pi
François Decomps	Michael Barré	Yong Sun
Fritz Venter	Michelle Martin	
I-Cheng Chen	Mike Ma	

We also want to thank our colleague and friend Bob McArthur, for being our sounding board, for sharing with us his wisdom about the meaning of being a Canadian and for twenty-six years of friendship with Caroline. To all the people who have shared our journey, whether your names are mentioned here or not, this book would not have been possible without your support. Thank you!

Preface

Lionel was born in France and went to the United States to study in 1986. Caroline was born in China and went to Canada to study in 1986. We went through two unusual, yet similar, professional and personal journeys and met twenty-two years later in Toronto.

Lionel's Journey

I had a great passion for mathematics and always had top grades in that subject, all the way through high school and university. When I was fourteen, I brought my mathematics textbook on a school ski trip and took a day off skiing to do mathematics exercises. In France, career paths for students are based on their grades and on the recommendations of teachers. Since I was good at mathematics, it was obvious to everyone that I should become an engineer or a scientist.

My father was a nuclear engineer. His career stopped at a certain point because, as he puts it, he "graduated from a third tier engineering school"; in France, the glass ceiling is based on education more than anything else. He really wanted me to graduate from the best engineering school so I would not run into the same career limitations. I graduated from the École Polytechnique de Paris with top grades.

At that point, the obvious next step was to go into the Corps des Mines and become a top civil servant in the French government. My mother had obtained a bachelor's degree in business administration from the University of Washington, Seattle, and the pictures she brought back made me want to experience the American way of life. Going against the grain, I chose to study chemical engineering at the California Institute of Technology. There I met the woman who became my first wife, Diane Michelangeli. Diane was Canadian; her mother was English Canadian and her father French (from Corsica). To my parents' chagrin, we decided to move to Canada after graduation. With a Ph.D. in chemical engineering, I started a career as an engineer.

Then something unusual happened—I decided to become a cross-cultural trainer. It was a gradual process that came about because of my work experiences and my evolving interests.

First, when I worked for Procter & Gamble and Xerox, I found that adapting to the Canadian workplace and working with people who thought differently was very difficult. I also went on international assignments to Italy and Germany, and I realized that many misunderstandings, missed deadlines, rework and frustrations came from interpersonal issues, not from technical problems. I tried to talk to my managers and colleagues about addressing these differences, but no one seemed interested. I now understand why, but at the time, I did not know how to frame the problem, let alone how to solve it.

Second, I realized I had become more interested in resolving people issues than in solving mathematical or technical problems. It struck me one Monday, when my colleagues and I were discussing what we had done that weekend. It was then that I realized my interests were quite different from theirs. My coworkers had spent the weekend using their lawn mowers, computers, stereo systems, cars and so on. They had all worked on some kind of machine. What did I like doing on weekends? My interests centered on communication and personal issues: I spent time trying to understand how people think. I talked to my relatives and friends in France. Diane and I spent hours talking about relationships. After receiving a Ph.D. in chemical engineering and working for eight years in the field, I realized I was not meant to be an engineer. But I am certainly glad I came to this realization when I did—better late than never!

Diane was very supportive of my pursuing my passion, which had now changed from mathematics to studying cultural differences. I researched the market and found there was no matching job title in any organization. The closest positions were learning and development specialists or diversity officers in human resources departments; however, no one would consider me qualified for them. I realized the only way forward was to start my own business. It was a long and difficult journey. When I started in 1998, I first bought a license from an American company and did many projects for IT companies in the US and Canada. After September 11, little work came from the US; the dot-com bubble burst, and there was even less work from IT companies. While continuing to look for new clients, I wrote my first book, *Managing Cultural Diversity in Technical Professions*.

Things went from bad to worse when Diane was diagnosed with cancer in 2002—she passed away five years later, leaving me with two young children. In early 2002, I had been in Canada for eleven years. I had left a well-paid engineering job, I had no steady clients and income and my wife had cancer. I felt a tremendous need to earn a predictable income, so I found a job in an outplacement company. My first book was published in late 2002 but did not generate the kind of revenue my employer and I had expected. The outplacement counseling business went through difficult times in 2004, and I was laid off.

By then, I had six years of experience working as a cross-cultural trainer and consultant and had gained the confidence I needed to make my business a success. In particular, I had made more than 120 presentations in one year. With the name recognition created by the book, I made significant progress and became a recognized speaker and trainer. My first break was signing a contract with the City of Toronto to help highly skilled immigrants (who often had a Ph.D. or a master's degree in a technical field and were on social assistance) find a job. An accounting firm then asked me to coach their international assignees. Business took off from that point.

I met Caroline at a time where the business had reached a plateau. I was providing advice to people at the individual level; it was clear to me that more needed to be done, but I had no idea what that was. Caroline gave me the key—we needed to work at the organizational level. Patiently, she showed me how to think, communicate and act at that level.

Caroline's Journey

I grew up during the Cultural Revolution, a very turbulent time in modern Chinese history, though my parents grew up during World War II, so their experiences were certainly worse. During my school years, I spent a lot of time working in rice paddy fields and factories— "educated by the farmers and workers." I marched in the streets, waving Mao's red book and denouncing whomever was not politically in favor at the time.

In my last two years of high school, the tide turned. Deng Xiao-Ping and his more liberal-thinking comrades started the "reform and opening" of China. Universities started to recruit students through a national examination. Between 1966 and 1976, universities completely closed their doors for the first five of those years, and then enrolled workers, farmers and soldiers based on political correctness for the next five. In 1977, overnight, the whole country went back to school. Teachers were eager to teach after being sidetracked for ten years, and provided free extra classes and tutoring on evenings and weekends. The competition to get into university was fierce: ten years' worth of high school graduates were competing to get a higher education. The acceptance rate was 2–3 percent. A teacher discussed my situation with my parents, and it was decided that since I was good at English, I should try to get into an English program rather than compete with the much larger science and arts crowd. At the time, the popular programs were mathematics, physics, chemistry and Chinese literature. English was popular, but few were good at it; I had better odds this way.

The strategy worked. I got into university and became an English teacher after graduation. I loved studying English. My dormitory room did not have a desk, so I sat on a little stool and used the bed as a desk to study English after work.

My hard work paid off. One day, in 1986, I was sent to write an examination in Beijing. The purpose of the examination was to select candidates to be trained in Canada as part of the Canadian International Development Agency's cooperation program with China. I came out with the top grades among others selected to take the test from the fourteen open coastal cities.

After many rounds of intensive examinations and interviews, I was selected for the Technical Interpreter's Program and studied at Malaspina College, in Nanaimo, and Simon Fraser University, in Vancouver. I also did two work placements with the City of Toronto and the Bank of Montreal. It was a steep learning curve, full of growing pains, but I fell in love with Canada in the process. On the plane going back to China, I felt a real, physical pain in my chest because I was leaving behind all the great experiences and the wonderful people I had met. At that time in China, going abroad was an exceptional event. Going once was extremely lucky. I did not dare to dream that I could ever go back to Canada. I went back to my teaching job at Yantai University and went through a long reverse culture shock.

I worked on an assignment to interpret/translate for a Canada–China project. The Federation of Canadian Municipalities and the Canada–China Trade Council worked with a Chinese Ministry to provide training for Chinese mayors and city managers. I accompanied the group to five Chinese cities and interpreted/translated for official meetings. I considered this the highlight of my career because it made me feel closer to Canada, but it did not cure my homesickness for Canada.

The Technical Interpreter's Program organized a seminar in Shenzhen for its alumni in 1990. The general manager of Nortel's joint venture in Shenzhen came to speak at the seminar. He invited me to work for him. I accepted the offer immediately because I felt the job would bring me closer to Canada, and it did. I came to Canada for training five years after my return to China. During that trip, the pain in my chest went away. I realized I could come back to Canada. The strange thing was, once it was up to me, not to the authorities, the urge to travel went away. I guess this is what freedom of choice means. Shenzhen in the 1990s had many opportunities. My first husband,

Paul, and I both had good jobs. We bought a condo, and our son was born. It looked as if we would settle down in Shenzhen.

In the late 1990s, Canada opened the "Independent Skilled Worker" immigration category to China. Many of my Nortel colleagues applied and often came to consult me in the process. Over time, Paul and I found ourselves discussing immigrating to Canada. Because I understood the difficulties of going abroad first-hand, and realized we had opportunities in China, I wanted to make sure that coming to Canada was a family decision, not only mine.

We ultimately decided to go, and arrived in Canada in 2000. The first few years of the lives of most immigrants in their new home countries are similar. Finding a job, finding the way in a new environment, raising children—it's not easy. Paul had a hard time finding work in his field and decided to go back to China. As with parenthood, no amount of reading and research can prepare one enough for the reality. We went our separate ways. I stayed in Canada with my nine-year-old son; he and I became Canadian citizens in 2004.

On the professional side, my integration was easier than Paul's. I found a human resources job with a high-tech company four months after arriving. My high-tech industry experience in China was a good fit for the company's fast pace and innovative culture. I enjoyed the job and the people with whom I worked. My manager and colleagues gave me rides when I was too scared to drive in the snow, taught me how to clean a snow-covered car and wished me a "hoppy" Easter. My work and the new community in which I immersed myself made the first few long winters more bearable, and the springs more beautiful, despite my difficulties at home.

Things became harder as time went by. I learned, after meeting Lionel, that when people move up in an organization, soft skills, which are measured by cultural standards, become increasingly important to success in Canada. (See Chapter 2 for more on soft skills.) When I felt my progress was slower than it should have been, I resorted to changing jobs. My good technical skills enabled me to find new positions relatively easily. I had the opportunity to work with a few top-notch Canadian organizations and developed expertise in several specialized areas of human resources, such as total rewards and global mobility.

When I met Lionel and read his book, I started to reflect on both my own professional journey and how HR professionals and managers can apply cultural knowledge to more effectively diagnose and resolve interpersonal issues in the workplace. As an immigrant, uprooting and transplanting oneself to a new work culture is a very painful experience. As an HR professional or manager in a multicultural organization, working with people from different backgrounds can be painful when things don't work out, even though everyone involved has the best intentions. However, the pain is part of the growth. We will all grow into better human beings if we keep learning despite the pain.

Our Journey Together

We met five years ago through a mutual friend and decided to work together, as our strengths complemented each other. We then developed a personal relationship, which led to marriage. On the personal front, we've merged our two families of three teenage children. We are learning together as parents how to support our children during a critical phase in their development. We are growing as much as they are through this experience.

On the professional front, we find that working together brings both challenges and opportunities. We are in the same situation as many organizations. We have learned that if we seek to understand how the other person thinks and keep an open mind, we can create a whole that is greater than the sum of the parts. For example, we both like to use diagrams to illustrate a point. However, Lionel has a hard time with diagrams in circles. (See Figure 1.4, for example.) Engineering diagrams are linear, with clear inputs and outputs. Many diagrams or models studying human behaviors or organizations are often circular, where inputs can also be outputs. From time to time, we would have some very stormy discussions, but we both remember that there is no teamwork without "storming,"[1] and we continue working toward a common goal.

Lionel has published two books, *Managing Cultural Diversity in Technical Professions* and *Recruiting, Reflecting and Promoting Culturally Different Employees*. Both books provide many practical solutions at the individual level (i.e., what individual employees, managers, HR professionals, immigrant servicing agency staff and recent immigrants can do to bridge the cultural gap and be productive). Through our five years of collaboration, we have created new approaches and materials. We find that North American organizations have made tremendous progress in becoming aware of cultural differences and want to go beyond "cultural sensitivity" to develop ways for everyone to work effectively together. This book builds on our work over the last five years and provides analysis and solutions at both the individual and the organizational level.

Our book is based on our work with real people (who are not perfect) in the real world (which also is not perfect), not academic studies. As an engineer who transitioned to become a human resources consultant, Lionel found that we cannot treat studies of human interaction in the same way as we do technical problems (where there is a much higher probability of finding *the* right answer). Similarly, Michael Adams, a noted researcher and commentator on social values and change in North America, stated that he strives to present a "big picture" that is "empirically defensible" and "makes at least some intuitive sense."[2] We know that not everyone will agree with everything we say, and that people take away different messages from a book, a workshop or a conversation. We ask you to look on our approach as a pragmatic analysis that will help guide you through real-world experiences in the global marketplace.

One of our clients designed a workshop evaluation which asks participants to respond these four qualitative prompts:

- My "aha" moments from this session are:
- I will share the following learning with others:
- Because of my increased awareness, I will . . .
- Questions to follow-up with my manager . . .

Our hope is that while reading this book, you have a few "aha" moments that make intuitive sense, that you share some of your learning with others and that you decide to implement some of our suggestions when you next go to work.

Notes

1. In Tuckman's team development model, every team goes through four stages: forming, storming, norming and performing.
2. Michael Adams: *Fire and Ice: The United States, Canada and the Myth of Converging Values*. Toronto: Penguin Canada, 2003.

Introduction

"What is different, is dangerous" is the title of Chapter 5 of Geert Hofstede's book *Cultures and Organizations: Software of the Mind*. It is human nature to view unfamiliar things as a danger or a challenge. The Chinese word *crisis* consists of two characters: the first means "danger" and the second "opportunity." As the workforce and customer base of North American organizations are becoming more and more culturally diverse, there will be many challenges, or dangers. There are also many opportunities for organizations that learn to manage cultural differences and increase the cultural competence of their employees. This book explores the challenges (or dangers) and opportunities brought by cultural diversity and discusses how to turn the challenges into opportunities.

Section 1.1: Key Messages of This Book

After delivering a training workshop, I was having an early dinner in a hotel lounge. This hotel is part of a chain that caters to business travelers. It was early, so the restaurant was not busy. There were three individual customers and a group of three at the bar. A staff member (a young white woman) went around the restaurant introducing herself: "Hi, my name is Amy. . . ." I overheard words such as *reception, business card* and *a draw*. She went around and talked to everyone except me. In the next thirty minutes, more customers came in and she went to talk to each new person or group. She did the draw and gave a gift certificate to someone.

She did not come to speak with me. I looked around; I was the only Asian, or visible minority, in the room. Was she afraid that I did not speak English? I was reading an English newspaper, so that was unlikely. I was reading. Did she want to let me read in peace? Yet she talked to a woman six feet from me who was reading a book.

I had never felt this visibly different before. I thought of three options:

- I could conclude that she was discriminating against Asians, never go back to this hotel chain again and tell all my Asian friends not to go there.
- I could ignore it because I had more important things to do.
- I could talk to her and find out what was going on.

I settled on the third option. I told the server that I would like to speak to Amy. When she came, I said that I wondered what she was telling others about and joked that I did not want to miss a good party. She introduced herself as the sales manager and said that the hotel was changing ownership and would be renovating in the next six months. She was very pleasant and positive. She asked what brought me to town and gave me her card, saying she would give me discounts for future visits. We parted on friendly terms.

(Caroline)

This situation illustrates how misunderstanding happens when people from different cultures interact with one another. Our guess is that Amy did not know how to connect with someone who looked different from her. It is easy for people on the receiving end to interpret this behavior as discrimination based on a visible or vocal[1] difference. One person has to take the first step to bridge the gap by giving the other the benefit of the doubt. Our hope is that Amy now feels more comfortable talking with Asians. But taking that first step is not easy. Caroline readily admits that she has chosen one of the first two options on many other occasions. It took thirteen years of working and living in Canada for Caroline to have the confidence to ask to speak with Amy and the skill to clear the air in a constructive way. Here are a few key messages we hope to draw from this story.

The first key message of this book is to give people the benefit of the doubt. We believe most people have good intentions at heart. Most people do not want to discriminate, to be unfair or to be disrespectful. They simply do not have enough knowledge or experience of interacting with people from different cultures to initiate a conversation or to recognize a certain behavior as cultural.

Most immigrants in North America come from homogeneous societies, where 90–99 percent of the population look the same and speak the same language. When we visited Beijing together, Lionel mentioned that he expected to see more foreign tourists, as in Paris or New York City; Caroline joked that the few foreign tourists like him are drowned in the human sea of 1.3 billion Chinese. While immigrants are learning how to interact with Americans, Canadians and other immigrants in North America, Americans and Canadians are also learning how to interact with immigrants and the rest of the world. Giving each other the benefit of the doubt and not assuming people are discriminating puts us on a positive path toward mutual understanding.

The second key message is to make it safe to discuss cultural differences in a constructive way. In many workshops, participants say it is their first opportunity to talk about cultural differences because they are concerned about offending people inadvertently. Many human resources (HR) professionals and managers[2] do not feel comfortable discussing cultural differences with their employees; if you do not say anything, you cannot say anything wrong.

When people do talk about cultural differences, they spend a lot of energy on semantics or political correctness. Caroline was interviewed by a social studies student doing a project to analyze the negative impact of the term *visible minority*. Caroline, a visible minority who has no problem being referred to as one, did not understand why this analysis was valuable. "I am visibly different from most people in Canada, and I am a minority. When Lionel goes into a Chinese supermarket in Markham, he is a visible minority." Unfortunately, focusing on semantics makes people even more uncomfortable and reinforces political correctness. It does not foster an environment where people are looking for constructive ways to work together. We want to promote discussion of cultural differences in a constructive manner.

The third key message is to focus on what we can each do to bridge the gap. We have attended workshops and conferences where the focus is on identifying who discriminates against whom under what circumstances. By the end of the day, everyone feels down because they either feel someone discriminated against them or someone considered that they discriminated against others. At one conference, the entire closing keynote address reviewed studies analyzing why immigrants were earning less than the rest of the population and concluded that discrimination was the main reason. How do participants feel walking away from such a message? Are they going to do anything differently the next day? Chances are many people feel powerless because they are relying on others to change.

Similarly, in internal workshops or meetings, employees often complain that management or other departments are not doing what they should. We have heard managers complain that "senior management" needs to change. We have also heard managers in the same meeting say that "we are part of the management; we must demonstrate leadership and initiate the change." We want to focus people's attention on what they can do differently to improve the situation, as opposed to waiting for others to change. Gandhi said, "Be the change you want to see in the world." Let us empower ourselves and lead the change.

The fourth key message is that HR professionals and managers need to lead changes at the organization level. Within any organization or any group in North America, there are a few people who are very knowledgeable and interested in cultural diversity and inclusion. There are probably also some who have a narrow, fixed view of the world, openly discriminate against people who are different from them and who think their cultural positions are always right. The majority of people are probably not aware of cultural differences in the workplace or do not have the skills to manage them, like Amy in our opening story. Focusing on discrimination will shut down not only the minority that discriminates, but also the silent majority. We want to help HR professionals and managers bring the silent majority on board by teaching people how to manage cultural differences and develop cultural competence. When the overwhelming majority of an organization embraces diversity and is actively involved in building an inclusive environment, it becomes socially unacceptable to discriminate.

The key is to take the analysis of cultural differences to the organizational level. Let us return to the situation described at the beginning of this chapter. After her encounter with Amy, Caroline looked on the career Web site of that hotel chain and reviewed the job descriptions of sales and guest service positions in culturally diverse metropolitan areas. There was no requirement for the ability to service customers from diverse cultures. Shouldn't such a requirement be included in the job description? How does the organization decide whether candidates have that skill or not? What kind of training does the organization offer its employees to develop those skills? Many organizations already have effective talent management systems and processes. We discuss how to build cultural diversity and inclusion into the existing system throughout this book, and specifically in Chapter 4.

Section 1.2: Structure of This Book

The following is the approach we take in this book:

1. First, we describe the cross-cultural challenges that professionals[3] and organizations experience as they work with people from diverse cultures. We focus on real-life situations that we have experienced personally, that our workshop participants have shared with us or that our clients have asked us to help them deal with.
2. Next, we analyze these challenges in order to identify their root causes. We refer to well-known cross-cultural concepts researched by experts in the field, such as hierarchy, individualism and risk tolerance, as well as concepts we have developed, such as the relative importance of technical skills and soft skills and the dynamics of cross-cultural feedback.
3. From there, the main focus is on practical solutions that readers can implement in their organizations, both at the individual level (by HR professionals, managers and employees) and at the organizational level (in the form of policies or programs).

Figure 1.1 graphically represents the structure of the book. In the center circle, there are six cultural factors that are the basis of our analysis because they have an extensive impact in North American organizations:

• Relative importance of technical and soft skills
• Cross-cultural communication

- Cross-cultural feedback
- Hierarchy
- Individualism
- Risk tolerance

While the analysis of cross-cultural issues could fill the entire book, we have decided to limit our descriptions to the minimum amount of material needed to understand the true nature of these issues and to focus our attention on the solutions that can be brought to bear on these problems.

The second circle in Figure 1.1 corresponds to the business contexts in which North American organizations deal with cultural differences. The projects in which various organizations have involved us can be divided in four categories:

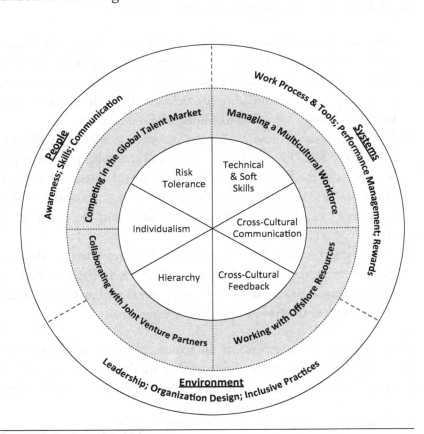

Figure 1.1 Roadmap of the Book

Managing a multicultural workforce: This corresponds to the "United Nations" workplace, which is so common in North America; because of immigration, many North American organizations employ people who were born in many different countries. Project teams often have fifteen people who, together, speak six different languages and were educated in nine different countries. Making such multicultural organizations run smoothly can be quite challenging at times. Since this is by far the most common challenge faced by our clients (probably 80% of our work is related to cultural diversity within North America), we examine this context more extensively than the others.

Working with offshore resources: Many North American organizations work with offshore resources that are either part of the same organization or part of a service provider. Offshore resources are usually located in developing countries because of skills availability and/ or salary differences. People involved in this process usually find it quite challenging, particularly at the beginning.

Collaborating with joint venture partners: When two organizations headquartered in different countries form a joint venture, they each bring their corporate and national cultures to the table. A new, joint corporate culture needs to be formed—and we have found there is the potential here for missteps that we hope to help you prevent.

Competing in the global talent market: In the last three decades, many North American organizations have made major efforts to expand. Doing business outside North America requires more than just translating the operations manual, however, as books such as *Blunders in International Business* (Malden, MA: Blackwell Publishing, 1974, 1993, 1999, 2006) document so well. Building a workforce in a culture that is very different from that in North American requires serious investment, in many senses of the word.

The outermost circle in Figure 1.1 corresponds to the **People– System–Environment (PSE)** framework we use to introduce the solutions we recommend. We describe this framework in detail in Section 1.6.

In summary, here is the content of each chapter:

Chapter 1 lays a foundation by addressing concerns that prevent people from discussing cultural differences, looking at the business case for cultural inclusion and describing our solutions framework.

Chapter 2 examines the relative importance of technical skills and soft skills, cross-cultural communication and feedback in the context of multicultural organizations in North America. Each of these three issues is analyzed, and solutions are provided following the PSE framework.

Chapter 3 covers hierarchy, individualism and risk tolerance, using a similar approach as that in Chapter 2.

Chapter 4 builds on Chapters 2 and 3 by looking at the impact of cultural differences and solutions throughout the talent management cycle in multicultural organizations in North America.

Chapter 5 looks at the challenges faced by North American organizations when they offshore work to developing countries such as India, and discusses solutions that help multicultural teams go through the four stages of team development.

Chapter 6 looks at multicultural joint ventures (JV) and the trials and tribulations some JVs go through.

Chapter 7 examines the challenges that North American organizations face on the human resources front when expanding outside their home turf through a series of case studies.

Chapter 8 concludes by looking at the competitive advantage organizations can achieve when they harness cultural diversity and foster an inclusive culture. It examines the process by which people change their individual behaviors and how change occurs at the organization level.

Section 1.3: Personality, Culture and Universality

When running into interpersonal issues that involve people from different cultures, we often hear people say, "Deep down we are all the same. We are all human beings," or "It's a personality conflict." In other words, people are uncomfortable talking about cultural differences. While we agree with both statements, where do cultural or group differences come in? Figure 1.2 shows the three levels at which we interact with one another.

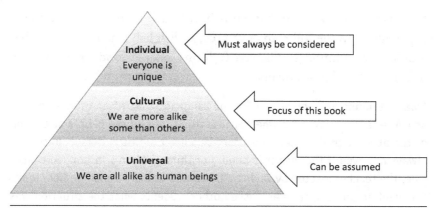

Figure 1.2 Three Levels of Interaction

- At the universal level, we are all the same—we are all human beings. Scientific research has proven that over 99 percent of human DNA is the same around the world.
- At the individual level, everyone is unique. Even identical twins have different aptitudes and personalities.
- Culture is somewhere in between; it makes us more similar to one group of people than other groups of people. The groups can be based on culture, language, gender, generation and so on.

Take food, as an example:

- At the universal level, we all need to eat to live. No one can survive long without food.
- At the individual level, each and every one of us has his or her own likes and dislikes, and some people have allergies.
- In the middle, we have Chinese food, Italian food, Mexican food, American food and so on, where each cuisine has features specific to that group, often based on the ingredients that are locally available.

Cultural and Universal

When dealing with cultural differences, the first challenge we face is the tendency to confuse cultural and universal traits. Because we are brought up in our own culture, we tend to think that everyone does things the same way and that our behaviors and belief systems are self-explanatory. In the following example, an English teacher realizes that a behavior common in Canada (offering people food or drink only once) is cultural, not universal:

I was attending an English as a Second Language class after arriving in Canada. The teacher asked me whether it is true that Chinese people offer food or tea at least three times to visitors because the initial default answer is always no, even if the visitor is hungry or thirsty. When I responded that is true, the teacher reacted by saying, "But that's so inefficient!" To her credit, she went around the class and asked other students what the situation was in their home countries. To her surprise, the answer was similar in most of the countries represented in the classroom. Students from the Philippines, India, Iran, Romania and Mexico all said that visitors wait to be asked at least a couple of times before accepting the host's offer.

There is a good reason for this: Many countries around the world experienced food and/or water shortage at various times in their history. As a result, the act of offering food or water communicates the utmost respect and hospitality, because it could mean that the host and his or her family may have to go without food or water the following day. For this reason, the default answer on the guest's part is no, as a way to show consideration for the host. The tradition has continued even though many of these countries do not have food or water shortages anymore.

(Chinese IT professional)

The challenge is that people interpret a behavior that goes against what they have been taught based on what this behavior means within their own culture. Quite often, the words that come to mind are *disrespectful* and *unacceptable*. Think about the Costco food sampling stations or subway stops in a North American city; people who do not observe the formal and sometimes informal line and try to push through before others usually generate a very unpleasant reaction. How do Americans and Canadians learn to wait in line?

Most American and Canadian children learn this behavior by repeating it throughout their kindergarten and elementary school years. Every time the recess bell rings, the teacher comes out, the kids line up in front of the teacher and everyone goes inside in line. American and Canadian kids repeat this behavior often enough and early enough that it becomes completely subconscious—to the point that people spontaneously form a line wherever they need to wait (e.g., at bus stops, coffee shops or airline counters).

By contrast, children in other parts of the world do not learn to wait in line. When the recess bell rings in France, everybody runs (most kids run to school, some run away from school—everybody is running). As a result, there is no expectation that people should wait in line. This behavior is especially visible in countries where there are not enough resources for everyone. If you take the bus in Mumbai at rush hour, you will have to push through the crowd in order to get on the bus. Because there is physically not enough space in the bus for all the people who want to get on it, the bus driver starts driving away before everyone has stepped onto the bus.

As the previous example illustrates, we learn our culture through a combination of the following:

- **Observation and mirroring:** When kids see their parents do certain things, they often reproduce these behaviors during play.
- **Teaching from parents, teachers and extracurricular activity coaches:** They teach us certain behaviors and attitudes that we end up integrating into our thought processes.
- **Sayings:** For example, the North American saying "The squeaky wheel gets the grease" clearly goes against the East Asian saying "The nail that stands out gets hammered down"; Americans and Canadians are rewarded for speaking up while East Asians are rewarded for being humble and preserving harmony within the group.
- **Repetition:** We repeat the same behavior many times, until it becomes second nature.

Learning to identify what is cultural and what is universal helps us give people the benefit of the doubt and allow people time to learn a new behavior.

Cultural and Individual

The second challenge is the tendency to confuse cultural differences with personality traits. When we see someone behave in a way that appears strange or inappropriate, many people are uncomfortable asking that person why he or she is behaving that way and end up judging without truly understanding. This misperception creates serious issues in the workplace. Here is an example:

I was engaged by an engineering firm to coach a Romanian engineer who gave feedback in a very direct way (more on feedback in Chapter 2). His colleagues found him "rude," "blunt" and "insensitive." His manager concluded it was a personality issue and put him on a performance improvement plan which, fortunately for him, included individual coaching. While he was successful in turning things around, we have met many people who were not given coaching in communication style; many employees who are put on performance improvement plans are eventually let go because the rationale is that people's personalities cannot be changed.

(Lionel)

As discussed previously, cultural differences are based on the fact that people in one country are taught to behave in a certain way in a given situation, while people in another country are taught to behave in a different way in the same situation. If we focus on personality differences, we will not be able to see the forest for the trees. In medicine, a correct diagnosis is critical to finding an effective treatment or cure. Separating cultural differences from personality issues helps the people involved avoid taking the issue personally; from there, they are more likely to discuss how they can adapt to each other.

If you see one of your employees/colleagues/customers do or say something you would never have thought of doing or saying, how do you determine whether it is driven by culture or by personality?

Observe. If you see three people of the same cultural background do the same thing in similar situations, the behavior is very likely to be culturally influenced. The odds that three people taken at random do the same thing in the same circumstances are low enough that you can conclude this behavior is cultural with a good level of certainty.

Ask the person. And ask in a way that shows you are trying to learn, as opposed to judging. If you want to discover if a behavior is cultural, remember the ESL teacher we discussed earlier, who asked,

"Do all Chinese people offer food three times?" In general, Americans are more likely than Canadians to ask directly what a behavior means when they do not understand—Canadians tend to pretend it did not happen and move on.

Ask other people who are familiar with the culture. For example, if you observe a Nigerian person behave in a way that appears strange to you, you can get a sense of whether it is cultural or not by asking either Americans or Canadians who have lived in Nigeria or Nigerians who live in North America. Having a good rapport with the person you are asking, and asking in a nonjudgmental manner, goes a long way. For example, if you say, "I saw my Nigerian colleague do this the other day. Is this behavior common in Nigeria? What does it mean? In what circumstances will Nigerians do this?" you will usually get a better response than if you say, "I can't believe what my Nigerian colleague did the other day! Do all Nigerians act in such crazy ways?"

Research books or Web sites. People who are interested in understanding one specific culture can look for books on the Intercultural Press Web site (http://www.nicholasbrealey.com/boston/subjects/interculturalpress.html). Intercultural Press sells books that examine the differences between the US and specific countries, such as Sweden (*Modern Day Vikings*), Mexico (*Good Neighbors*), France (*Au Contraire!*), Spain (*Spain Is Different*), India (*Speaking of India*), Japan (*With Respect to the Japanese*) and China (*Encountering the Chinese*).

Utilize cross-cultural consultants and coaches. These professionals can help organizations, their managers and HR professionals differentiate between culture and personality and determine the best course of action.

Section 1.4: Stereotypes and Generalizations

We will inevitably generalize to some extent when discussing any group difference, whether the group is based on culture, language, gender or generation, just to name a few. We need to feel safe to discuss the cultural differences that matter in the workplace; we also need to strive to understand each other's perspectives in order to leverage the strengths of these different perspectives. At the same time, we need to

Table 1.1 Difference between Stereotypes and Generalizations

STEREOTYPES	GENERALIZATIONS
Are based on assumption	Are based on observation
Present a fixed and inflexible image of a group	Provide general characteristics of a group based on cultural and social factors
Are judgmental	Inform rather than prescribe
Focus on the negative judgment of the behavior	Neutrally describe the behavior as observed
Ignore individual exceptions	Recognize that individuals within groups vary in their compliance
Example: "Mexicans are always late, so I will give my Mexican colleagues appointments 30 minutes before my target."	Example: "I know that time is more flexible in Mexico than in the US. I will use this knowledge to inform my observation of my Mexican colleagues' us of time."

avoid falling into the trap of stereotypes. Nobody likes to be judged preemptively based on their culture, gender, age or any other group factor. So where is the fine line between stereotypes and generalizations? Table 1.1 summarizes the key differences.

The key difference between generalizations and stereotypes is not in the information itself, but in the way people use this information:

- When we have information about people (we know they belong to a particular group or come from a particular country) and information about the group they belong to or the country they come from, stereotyping occurs when we use that information to anticipate their behaviors and act preemptively.
- By contrast, if we use the information we have about people and the group they belong to as a way to guide our observation and understanding of their behavior, we are using this information in a constructive manner.

This example related to gender differences illustrates that the principle works with any group differences. We know an employee is a single mother. We are considering an opportunity for an international assignment. If we conclude that, as a single mother, she probably cannot take this kind of assignment and therefore we do not offer her the opportunity, we are stereotyping—we are acting preemptively based on our knowledge of her situation. Instead, we need to use this information reactively and put ourselves in another's position. In this situation, we offer the assignment opportunity to all qualified employees. If this female employee comes forward and expresses interest in taking on this challenge, we can discuss with her what support the organization can provide based on her particular situation.

Section 1.5: Visible and Invisible Differences

When we talk about different cultures and cultural differences, the first things that come to mind are often food, music, dance, costumes—the visible artifacts of different cultures. While we enjoy exploring the fascinating differences between these visible cultural artifacts, what makes or breaks a person's career or a business relationship are rarely the visible differences—precisely because they are visible. People know they need to deal with them. For example, most Japanese people know that Americans and Canadians do not bow when they meet for the first time—they shake hands. Most Japanese people have seen this behavior in movies or heard about it from colleagues who travel to North America. As a result, many Japanese extend their hands to shake the hands of their North American counterparts; while their handshake may not be as strong as some Americans and Canadians might expect it to be, the expected behavior is clear in this case.

There are many examples where visible differences have created challenges in the professional work environment. In the late 1980s, a significant controversy surfaced in Canada when a Sikh Royal Canadian Mounted Police (RCMP)[4] officer asked to wear a turban with his uniform instead of the RCMP felt hat. After much debate, the conclusion reached was that religious belief trumps the uniform, and the officer was allowed to wear his turban with the RCMP uniform. While there are work contexts where wearing a turban might create a potential safety hazard (e.g., at construction sites or oil rigs, where wearing protective headgear is mandatory), we find that most North American organizations have found ways to deal with visible issues by now.

Most of the questions we field during workshops and in our consulting practice are related to invisible cultural differences. Imagine culture

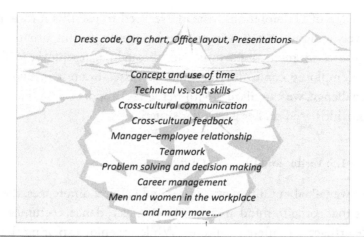

Dress code, Org chart, Office layout, Presentations

Concept and use of time
Technical vs. soft skills
Cross-cultural communication
Cross-cultural feedback
Manager–employee relationship
Teamwork
Problem solving and decision making
Career management
Men and women in the workplace
and many more....

Figure 1.3 Cultural Differences in the Workplace

as an iceberg, as shown in Figure 1.3. We find that the differences that create most of the challenges in the workplace are below the water line, meaning, it is the part that people do not see readily and therefore only identify through trial and error that causes the problems.

Here is an example of an invisible difference. When we have a regular team meeting every Tuesday at 10 a.m., at what time does the meeting actually start? The answer depends on where the meeting takes place:

- In many parts of Canada and the US, it often starts at 10:05 a.m. In other words, we give one another about five minutes of social grace time.
- In New York City, the meeting will likely start at 10:02 a.m. The pace is expected to be faster there.
- This social grace period is longer on the West Coast—such a meeting often starts around 10:10 a.m. in Los Angeles or Vancouver.
- In Germany, the social grace period is one second. Germans generally arrive five minutes early in order to start the meeting precisely on time.
- In Mexico, the social grace period is thirty minutes in northern Mexico and forty-five minutes in southern Mexico. Southern Mexicans consider northern Mexicans to be uptight.

When people educated in different parts of the world meet for the first time, at what time does the meeting start? We have heard many of our clients express significant frustration about working with people who manage time in very different ways. Think of the situation where a culturally different person joins an established team:

- If the new team member has a more flexible sense of time than the rest of the team, his or her teammates are likely to interpret his or her behavior as demonstrating a lack of respect for their time. Any suggestion from the new team member that his or her teammates "relax," "take it easy" or "chill out" is likely to backfire significantly.
- If the new team member is more punctual and shows up early at every meeting, his or her teammates are likely to wonder why this new team member is so uptight. More importantly, they are likely to react negatively if the new team member expresses frustration at what he or she may perceive as a lackadaisical approach to time on their part.

In this book, we focus on the invisible differences because they have the greatest impact on people's productivity and relationships in the workplace.

Section 1.6: People–Systems–Environment Solutions Framework

Once people understand the cross-cultural nature of the challenges they are facing, their next question is, "What is the solution?" There is no shortage of action steps that North American organizations and their employees can take. When we tried to list all the possible action steps that organizations could take in order to overcome cross-cultural issues, we found that many action steps ended up being repeated and the list became so long that it was hard to manage. We needed a framework to make these solutions more manageable. By looking at the common links between them, we determined that action steps could be divided into three categories that are interrelated, as shown in Figure 1.4.

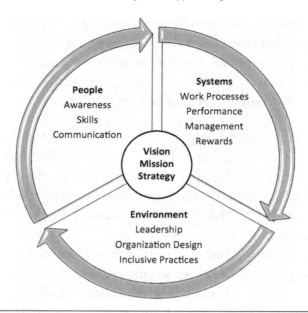

Figure 1.4 Diversity and Inclusion Solutions Framework

- **People:** Building awareness, increasing skill levels and improving communication between individuals or among teams are essential to bridge the cultural gap.
- **Systems:** At the organizational level, putting in place work processes, performance management and reward systems that are aligned with the organization's business strategy helps people "speak the same language" and work in ways that add up to achieving the organization's goal.
- **Environment:** To sustain the increased people capabilities and system effectiveness, we need leadership, effective organization design and inclusive practices to create an environment where cultural diversity becomes a true competitive advantage.

This framework is about inclusion. Diversity does not automatically mean inclusion. The overarching objective is to support the organization's business strategy and turn cultural diversity into opportunities through inclusion. As Royal Bank of Canada defines it, "diversity is the mix, inclusion is getting the mix to work together."[5] We apply this framework in later chapters in specific business situations and provide specific examples. Here is a general overview of each of these three components.

People—Awareness, Skills, Communication

Here we look at the individual and team level. When trying to assess the situation of a particular organization, the following are questions we often ask when it comes to *people*:

- Do people understand the root cause of the challenges they are facing? Are they *aware* of the impact of cultural differences on the issue at hand?
- Do people have the *skills* required to work with others from diverse cultures?
- Are people open to communication? Do they have the skills and processes needed to *communicate* effectively across cultures?

To answer these questions, organizations need to create awareness, build skills and promote effective communication:

Awareness: Create awareness throughout the organization.

Since many cross-cultural misunderstandings are misdiagnosed, a very important first step is to create awareness within the organization. This removes (or at least reduces) the chances of people taking the situation personally or blaming each other; it also encourages more open and honest communication. Workshops, presentations, facilitated discussions, videos and books are all great ways to help people identify the root causes of problems that are cultural in nature and provide a forum for people to discuss cultural differences in a constructive manner.

Skills: Build soft skills and cultural competence through personal development plans, training, coaching and mentoring.

Once people become aware that they need certain soft skills (see more on soft skills in Chapter 2) to be more effective when working with people from different cultures (in particular, better communication skills), the organization needs to provide the corresponding learning opportunities. One important step is to help employees create their own personal development plan. Many employees from hierarchical cultures do not understand that they own their personal development and do not know which soft skills are important in North American organizations. Managers need to help these employees set development goals and create action plans to reach these goals.

Communication: Promote ongoing communication and communicate effectively across cultures.

Open communication is the key to effectiveness for any organization. It becomes even more important for multicultural organizations because there are a thousand and one ways culturally different people can misunderstand one another, even when everyone involved has the best intentions. Helping everyone learn to interpret the messages they receive from others the way these messages are intended creates better communication within organizations. The benefits of ensuring that everyone works on communicating effectively go well beyond the improvements in cross-cultural communication and usually help the organization as a whole.

Systems—Work Processes and Tools, Performance Management, Rewards

These refer to solutions at the organization level. Once people have become aware of cultural differences and begin learning soft skills to collaborate and communicate more effectively across cultures, they need systems that reinforce their learning and encourage the desired behavior. The following are key questions organizations need to ask themselves when looking at their *systems*:

- Does the organization have work **processes and tools** to help people bridge the gap?
- Does the **performance review** process measure and develop people's soft skills?

- Does the **reward** and recognition program encourage the desired behaviors?

To answer these questions, organizations need to implement processes to facilitate better communication and decision making, align performance management and rewards systems to hold people accountable for targeted results and reward the desired behaviors.

> **Work processes and tools:** Provide employees work processes and tools that promote cultural inclusion and facilitate better communication and decision making across cultures.

Many organizations have set up effective business processes to ensure that work runs smoothly. In a similar manner, human interaction processes can help increase the productivity of people working together. For example, the tool in Table 1.2 can help managers and employees with a different sense of hierarchy (see more on hierarchy in Chapter 3) reach agreement on who makes what decisions by breaking down all the decisions they have to make into five categories, depending on who makes them.

Note that these examples are given for illustration purposes. The same decision types can be made at different levels depending on the industry, the organization and the people involved. The key is to have a tool for the manager and the employee to have the conversation. When the manager and the employee have ongoing discussions following this tool, it ensures that no decision gets left out (a situation where both think the other will make the decision) or that people do not "step on each other's toes" (because they both think they should make a given decision).

Table 1.2 Decision-Making Tool

DECISIONS MADE BY	EXAMPLES
Manager	Budget, performance management, promotion
Manager with input from employee	Workload, direction of a project
Manager and employee jointly	Vacation, training
Employee, but check with manager	Non-routine tasks, working with other departments, getting involved in a committee
Employee	Routine tasks

Performance management: Hold people accountable for desired results and behaviors.

Whenever an organization wants to see certain results and behaviors, it needs to consider people's motivation and ability and provide the tools and processes people need to achieve the desired results or demonstrate those behaviors.

Ability + Motivation + Tools = Desired Results and Behaviors

Building awareness and skills and promoting communication address the "ability" part of this equation. Work processes and tools complement them by addressing the "tools" part. Performance management and rewards systems focus on the "motivation" part. An organization needs to have a robust performance management system that aligns employees' efforts toward achieving the organization's goals and holds people accountable. In particular, if cultural competence is important to the organization's success, it needs to be measured through performance reviews, because what is measured gets done.

Rewards: Ensure that the total rewards program drives the desired behaviors.

In line with the performance management system, the rewards program also needs to drive the desired behavior. For example, when employees see that people who have great soft skills and work well with people from diverse backgrounds are rewarded through financial gain and good career progression, they get the message that these skills are important to the organization and their own success and are more likely to invest in learning those skills.

Environment—Leadership, Organization Design, Inclusive Practices

People with cultural awareness and competence, committed to open communication and equipped with systems that facilitate effective collaboration, can create an environment that turns cultural diversity into a competitive advantage. The following are key questions we ask when examining the **environment** of an organization:

- Do **leaders** lead by example? Have they created a common goal and communicated it to everyone?
- Is the **organization's structure** conducive to effective collaboration and communication across cultures?
- Are employees encouraged to reach out and share their cultures and perspectives? Does the organization have **inclusive practices**?

To answer these questions, organizations need inclusive leadership; they also need an organization design that aligns the work flow with the common goal and encourages inclusive practices to bring people together. Again, we are looking at solutions at the organization level.

Leadership: Start from the top and lead by example.

The culture of the organization reflects the values of its leaders—employees learn what to do and what not to do by emulating their behaviors. Leadership styles are also cultural. An executive who has worked in many parts of the world shared the following with us:

An American leader must raise enthusiasm. A German leader has to be an expert. A Japanese leader is discrete, but must create consensus. A French leader is a brilliant speaker. A Russian leader is tough and strong, and dictates his decisions. Someone who is a leader in one country will not be in another country. We need to adjust our leadership style based on the cultural environment we are in.

In this respect, leaders need to educate themselves on cultural differences and display the inclusive behaviors they want to see within the organization. Leaders also need to set and articulate common goals for the organization that embed cultural inclusion, since shared goals are the key to resolving differences of any nature (e.g., culture, gender, generation, personality). People who have the ability to identify and focus on a common goal have higher success rates in resolving their differences.

Organization design: Align the organization structure to foster collaboration.

Even when people are willing and able to collaborate, if the organization structure is not designed to promote information flow and teamwork, there will be communication breakdowns. Therefore, organizations need to become conscious of this need and be deliberate in their attempts to ensure the organization structure is conducive to collaboration and communication across cultures.

Over the last few decades, North American organizations have striven to make their organization more flat and empower their employees. There is less emphasis on titles and dependency on managers' formal power. At the same time, organizations in hierarchical countries still have a "tall and narrow" structure, with more job levels and emphasis on titles. They rely more on the managers exercising formal power. When working with multinational joint ventures or expanding into the global market, North American organizations need to continuously adjust their organization structure to align their business model and culture with the partner's or the local national culture. (See more on this in Chapters 6 and 7.)

Inclusive practices: Organize events and create opportunities to encourage employees to build good working relationship with their colleagues.

Compared to many other countries around the world, Canada and the US have done a great job in embracing diverse cultures and celebrating differences. Many North American organizations have progressive practices, such as multicultural potluck and employee resources or affinity groups, where people sharing characteristics such as coming from the same country, speaking the same language or sharing the same culture get together to discuss the challenges and opportunities they have as a result of this common characteristic. These events and activities communicate a clear message to employees that they can be proud of their cultural heritage and share it with their coworkers; in turn, they are also expected to be respectful of other people's cultural heritage and learn other cultures.

Section 1.7: Business Case for Building Cultural Competence

As the examples mentioned so far demonstrate, cultural differences often generate major challenges in the workplace, and bridging the gap requires a lot of hard work. Readers may wonder whether the pain is worth the gain.

The business case for building cultural competence at the individual level is, "Because this is critical to your success." If you are an HR professional or manager in North America, it is easy to see that the main business and demographic trends all point in the same direction—in the coming years, all North American professionals will work more and more frequently with people who are culturally different from them. Whether your culturally different employees, colleagues, managers, suppliers or clients are down the hall or halfway around the world, having the ability to understand and influence them will make a major difference to your success as an HR professional or manager.

At the organizational level, the benefits of building cultural competence are obvious. According to US Department of Homeland Security, about 32 million (or approximately 10% of the US population) obtained legal permanent status in the last thirty years. The latest Canadian Census shows that over 20 percent of Canada's population are immigrants, and they come from 130 countries. First, North American businesses cannot afford to ignore this population segment as potential customers. Second, North American organizations want to leverage the talent and skills immigrants bring. Third, North American organizations have been looking for ways to sell products or services, source parts or services or find business partners all over the world. Many Fortune 500 companies do over 50 percent of their business outside of their "home" country (the country where their headquarters is located). Cultural competence will become a competitive advantage for North American organizations in all these situations.

One of the biggest benefits of cultural diversity and inclusion, in our experience, is the creativity brought by the diversity of thought. When culturally different people work together, they see the same problems from different angles; they also know different techniques and have learned different approaches. Together, they can come up with solutions that no single individual would have been able to come up with on his or her own.

There is one big caveat here. In order to brainstorm ideas together, we need to trust one another; more specifically, we need to trust that our colleagues' ideas—which may initially seem so far out of our range of experience that they seem to come from Mars—could solve the problem we are facing. We also need to believe, deep down, that we are better off together than separate. This is what this book is about— we want to help people learn to work together effectively so they can develop the trust they need to innovate together and help their organization respond to a rapidly changing world.

Notes

1. Some recent immigrants do not look visibly different but may speak English with an accent that indicates they come from another part of the world. A woman who immigrated to Canada from the UK at the age fourteen said that she worked hard to "lose" her accent.
2. We use *manager* as a general term for anyone who makes hiring and firing decisions and conducts performance reviews. It can mean a CEO or president leading a private company, a director or agency head leading a government department or a nonprofit agency or a frontline supervisor and any other levels of managers in between, regardless of the titles in their particular organization or sector. We use *HR professional* as a general term for anyone who works in a human resources function in any capacity, such as chief HR officer, HR business partner, compensation specialist, recruiter, diversity and inclusion officer, training specialist and so on.
3. In this book, we define *professionals* as people who have the equivalent of a college or university degree, regardless of the profession or sector in which they work—for example, engineers, accountants, pharmacists, teachers and so on.
4. The closest US equivalent of the RCMP is the Federal Bureau of Investigation (FBI).
5. Retrieved from RBC's Web site on April 26, 2013: http://www.rbc.com/ diversity/what-is-diversity.html.

Cultural Factors and Concepts—Part I

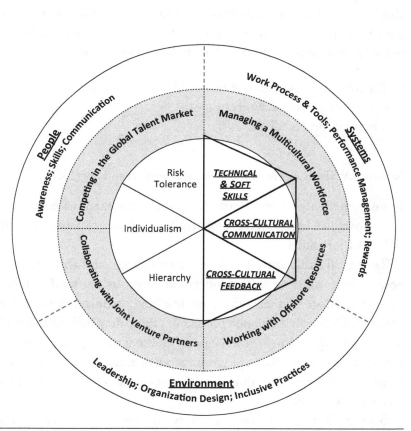

Figure 2.0 Roadmap of the Book

Cultural differences have been studied extensively by a number of researchers and social scientists. Readers who are interested in learning more about the foundational concepts and works in this field are encouraged to look at the bibliography of this book for suggested reading. Chapters 2 and 3 describe a number of cultural factors and fundamental concepts that we apply when analyzing cross-cultural challenges in specific business situations in subsequent chapters. This chapter examines three concepts that HR professionals and managers need to keep in mind when dealing with cultural diversity in the context of immigrants working in North American organizations:

- The relative importance of technical and soft skills
- Cross-cultural communication
- Cross-cultural feedback

Section 2.1: The Relative Importance of Technical and Soft Skills

In our experience, many North American organizations break down their workforce based on their relative strengths on two axes, technical skills and soft skills.

Technical skills correspond to the knowledge and abilities people need to perform their work. Colleges and universities tend to focus a large percentage of their efforts on teaching technical skills to their students. Depending on one's profession, these may include the ability to do load calculations (in the case of civil engineers), calculate taxes (accountants), write code (programmers), operate medical equipment (medical lab specialists), draw blood (nurses), fill prescriptions (pharmacists) and so on.

Soft skills refer to people's ability to manage themselves (their time/emotions/energy, and so on); manage interactions with their customers, peers, managers and reports; and navigate the system or get things done within or outside their organization. Different organizations/sectors use different words for soft skills. In health care professions, soft skills include "patient counseling skills" (in the case of pharmacists), "bedside manners" (nurses), "chair-side manners" (dental hygienists) and so on. In professional service firms they include "client

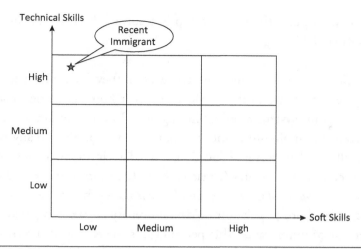

Figure 2.1 Talent Management Grid

relationship management." Interpersonal skills and communication skills apply to many organizations.

Many organizations have talent management tools similar to Figure 2.1, where they rate their employees' technical and soft skills at low, medium and high. The definitions of each axis may be different, but the idea is the same.

Technical skills and soft skills are independent. Some people may have amazing technical skills yet are really difficult to work with, or have no common sense, while other people are easy to get along with but may find basic arithmetic challenging. Most organizations have people in all squares of this grid. Organizations attempt to minimize the number of people in the bottom left corner (by placing people who are rated low on both scales on performance improvement plans) and try to increase the number of people in the top right corner (people who are ready to take on additional responsibilities) through training and development programs.

Immigrant Employees: High Technical but Low Soft Skills

Where does the average immigrant end up on this diagram by North American standards? Most managers or HR professionals we have worked with place them in the top left corner (high technical skills, low soft skills) in Figure 2.1.

- In Canada, most immigrants come after they have obtained their degrees and some work experience in their home countries. Canada uses a point system to select immigrants. Immigrants must meet or exceed the minimum number of points required. Since many points are allocated to formal education, Canadian immigrants are usually well educated. Statistics Canada's *2008 Canadian Immigrant Labour Market: Analysis of Quality of Employment* shows that 24 percent of the Canadian-born population holds a university degree compared to 40 percent of immigrants. This percentage is increasing: It jumps to 52 percent among those who arrived between five and ten years ago and 57 percent among those who arrived within the last five years.
- In the US, many immigrants go through the American education system—they come to the US to study, either at the undergraduate or graduate level, and end up staying in the US after their graduation. Americans consider these immigrants technically competent because they have American degrees.

An important difference between the two countries is the number of unauthorized immigrants; on a per capita basis, the US has a much higher number of unauthorized immigrants than Canada does. While it is challenging to come up with an accurate estimate, in the US, the number quoted by the *Economist* is 12 million people; in Canada, Auditor General Sheila Fraser stated in a 2008 report that Canada lost track of 41,000 unauthorized immigrants. This difference is easily explained by geography—Canada is much farther from any potential source of unauthorized entry than the US, and its climate is far less appealing than the US climate. As a result, while the US has a sizeable number of immigrants in the low technical skills/low soft skills square on Figure 2.1, the number of immigrants in this category is much smaller in Canada.

This has one major consequence on the attitude of locals toward immigrants: When the average Canadian meets the average immigrant, he or she assumes the immigrant is in the country legally and has skills. The situation is different in the US, where there are far more immigrants with low technical skills. Most Western European countries have similar challenges—the proportion of unskilled and unauthorized immigrants relative to their population is similar in these countries to that in the US. The Conference Board of Canada compared Canada with sixteen other developed countries on overall social performance.[1] One of the seventeen measurements is "Acceptance of Diversity." Canada scores the highest on this indicator—82 percent of Canadians said "their community was accepting of people from different racial, ethnic, and cultural groups"—while 79 percent of Americans and only 59 percent of Italians and 52 percent of Japanese agreed with the statement. Our book is not about the general population's attitude toward immigrants; instead, we focus on people with professional expertise—people with high technical skills relative to the rest of the population.

Most immigrant professionals appear to have low soft skills when they first interact with their North American colleagues because soft skills are measured by cultural standards. By their home country standards, some have excellent soft skills, others have average soft skills and some have poor soft skills. In the Canadian immigration point system, no point is allocated to soft skills—Canada welcomes immigrants whose soft skills are anywhere along the soft skills scale by their home country's standards. However, when these immigrants arrive in Canada, their soft skills are measured by Canadian standards, and such skills may be judged as low by their Canadian colleagues. As a result, immigrants end up in the top left corner of Figure 2.1.

Lionel's situation illustrates this point very well. In France, his soft skills were considered excellent—he was the captain of his university's rowing team, he was one of the two founders of the first career fair in the same university and he was chosen by his peers to act as maître d'hôtel in a restaurant. When he arrived in the US, the rating of his soft skills went overnight from high to low because Americans did not appreciate the way he formulated his questions and comments—by American standards, he came across as putting others down. When he moved to Canada, he experienced further challenges. Both in the US and Canada, the negative comments he made to his colleagues were interpreted as harsh because French negative feedback is worded much more strongly than North American negative feedback (see more on feedback in Section 2.5). Where Canadians or Americans say: "This is a good report. You may want to look at section three some more, but overall good work," a French person says: "Rewrite section three—it is wrong!" It was the same message—"You need to work some more on section three"—but in Lionel's case it was delivered so differently that no Canadian or American technician wanted to report to him. With a Ph.D. from Caltech, his peers were clearly placing him in the top left corner of Figure 2.1.

Which Is More Important: Soft Skills or Technical Skills?

The crux of the matter is the relative importance various countries or cultures place on technical skills and soft skills. If we express this importance by allocating percentages that add up to 100 percent, we find that the relative weights of technical skills and soft skills are essentially 50/50 in North America. In both the US and Canada, soft skills matter quite a bit more than they do in most countries where immigrants come from. Lines of equal value (Line B) are diagonal— the three people represented by the star and the two dots on Figure 2.2 bring the same value to the organization.

Most Asian, African, Eastern European, Latin American or Middle Eastern countries are significantly more hierarchical than either the US or Canada (see more on hierarchy in Chapter 3). Outside of North America, being a good manager does not require convincing your employees to do things the way you tell them to—they will do it your way because you have a higher title. By contrast, managers in hierarchical cultures need to be able to tell their employees in detail how to do their work because employees will either stop or go off track if they are not told what to do next.

One of the easiest ways to quantify this difference is to compare the importance of the ability to make good presentations in North America with the importance of that skill in other parts of the world. We can measure the importance of a skill in a culture by looking at the age at which kids start learning the skill through the educational system:

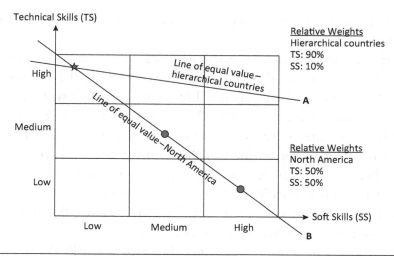

Figure 2.2 Relative Weights for Technical and Soft Skills

- On average, American and Canadian kids make their first public presentation when they are between three and five years old—"show and tell" is usually their first practice. And they continue to apply this skill throughout elementary and high school.
- By contrast, many kids from hierarchical countries often make their first public presentation much later in life. When we ask workshop participants who grew up outside North America at what age they made their first public presentations, the answers range from "high school" and "university" to "in the workplace," "when I moved to the US/Canada" or even "never." For example, Caroline's first public presentation was the defense of her undergraduate thesis while Lionel made his first presentation in high school.

In many cases, kids growing up in hierarchical cultures stand in front of the class before making their first public presentations. However, in these situations, they recite things they have learned by heart (like songs, poems, plays or multiplication tables). The first time they choose the topic, prepare the materials and present the results happens much later in life. The Chinese company Caroline worked for in China did not use PowerPoint presentations at all. Instead, employees wrote long reports. Each level of the organization employed professional writers who specialized in writing reports to superiors. People then read those reports in meetings.

In the home countries of North American immigrants, the relative weights of technical skills and soft skills range from 90/10 to 80/20. The line of equal value is very flat (Line A in Figure 2.2), with most of the emphasis on technical skills. One approach is not inherently better than the other—they are just very different. For example, Chinese kids do much better on mathematics exams than North American kids because the Chinese educational system places significantly more emphasis on mathematics skills; by contrast, North American kids are much more at ease when presenting since they practice that skill to a much greater extent than Chinese kids do.

The practical consequence of this difference is usually devastating for immigrants. Figure 2.3 illustrates a situation many immigrants have encountered. Candidate A and Candidate B are competing for a job or a promotion:

- Candidate A is a recent immigrant who has better technical skills than Candidate B (e.g., Candidate A may have a master's degree when Candidate B has a bachelor's degree) but lower soft skills by North American standards.
- Candidate B has spent many years in North America and is very familiar with the North American business culture (e.g., B may have been born in North America or immigrated at a young age).

Who brings more value to the organization? In the situation represented by Figure 2.3, the answer depends on which criteria the person or people making the decision are using. By North American standards, B clearly brings more value to the organization than A does. Consider the following example.

A high-tech company employs many highly skilled engineers and scientists. One of the recruiters in the company is a recent immigrant. Her technical skills are excellent; she had an engineering degree and is able to understand the technical requirements of the positions and assess the technical backgrounds of candidates better than other recruiters. However, she comes

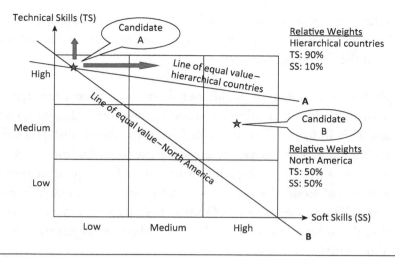

Figure 2.3 Which Candidate Gets the Job or the Promotion?

across as very blunt by North American standards. When the position of recruiting team leader became open, she thought she was the most qualified candidate because of her superior technical skills. However, her managers concluded that another recruiter, who had better soft skills, was a better choice for the position.

How does A interpret the situation? In most cases, A sees the situation as unfair and usually blames a visible difference between him- or herself and B, such as favoritism, racism, sexism, nepotism and so on. In the previous example, the successful candidate was a visible minority woman, so the immigrant employee could not blame management's decision on sexism or racism. Had the successful candidate been a white male, that could have been her interpretation of the situation.

While favoritism, racism, sexism or nepotism certainly do exist in North American organizations, the key issue here is that **A does not understand the criteria that people around him or her use to measure performance**. Specifically, A is not aware of the importance of soft skills in North American organizations.

A's analysis of the situation tends to follow these lines: "I have been bypassed for a job/promotion; I deserved this position since I am more

qualified than [the successful candidate]. This is unfair. This is ___ism."
What does A do at this point? Many immigrants to North America
react in the following manner:

1. First, they complain to people they know. Since most immigrants
   network within their cultural groups (Russians with Russians, Indians with Indians, Mexicans with Mexicans, and so on), and since
   their cultural peers are very likely to see the situation from the same
   vantage point, this complaint often intensifies a general feeling
   within the group that favoritism/racism/sexism/nepotism is alive
   and well in the organization. From an HR or management perspective, this often contributes to lower employee engagement among
   immigrants.
2. A common next step for A is to look for another job. The thought is,
   "If this company is unfair, I'll find a merit-based organization that
   will reward my qualifications appropriately." While the individual
   rarely benefits from this change (people often go from one organization to the next and experience the same problems with different
   sets of people), this approach often creates a retention problem for
   organizations when the labor market is in favor of employees (think
   of Alberta, Alaska or Texas between 2005 and 2008, accounting
   firms between 2002 and 2007 or IT firms between 1997 and 2001).
3. In most cases, A has difficulty finding another job and remains in
   his or her position. Since A wants to become more employable or
   promotable, A's logical next step is to obtain a higher degree, desig-
   nation or certification as represented by the vertical arrow pointing
   upward in Figure 2.3. For example, if A has a bachelor's degree, A
   goes back to university and obtains a master's degree. If A comes
   with a master's, A obtains a Ph.D.; if this does not work, A goes to
   obtain an MBA as a way of establishing superior technical skills.
   Unfortunately, this does not solve the problem because he or she is
   not working on the root cause—the issue is not a lack of technical
   skills, it is a **lack of soft skills by North American standards**. However, the employee does not know this and doesn't know he or she
   doesn't know. We once met a Ph.D. who had gathered ten different
   designations and/or certifications and was still unemployed.

When immigrants come to North America, the challenge they face in understanding the relative importance placed on soft skills is compounded by the fact that good soft skills look quite different in different cultures. Going back to the example of presentations, anyone who attends an international conference quickly notices that presenters from different countries have different approaches to presentations. One easy way to illustrate this point is the joke about five journalists from different countries who have been asked to write an article on elephant mating:

- The French journalist wrote "The secret love life of elephants."
- The German journalist wrote "The sociological and psychological dynamics of elephant couples—Part 1: From Karl the Great to Bismarck."
- The Chinese journalist wrote "Chinese were the first to mate elephants during the Qin Dynasty."
- The American journalist wrote "How to make a million dollars by mating elephants."
- The Canadian journalist wrote: "Elephant mating: A federal, provincial or municipal responsibility?"

As this joke demonstrates, people have to adapt their approach to any topic, depending on the cultural background of their audience. This applies to North American immigrants, who need to learn the importance of making good presentations here, as well as what makes a presentation good.

Section 2.2: Applying the PSE Framework to Bridge the Soft Skill Gap

The key to integrating immigrants into North American organizations is to make them and their North American colleagues **aware** of this difference, help them **develop their soft skills, set up systems** that encourage them to move in this direction and create a **supportive environment**. Successful approaches typically combine some of the following elements.

People—Creating Awareness and Developing Skills

Creating Awareness

In our experience, only a small percentage of immigrants and an even smaller percentage of professionals educated in North America are aware that the relative importance of technical skills and soft skills is not the same in North America as it is in other countries. Therefore, making everyone aware of this difference comes first. Here are some action steps and considerations:

Organize live workshops. While a number of men may wake up on a sunny Saturday and decide to go shopping for a big-screen TV or a new set of golf clubs, few people wake up on a sunny Saturday and decide to go shopping for a life insurance policy. It is the same with cultural awareness: Very few managers or employees go to work on a Monday and decide to work on their understanding of cultural differences. As a result, building cultural awareness may require some push on the organization's part. In our experience, the fastest and most effective approach to generate awareness is via a live workshop that mixes professionals educated both outside and in North America.

The key advantage of holding it live is to create a forum where people have a chance to discuss this topic with others. When they do, they realize this difference is real and goes to an unrecognized heart of cultural difference, deeper even than food, music and language. Participants recognize that people think differently because they have been taught to think differently.

Offer e-learning courses or resources. These may require some up-front investment, but providing courses to a large audience helps amortize the cost. They allow flexibility: people can access them anytime and anywhere. A key limitation is the fact that many immigrants do not see value in soft skills training and therefore may not feel the need to watch a podcast on cross-cultural communication by themselves, whereas they may go on the Internet to search for technical information on a regular basis. Launching an online course with live promotion and senior management involvement helps employees put more value on the course. Managers can also organize a whole team to watch e-learning videos or podcasts at the beginning of team meetings on a regular basis to promote awareness and create a forum for the team to have a conversation.

Make books available to employees through an internal library. Through LinkedIn, Lionel has received many comments from immigrants who said that reading the book he coauthored with Don Rutherford, *Recruiting, Retaining and Promoting Culturally Different Employees*, has made a significant difference in their careers.

There are two categories of books that are really helpful to immigrants and their colleagues/managers:

1. Books examining the impact of cultural differences in the workplace. In Chapter 1 and the reference section of this book, we list a number of cross-cultural titles that organizations may want to include in their libraries.
2. Business books covering a range of soft skills important in North American organizations, such as *Getting to YES: Negotiating Agreement without Giving In* by Roger Fisher and William Ury and *The Seven Habits of Highly Effective People* by Stephen Covey, as well as biographies of influential people/business leaders, such as *Straight from the Guts* by Jack Welch.

Provide training to HR professionals on how to diagnose cross-cultural issues accurately. Since HR professionals are often at the forefront of employee issues, when they see an immigrant whose soft skills are considered poor by North American standards and will likely prevent the employee from reaching his or her professional goals, they can help that person through coaching, recommending books and training.

Developing Skills
While awareness is 50 percent of the solution, once people become aware, it takes a lot of hard work to develop the soft skills they need to succeed in North American organizations. Here are some action items immigrant employees can take to learn soft skills:

Observe how others handle a wide range of interpersonal situations in the workplace. How do you express disagreement with a colleague during a meeting? (See more on this in Section 2.5.) How do you manage a sudden high volume of workload in the organization? How do you handle a delay or a change of scope in a project? How do you delegate a task to an administrative assistant? For many immigrants, careful observation will help them realize that there is a difference and that they need to learn how to handle these tasks in a way that works for their North American counterparts.

Emulate the behavior of role models or people who have the soft skills the immigrant is trying to learn and who are clearly recognized by everyone as demonstrating these soft skills in a wide range of situations. This can be a precursor to mentoring or a step on its own.

Attend training sessions. Many soft skills are related to human interactions, so immigrants need to learn how Americans and Canadians interact with others by seeing them in action. In many cases, they need to take these courses even if they have already taken similar courses in their home countries. For example, taking a communication course enables them to work on communication skills with their colleagues educated in North America, who are very different from colleagues in their home country.

Read books or watch online learning modules. For example, Lionel worked on his soft skills by borrowing books on tapes from his company library and listening to a number of recorded courses while commuting to work.

It is clear that people do not change behavior overnight after taking a course or reading a book. Managers play a major role in helping immigrant employees transfer their learning into day-to-day work through feedback and coaching. Positive reinforcement is as important as negative feedback. Whenever immigrant employees demonstrate a soft skill that is valued by the organization, managers need to provide timely encouragement so the employee knows to repeat that behavior.

Systems—Driving Behavioral Change through Performance Management

Once people have built awareness and skills to bridge the soft skills gap, the organization needs to reinforce the behavior and encourage ongoing skills building through performance management and rewards systems. A good performance evaluation system does not benefit only immigrants—it benefits everyone. From time to time, workshop participants tell us that they have not had a formal performance evaluation in years—that is clearly an issue for the whole organization. A robust performance management system should have the following characteristics to be effective.

Explain clearly how performance is measured by using concrete examples to illustrate what good, average or poor performance looks like in your organization. Both immigrants and managers need to communicate and clarify the expectations up front and on a continuous basis to avoid unpleasant surprises at performance review time.

Measure not only WHAT is achieved, but also HOW people achieve the results. We see a number of organizations that measure performance based on a competency model or key behaviors or values (i.e., soft skills) that are embedded in the performance evaluation. Employees receive ratings on both business results and behaviors in alignment with the organization's values. Going back to the technical recruiter example in Section 2.1, when immigrant employees understand that they will not be promoted because of the way they communicate with colleagues even though they have achieved their targets, they will have to make a decision on either developing their communication skills or staying on a technical career path.

Help immigrant employees understand which soft skills should be their focus. The list of soft skills people can work on is very long; however, each is not critical to everyone. For example, client relationship-management skills are not as important to people who work in the back office as they are to client-facing employees. Immigrants working in a North American organization need help determining which soft skill(s) they should work on first. Our coaching experience suggests it is difficult to make much progress if they try to improve more than three soft skills at the same time. While individual immigrants are ultimately responsible for their own personal growth, managers and/or HR professionals should help them determine the following:

- Which soft skill gap limits their ability to influence their colleagues the most

- Which soft skills are most important in their current position
- Which soft skills they need to develop in order to be ready for their next career move

Help immigrant employees create personal development plans. Once employees have identified which soft skills they need to focus on initially, they need to create an action plan. Since the majority of immigrants to North America come from hierarchical cultures, many have never gone through such an exercise. Guidance from their managers and/or HR professionals ensures they create SMART (Specific, Measurable, Ambitious, Realistic and Time-bound) goals and then design and implement the corresponding action plans.

Identify ways to develop soft skills above and beyond formal training. In the minds of many immigrants, personal development is the same as formal training. For example, they tend to equate "improving my project management skills" with "taking a project management course" or, even better, "getting a PMP certification." Managers and HR professionals can help them find other on-the-job or volunteer opportunities to develop their soft skills. For example, a manager could ask them to manage a small project or volunteer for a holiday fund-raising committee in order to apply the project management skills they learn in a course.

Reinforce ownership. In many organizations, making the most of the personal development process requires educating both employees and managers on how to use it effectively. Immigrant employees need help and support from their managers and HR professionals to assume ownership for their own development.

Environment—Implementing Inclusive Practices

Most North American organizations want to be merit based; they want to hire and promote the best person for each position. Many organizations have incorporated cultural diversity in their values and communicated with their workforce that everyone has an equal opportunity to reach their professional goals, no matter what they look like or where they come from.

To take this vision further, many organizations have implemented inclusive practices that communicate with employees in general, and immigrants in particular, the unwritten rules of career management in the organization:

Explain the rationale of hiring and promotion decisions to everyone. This helps ensure that employees interpret these decisions accurately and draw the right conclusions when it comes to managing their own careers. This is especially helpful for immigrants since they are likely to misunderstand how performance is evaluated for cultural reasons. In particular, announcements that describe both the position requirements and the specific accomplishments of the successful candidate that demonstrate why he or she is the right person for the position help immigrants learn what they need to be able to do if they want to have such a position.

Provide career management courses. In order to ensure that these courses address the specific needs and situations of immigrants, the content and facilitation of these courses need to cover the specific challenges immigrants face when managing their careers in North American organizations (see more on this topic in Chapter 4). In the case of large organizations that employ many recent immigrants, providing career management courses that are specifically designed for immigrants can be very beneficial.

Create and provide mentoring programs, particularly those specifically designed to help protégés work on their soft skills. We have seen large organizations create their own internal mentoring programs, while smaller organizations make use of programs that are available publicly through professional associations or nonprofit organizations. The mentoring program of the Association of Professional Engineers and Geoscientists of Alberta is a good example. Protégés are matched with mentors from the same profession and can learn from more experienced mentors how to tackle a range of difficult interpersonal situations they encounter in their work.

In our experience, making such programs successful requires three key elements:

• A dedicated program manager who tracks the progress of mentor–protégé pairs to ensure that mentoring is taking place

- Preparation for mentors so they are aware of the cultural challenges they are likely to experience and know how to deal with these challenges
- A distance between mentors and protégés that makes it obvious that mentors have no vested interest in the feedback they give to protégés (in particular, a mentor cannot supervise, directly or indirectly, his or her protégé)

Choosing the right mentor is quite important for immigrants; this mentor should be someone who is intimately familiar with the organizational/professional culture in which the immigrant operates and has been able to successfully integrate into the North American work culture. Protégés need to find mentors that make them comfortable—they need to be able to let their guard down and admit that they do not understand what is happening or that the impact they had was not the impact they wanted to have.

Many immigrants spontaneously choose mentors within their cultural group. While this choice usually helps the communication between the mentor and the protégé, there is a downside. If the mentor has not integrated well and interprets the situations that stump the protégé from the same perspective as the protégé and therefore reinforces his or her negative behavior by North American standards, it does not help the protégé learn soft skills by North American standards. Lionel experienced this problem at one point in his career—he kept seeking advice from another French person who, despite having been in the US longer, did not have particularly good insight into the American concept of teamwork; as a result, the more Lionel followed her advice, the worse his relationship with his teammates became.

Offer cross-cultural coaching by an external coach to new hires who have never worked in North America before. Such coaching programs work both on creating awareness and on building skills. They help immigrants understand better how their performance is evaluated, determine which soft skills they need to work on and learn how to improve these soft skills. Several North American organizations that have used this approach have seen a significant increase in the success rate of immigrant new hires. In one organization, the percentage of international new hires and transferees who were terminated or left the organization before the end of their first year dropped from over 10 percent to 1–2 percent after cultural integration coaching was offered to all international new hires and transferees.

Section 2.3: Cross-Cultural Communication

Cross-cultural misunderstandings resulting from both verbal and nonverbal communication style differences have been studied extensively by many social scientists and researchers. In our workshops, we find that many managers and HR professionals have clearly identified these issues as cross-cultural. We encourage readers to familiarize themselves with some of the work referenced in this book. For example, Chapter 6 of *Recruiting, Retaining and Promoting Culturally Different Employees*, by Laroche and Rutherford, contains a description of many potential cross-cultural communication pitfalls. In this chapter, we focus on two cross-cultural communication challenges that are frequently encountered in many organizations.

Message Received vs. Message Intended

When communicating across cultures, the message people receive may be quite different from the message that is meant to be sent. Many cross-cultural communication misunderstandings can readily be overcome when we realize we typically interpret the words, body language or behaviors of our culturally different counterparts based on what these words, body language or behaviors mean in our culture. When a person is culturally different from us, there can be a significant gap between message sent and message received. These words, body language or behaviors may mean something different to him or her than what we take away.

We illustrate here this general principle with one specific example: The amount of silence people leave during conversations.

Figure 2.4 is a graphic illustration of how much silence is in a conversation between two people compared across three groups of people. Americans and Canadians tend to speak in turn and leave a small silence in between them; by contrast, Latin Americans tend to over-lap significantly, and East Asians tend to leave significantly longer silences. These differences have a significant impact on cross-cultural communication in many professional situations (such as global conference calls or face-to-face meetings):

- Everyone interprets the behavior of people who leave shorter silence than they do (or jump in before they would) as "rude"/ "interrupting"/"finishing my sentences"—East Asians consider that Americans or Canadians do not give proper consideration to what they said, while Americans or Canadians consider that Latin Americans interrupt them.
- Similarly, everyone interprets the behavior of people who leave longer silence than they do (or do not jump in as quickly as they would) as "not interested"/"not engaged"/"not participating enough"/"cold"—Latin Americans consider that Americans or Canadians are not interested in what they have to say, while Americans or Canadians consider that East Asians are not engaged in the conversation.

The impact of cross-cultural misunderstandings on organizations is often quite significant:

- They often lead to poor working relationships. When people interpret the behavior of one of their coworkers as disrespectful, they are unlikely to volunteer information or help that person.

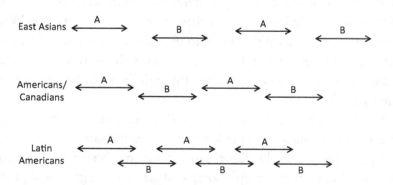

Figure 2.4 Silence Gaps in a Conversation in Different Cultures

When people refrain from making discretionary efforts, cross-cultural misunderstandings decrease organizational effectiveness significantly.

• Miscommunication is often interpreted as a lack of respect and sometimes results in people losing their job. For example, a contract Russian IT specialist who worked at the internal help desk in the head office of a large American corporation was called for help by an employee. He went to her office to provide support and initiated the conversation by translating literally into English what he would have said in Russian. It came out as "What's wrong with you?" when he meant "What problem are you experiencing?" The employee interpreted this sentence based on what it would mean if it was said by the average American—"You are an idiot. You messed up your computer and now I have to fix it for you." She complained to his manager and HR. Since this was not the first time people had complained about this IT specialist behaving in a rude manner and he had been given feedback several times before, this was the last straw, and his contract was terminated. In this situation, neither the IT specialist nor his colleagues were aware that the problem was the result of cross-cultural misunderstanding and poor soft skills by North American standards.

Different Languages Spoken in the Workplace

One issue most commonly faced by many organizations is language—what should we do when people speak a language other than English in the workplace? Consider the following situation, which has happened in many organizations:

Bob, Mike, Jose, Maria and Gustavo work together. They are in the staff room to get a coffee. While waiting for their turn to get their coffee, they start chit-chatting. First, they talk about the weather. Then the conversation moves on to the Super Bowl—Bob and Mike discuss passionately which team has the best chances to win this year. For a minute, Jose, Maria and Gustavo remain silent, and then they start a conversation in Spanish. By the time they all have their cup of coffee, Bob and Mike have stopped their conversation; they watch the animated discussion in Spanish between

Maria, Jose and Gustavo for a minute, then drift away from the staff room back to work.

No one in this situation intends to create a problem. But everyone involved feels excluded by the other group. In order to understand the dynamics behind this issue, we first need to look at what is happening in the mind of the people on both sides, namely the people who speak English as a second language (ESL) and people who speak English as a first language (whom we will call native English speakers).

For ESL speakers, speaking English all day long takes an incredible amount of additional energy above and beyond doing their regular work. Most people who grow up in the US or Canada have learned some French (if you grew up in English Canada) or Spanish (particularly if you grew up in the southwestern United States). If you speak English as a first language and learned French, Spanish or any language other than English at some point, try to remember what happens when you are trying to speak that language. Chances are, you make sentences in English in your head and then translate these sentences word for word into the second language you are trying to speak.

When we learn a second language, we initially think in our first language and translate back and forth continuously—we translate what we hear into our first language, formulate a response and then translate that response into the second language we are speaking.

Because this mental gymnastics takes a lot of energy, ESL speakers are usually exhausted at the end of the day. Some seize opportunities they might have to bypass this whole process by speaking their first language with other people who speak the same first language. When they do this in private, there is no impact. The trouble usually starts when ESL speakers start speaking Chinese, Tagalog, Spanish or Russian in the office. When this happens, some people who do not speak this language react quite negatively by thinking the following:

- "They do not want to integrate."
- "They are excluding us."
- "They speak their first language because they don't want us to understand."
- "They are talking about us."

This problem is particularly acute when people who speak a language other than English start laughing. At that point, some people who are around them wonder, "Are they laughing at me?" Native English speakers are not the only ones reacting this way. An HR professional said that one employee who complained most vehemently about people speaking Chinese in the workplace was someone who spoke English as a second language (and who, incidentally, also spoke Hindi in the office on a regular basis).

In our experience, ESL speakers who operate in English have to overcome several professional hurdles because they operate in a second language:

- People are usually perceived as being less competent if English is their second language. When people look for words or mispronounce them by North American standards, their colleagues often mentally downgrade their technical skills. This is particularly true if immigrants stumble on the technical words that are specific to their fields. In this case, many North American professionals interpret this behavior as implying "they don't know what they are talking about" instead of realizing that they know this subject in their first language, but the English words don't come out that readily. In Japanese, Korean, Chinese and Vietnamese, there is a word to say "ten thousand," and one hundred thousand becomes "ten ten-thousand," one million will be "one hundred ten-thousands" and so on. As a result, Asians may be quick calculators although they give Westerners the impression they have difficulties handling large numbers.
- People speaking in their non-native language may use a word that means roughly what they are trying to say without realizing this word has an additional meaning they did not intend to communicate. Again, the message received can be quite different from the message they meant to send. A good case in point is the Spanish word *molestar*, which means "disturb" or "bother" in English while sounding very close to the English word *molest*. Some Spanish speakers may end up telling their managers when they walk into their office without an appointment, "I am so sorry for molesting you."

- Because speaking English takes so much effort, many immigrants participate a lot less in meetings than they do in meetings held in their first language. They may be perceived as being less engaged or having less to contribute; both interpretations are perceptions, not reality. This results in a loss of ideas—they may have suggestions that can lead the team to the solution of a problem in question, but they do not verbalize these suggestions because it takes so much effort.

On the flip side, one common complaint we hear from ESL speakers goes along the following line: "We ask native English speakers to give us a chance to participate by slowing down. They slow down for one or two minutes and then get back to normal speed. They do not want to help us." In our experience, this description looks at the situation from only one vantage point. To understand what happens in the minds of native English speakers at that point, we need to turn the situation around—what happens to people when they are asked to speak their first language slowly?

Lionel, who speaks French as a first language, experiences this situation when meeting with some of his English Canadian clients. One HR manager, who speaks French as a second language, wants to speak French with Lionel because she does not have many opportunities to practice her French. That situation is quite uncomfortable for him—speaking French slowly is very unnatural. He would prefer switching back to English, since this would considerably speed up the meeting. The key point is that everyone experiences major difficulties when trying to speak their first language slowly in an environment where most people speak this language fluently.

Section 2.4: Bridging the Gap in Cross-Cultural Communication

Effective cross-cultural communication requires continuous and deliberate effort in many areas. Here are some of the action steps that North American organizations can implement following the PSE framework.

Building Awareness and Skills for Cross-Cultural Communication

Putting Ourselves in Others' Shoes

One of the most powerful tools we have found is an exercise that helps people put themselves in the shoes of the others. The exercise goes like this:

- People who speak English as a first language are asked to describe their morning routine to another person with a twist—they have to double every verb with a synonym. It sounds like this: "I woke up, rose at 6:30. I brushed, cleaned my teeth. I turned on, powered up my computer."
- People who speak English as a second language are asked to describe their morning routine to someone who speaks the same first language as they do (e.g., native Spanish speakers pair up together; native Mandarin speakers pair up together, etc.) with a different twist: They have to pause after every word; for example, a native French speaker might say "Je . . . me . . . suis . . . réveillé . . . à . . . 7 . . . heures."

In our experience, this exercise opens up people's minds in 99 out of 100 cases. Native English speakers find doubling the verb exhausting and gain an appreciation for the difficulties ESL speakers face when operating in English all day long. ESL speakers come to understand why native English speakers cannot speak slowly for very long.

In one organization, a senior HR professional said it helped her understand why the HR representative of their Quebec City office (who speaks French as a first language) was not participating as much as representatives of other (English-speaking) offices during conference calls. On the other hand, through this exercise and discussion ESL speakers also realize the impact they have on English speakers when they start to speak their first language. This mutual understanding forms a foundation for both groups to look for ways to create a common communication protocol.

One of our clients, a large bank, trained all their multicultural ambassadors to do this exercise in the Monday morning huddle in their various offices and branches. Other organizations train their managers to do this exercise at the beginning of their team meetings. Having everyone go through this exercise clearly multiplies its impact on the organization—particularly if the person leading the exercise is a senior leader. It also can create a forum for the team to clear any misunderstandings and discuss how to communicate more effectively with one another.

Awareness training sessions also help distribute the necessary knowledge throughout the organization. Please refer to Section 2.2 for more detail on the various ways of building awareness. No matter what approach is used (live/Web-based/online/etc.), these sessions need to emphasize the following points:

1. **Remember that communication is not just about sending messages, it is also about making sure that the message received is the message that is meant to be sent.** The more culturally different two people are, the likelier they are to misinterpret each other's messages. This applies both ways—when they send messages and when they receive messages.

2. **Patience is a virtue.** People who come from culturally similar backgrounds fill in the blanks of the conversation with the same information and are likely to interpret messages the same way. Communication between culturally different people is usually slower than communication between culturally similar people, particularly at the beginning of a new working relationship. When people do not know one another and start working together for the first time, they have to spell out everything to ensure that culturally different people do not fill the blanks with information that is not intended.

3. **Awareness is 50 percent of the solution.** When we know we are dealing with a cultural difference, we react differently. Rather than blaming (the other person or ourselves for not measuring up), we look for solutions to a common problem. Showing interest for and learning about our counterpart's cultural background usually helps smooth relationships.

4. **The golden rule needs to be replaced by the platinum rule.** Instead of "do unto others what you want them to do unto you," we should learn to "do unto others what they want you to do unto them." Behaviors that may be helpful or respectful in one culture may be interpreted as unhelpful or disrespectful in other cultures. If you

want to help or show respect and are not sure how to do it, we recommend that you ask your counterpart. This principle applies not only to cultural differences, but also in many other situations. Lionel's experience illustrates this point very well:

One of my colleagues was visually impaired. He figured out how to go from his home to the office and back by counting paces—from his desk to the elevator, from the elevator to the front door, from the front door to the street corner and so on. From time to time, he would run into difficulties: A good soul saw him at a street corner, grabbed him by the arm and took him to the other side. While this person was clearly well-intentioned, the outcome was that he had lost his count and needed help from this point on whereas he usually did not.

One morning, I heard him complain about this behavior. Since I could see myself doing that, I asked him what was the best way to help him. His answer was a complete surprise to me. He told me that the best way to help him was to put my left hand, like a hook, behind his right elbow, and walk 45 degrees behind and beside him. As we walked along, he was scanning the ground with his cane in his left hand, and he wanted me to tell him when the ground was not level—one inch was enough for him to fall or twist his ankle. I would never have anticipated his answer, so I learned to ask when trying to be helpful to people.

Learning to Walk in Other People's Shoes

How do we deal with cross-cultural misunderstandings? Because the workforce of many North American organizations includes people from a wide range of cultural backgrounds, we find it is not practical to provide information on every cultural group involved. Nor is it desirable—in most cases, this approach can be counterproductive since it often leads to stereotyping; people may interpret it as "the ten-point plan for dealing with Chinese/French/Mexicans/etc." A more productive approach is to provide practical solutions that can be applied to anyone, no matter their cultural background. Some workshop participants said jokingly that these points also apply to communicating with their in-laws.

In our experience, it is important to help employees develop the skill of separating impact from intention. Indeed, the impact people have on us may not be their intention, and the impact we have on them may be quite different from our intention. Here are the two steps to learn to differentiate between impact and intention when you **send** messages to others:

1. **When sending messages to culturally different people, continuously monitor the impact you have on them.** The key here is to try and notice if and when your counterparts react in an unexpected manner since this is a likely indicator that what they understood is different from what you mean.
2. **When you have noticed that your counterpart's reaction is not in line with your expectations, stop and clarify.** It is very tempting at that point to pretend everything is fine and move on to the next topic as if nothing happened; unfortunately, in many cases, the misunderstanding that took place will likely increase over time, rather than disappear.

Here is an example of how to put these suggestions into practice: Toward the end of the movie *Outsourced*, Todd (an American manager) is saying goodbye to his Indian counterpart, Puro. He uses an expression that is common in North America—he says, "Break a leg!" Puro takes this expression literally—"Why do you want me to break my leg?" At that point, Todd realizes that the impact he has is not the impact he wants to have (Suggestion #1), so he stops and clarifies (Suggestion #2). He explains to Puro that this expression is meant to wish people good luck in North America, to which Puro responds: "I wish both of your legs get broken!"

On the **receiving** end, it is important to remember that the way you feel may not be the way your counterpart wants to make you feel. Here are the four steps to learn to deal with this issue:

1. **When receiving messages from culturally different people, continuously monitor your own emotional state so you can determine when you are reacting negatively.** When you work with culturally different people, there will be times when you find yourself feeling offended, annoyed or disrespected—keep in mind that this does not imply that they mean to make you feel this way. Since

you may interpret their message differently from what they mean, you first need to monitor your own emotions and realize when you are reacting negatively. Usually, the problems are on the negative side—if you react positively to something your counterpart meant neutrally, it does not create nearly as much of a challenge.

2. **When you realize you are reacting negatively, don't act on this feeling.** This part is easier said than done, but it is critical to at least try to put some distance between yourself and your own emotions. The analogy is the advice many communication courses provide on e-mail communication. When we receive an emotionally charged e-mail, we should write the response but wait until later in the day to decide whether we will send it or not; we may also want to pick up the phone and talk to the e-mail sender to understand his or her intentions and clear the air. In verbal communication, we also need to train ourselves to pause before responding to an emotionally charged situation.

3. **Look for the trigger of that negative feeling.** What is the word, body language or behavior that triggered that feeling? This step is straightforward when it comes to e-mail or voicemail messages— you can read or listen to them over and over again until you find what triggered your negative reaction. Sometime it is easy to pinpoint. An ALL CAPS e-mail message usually generates a strong negative emotion in the US or English Canada because it is interpreted as shouting at the message recipient. But it does not have that meaning in Quebec. In this case, it is easy to see where the emotion comes from. In verbal communication, it may take a while for you to pinpoint the exact cause of your negative reactions, particularly in conference calls—you hang up with a negative feeling and cannot really determine where that comes from. Don't hesitate to ask colleagues you can trust to debrief such calls with you in order to identify the root cause of these negative feelings.

4. **Determine what that trigger means to the other person.** You may have interpreted a word, body language or behavior differently from what the person meant. You can find out what the person meant by asking people who are familiar with your counterpart's culture.

Helping employees develop their communication skills through training, coaching and mentoring has proven to be beneficial to everyone involved.

Good Communication Is Good Cross-Cultural Communication

In our experience, virtually all the skills taught through regular communication workshops can be applied when working across cultures. The key is to continuously remember that misunderstandings across cultures take place more often and require more work at preventing and identifying them. Here are a few suggestions:

Write meeting minutes. We all know we should prepare an agenda and write minutes for every meeting, but most of us do not do it on a regular basis. When working with recent immigrants, meeting minutes greatly decrease the magnitude and frequency of misunderstandings. One Canadian professor who worked with students from all over the world developed the habit of asking them, at the end of every weekly meeting, "Please tell me, in your own words, what you are taking away from this meeting and what you are going to do before our next meeting."

Go around the table. During a meeting, the meeting leader goes around the table and asks all participants their thoughts on the topic at hand. In a multicultural team, this approach gives those who are waiting for a long silence to voice their opinions a chance, while people who are used to jumping in know this is time to listen.

Schedule ESL speakers' presentations in the early part of the day or meeting. This allows them to present when their ability to speak English is better, and therefore they have a better chance of getting their points across than later in the day/meeting, when they are likely to be more tired and have more difficulty finding the right words.

Listen actively. Ask clarifying questions, rephrase or paraphrase when speaking with an ESL speaker with a strong accent. State what you understand and what you do not. ESL speakers become more fluent when the listener is supportive and patient.

Mirror people's behavior. For example, when speaking with people who leave longer silences than you are used to, refraining from speaking as early as you normally would helps put the other person at ease. This approach is particularly useful in job interviews when North American recruiters interview East Asian candidates—in extreme cases, recruiters do all the talking while candidates listen the whole time if neither pays attention to bridging the gap. Mirroring our counterparts' behavior is a very effective approach in many areas—not just in the amount of silence people show, but also in terms of vocabulary, range of emotions displayed, body language, presentation style and so on.

Teach immigrant employees to choose an appropriate medium. As Marshall McLuhan states in his famous aphorism "the medium is the message,"[2] one critical aspect of communication is the choice of medium. How do we communicate? Do we meet by telephone, videoconference or in person? Do we make a presentation or write a report?

Most immigrants come from cultures in which a higher percentage of the message is communicated nonverbally than it is in North America (people familiar with the work of Edward T. Hall[3] will recognize them as high-context cultures). As a result, they tend to prefer higher bandwidth communication—face-to-face meetings compared to phone calls, phone calls compared to e-mails—since higher bandwidth communication tools give them better access to these nonverbal messages. For example, one of Caroline's friends recently joined a local Hong Kong company after working for a multinational company for many years. She was told that she should never send people an e-mail without first having had extensive verbal communication with them.

In general, HR professionals and managers need to teach immigrant employees to consider the purpose and the audience of the communication, as well as the interaction required for the topic at hand or the speed required to pass the information, before choosing the appropriate medium. Specifically, many immigrants need to learn how to leave a proper voicemail message and how to write an e-mail because these media are not used as frequently in their home countries.

Implementing Systems to Improve Communication

Work Processes and Tools
Teach immigrant employees how to use the organization's communication processes and tool. Most North American organizations

have designed and implemented many communication processes and tools, such as one-on-one manager–employee meetings, manager-once-removed meetings, groups meetings, conference calls and online collaboration tools. Immigrant employees may not be familiar with them. In their home countries, managers usually initiate the meeting, and so they may not be comfortable initiating or organizing a meeting. They may not be used to leveraging technology to the extent of their North American colleagues.

Establishing Communication Protocols

We have seen work teams actively engaging in conversations to establish communication protocols among themselves. Returning to the issue of different languages spoken in the workplace, many organizations resolve the issue by agreeing on communication protocols as follows:

Differentiate between personal time and company time. English is the default language to use on company time, while people are free to "blow off steam" by speaking their first language when they are on their lunch break.

Encourage mutual accommodation in both situations. For example, if two Chinese speakers are heating their lunches in the kitchen and speaking Chinese when a third person who does not speak Chinese steps into the same space, they should switch back to English in order to make everyone feel included. On the other hand, if two Russian speakers go into a meeting room and close the door, no one should care whether they speak English or Russian as long, as they get work done.

Being inclusive does not stop at the choice of language—selecting topics that are of interest to everyone and giving people chances to participate in the conversation helps increase the sense of belonging. Another example where the same principle applies is gender difference. Men are sometimes more interested in sports-related topics and need to be cognizant when their female colleagues are involved in the conversation, while women are sometimes more interested in family or children-related topics and need to be cognizant of the presence of their male colleagues.

Creating an Environment for Effective Communication

Leadership

When working with multicultural teams, we find that the quality of their communication is usually both an indicator and a driver of their effectiveness as a team. Team members should want to communicate effectively with one another; they also need to make it possible to address communication issues within the team.

Leadership is key in driving the effectiveness of cross-cultural communication. When leaders lead by example and take the time to understand immigrants and their issues, the whole organization benefits. They create an environment where people feel empowered to seek ways to communicate more effectively. For example, David Miller, the former mayor of Toronto, showed his understanding of immigrants' issues by being the keynote speaker at a conference organized for internationally educated professionals and staying at the conference after his address, answering questions from conference attendees. His commitment sets a great example when it comes to integrating immigrants into the economic and social fabric of a city where immigrants account for close to 50 percent of the population.

Inclusive Practices

Effective communication does not come from implementing a ten-point plan—it comes from doing a lot of little things better. There are many things people and organizations can do to create a positive environment:

Lunch and learn presentations: In these get-togethers, people of different cultural groups make a presentation on elements that are meaningful to them (e.g., how the educational system works in their home country). This can help people learn more about the way specific cultures think. Alternatively, they may show movies from different cultures as a way to spark a discussion about cultural differences between this culture and North American culture. Discussing movies such as *Not One Less/Lagaan/L'Italien* helps North American colleagues understand Chinese/Indian/French culture, respectively.

Multicultural potlucks: Everyone brings food that is typical of their own culture to these events. While it is important for organizations to go beyond this step (food is part of visible differences, and learning about sushi only goes so far in improving communication with Japanese people), we find it is essential in the sense that it gives people an opportunity to showcase their culture in a way everyone can readily appreciate. The best demonstration of this point came from the pride one Moroccan researcher (who had obtained a Ph.D. in an American university) displayed during such a potluck in his research center: He and his wife prepared a couscous dish for forty people, and he changed into traditional Moroccan clothes when serving the food; he was beaming during that potluck. Such events have a high return on investment since the only cost to the organization is the time of the person who organizes it.

Section 2.5: Cross-Cultural Feedback

Nowhere is the difference between the message sent and the message received more critical to the career of immigrant employees than in the case of feedback. In our experience, this is the biggest issue. In one large accounting firm, we found that approximately 30 percent of immigrants and expatriates were surprised when they received their first written performance appraisal—they expected an "above average" rating and received a "below average" rating; even more striking, 5 percent of immigrants and expatriates thought they would receive an "exceeding expectations" rating when they were rated "unacceptable" by their managers and peers. Figure 2.5 graphically represents the dynamics that lead to this critical issue.

Direct vs. Indirect

Feedback can be positive or negative, so we can represent it like an axis; in the middle, there is 0. Figure 2.5 implies that the farther a

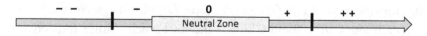

Figure 2.5 Graphical Representation of Feedback

comment falls from 0, the stronger the feedback. On the very right of the axis, we have very positive feedback—when managers give feedback that falls in this area to an employee, it means he or she has done something really well and will soon get a raise, a promotion, an award or a bonus. Conversely, on the very left of the axis, we have very negative feedback—when managers give feedback that falls in this area to an employee, it means he or she has done something terribly wrong and will be given a written warning, put on a performance improvement plan or terminated. In the middle, there is a neutral zone, when the comment is neither positive nor negative. The most famous English word in the neutral zone is *interesting*, which is neither good nor bad.

While some employees are more sensitive to feedback than others, these personality differences are compounded with cultural differences. As shown in Figure 2.6, relative to Canada and the US,[4] many European, Middle Eastern and African countries have a much bigger neutral zone (the bar at the bottom). When an American or a Canadian gives people from these countries slightly negative feedback, the words are heard but the message is not understood (Arrow A goes into their neutral zone).

Here is an example an IT director from Israel who was working with a team in Israel shared with us:

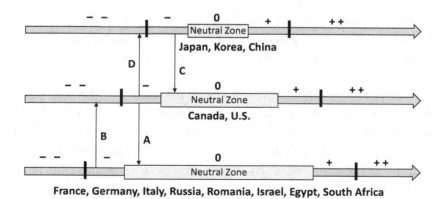

Figure 2.6 Cross-Cultural Feedback

A programmer in Israel wrote a specification. His Canadian colleagues sent him e-mails to give him feedback. But he did not understand their feedback. I had to pick up the phone and tell him, "Look, this specification does not work. You will have to rewrite it." The programmer in Israel was very surprised and responded by saying, "Why do you say so? I had three people sending me an e-mail thanking me. If they don't like the specification I wrote, why do you thank me?"

On the other hand, when people from France or Romania give slightly negative feedback to Americans or Canadians, it sounds much stronger than intended (Arrow B goes into their double negative zone). Here is a situation we have observed in many organizations: A North American presenter is presenting data to an audience of peers. If a member of the audience disagrees with one of the numbers, what will he or she do?

- The average American or Canadian audience member usually chooses between two options: The first is to say nothing, wait until the end of the presentation and discuss the number one on one with the presenter; the second is to raise his or her hand and say something such as, "How did you arrive at this number?" (Canadians tone down their disagreement even further by starting with an apologetic comment, such as, "Correct me if I am wrong," or "I may have missed something.")
- The average South African, Israeli, German, French or Russian audience member typically makes one of three comments: "I disagree," "That number is wrong" or "You are wrong."

When the average North American presenter hears these comments, the message received is quite different from the message that is meant to be sent. By South African or Israeli standards, this is a disagreement on a number—there is nothing personal about it and no attack is intended. By North American standards, this is an unwarranted personal attack in public. For example, Lionel made this kind of comment a number of times when he worked with a large consumer product company. His colleagues found his comments offensive, and, in one case, a colleague avoided collaboration for six months. Obviously, this has a significantly negative impact on both the performance of immigrants and on the effectiveness of the organization as a whole.

As Figure 2.6 suggests, North American organizations also experience the reverse issue, where North American feedback comes across much more strongly to East Asians than intended (Arrow D goes into their double negative zone on the bar at the top) while lightly negative feedback by Chinese or Japanese standards is often interpreted as neutral by North American standards (Arrow C goes into our neutral zone).

Again, this cultural difference causes many misunderstandings, as the following situation demonstrates: When North American organizations work with colleagues in East Asia, the messages sent by East Asian colleagues are often misunderstood by their North American counterparts. For example, Caroline worked in a Canadian technology company that has a subsidiary in Taiwan. Her Canadian colleagues came to her on several occasions to ask for advice; the conversation went like this:

COLLEAGUE: I don't understand. We had a conference call with Taiwan and asked people there to do a number of things. They said, "Yes, yes" all the time, but nothings happens afterwards. What's going on?

CAROLINE: In Chinese, there are four kinds of yes—Yes, I hear you; Yes, I understand; Yes, I agree; and Yes, I will do it. Which yes did you hear?

COLLEAGUE: What do you mean, "there are four kinds of yes"? How do I know which yes I am dealing with?

CAROLINE: You have to listen to what else they say besides yes. If they say yes and bring up a glitch like "It will be disruptive," "It will be difficult" or "We will have to [do something really unusual] to make it happen," they are really telling you that it won't work. In order to understand the message they are sending you, you need to listen carefully and read between the lines—the range of signals they use is smaller, so you need to increase the gain of your receiver.

Misinterpreted cross-cultural feedback usually has significantly negative consequences on the relationships between the individuals involved (Caroline's Canadian colleagues considered their Chinese counterparts unprofessional until they understood the real issue) and on the organization's effectiveness (some of them made commitments to their clients based on what they interpreted as commitment from their Taiwanese colleagues).

How Bad Is the Situation?

When employees, suppliers or service providers receive negative feedback from their managers, colleagues, customers or clients, it is critical for them to understand how unhappy the feedback giver is with their performance because this will drive both the amount of corrective action they need to take and the speed at which they need to take that corrective action. The unhappier the feedback giver is, the more corrective action the feedback receiver needs to take and the faster he or she needs to implement the corrective action. In one workshop delivered to a service sector organization, one participant phrased it as "the unhappier the client, the bigger the gift basket I send." The challenge is that the indicators people use to tell one another how unhappy they are vary from culture to culture:

- In Italy, the two best indicators of the severity of a situation in the mind of a manager are the volume of his or her voice and the movement of the arms; the louder the voice and the more arm movement, the worse the situation.
- In France, the two best indicators of the severity of a situation are the volume of the manager's voice (such as in Italy) and his or her tone modulation—the voice of an unhappy French manager goes from low pitch to high pitch to low pitch again, and the more frequently he or she does that, the unhappier he or she is.
- In Japan, the key indicators of the severity of a situation in the mind of a manager are the length of the silence (the longer the manager remains silent, the worse the situation is) and the negative vibes from the manager (watch his or her face, in particular—unhappy Japanese frown ever so slightly, so you have to really pay attention to pick it up if you have limited experience of the Japanese culture).

Most Americans and Canadians are able to tell that a recent immigrant from Italy is unhappy; however, they are often unable to determine to what extent this person is unhappy because he or she appears to be "off the charts" by their standards, no matter what the situation. North American employees are also unable to pick up the signals sent by French managers or customers because they are not looking for the indicators used by French people (they are not "on the same wavelength").

The same is true in reverse—many immigrants to North America have difficulty decrypting the intensity of the feedback signals they are receiving from their North American colleagues, managers or clients and even more difficulty sending the right signal when trying to describe the severity of a situation so that their North American counterparts understand it as they see it.

North American managers typically use two specific indicators to communicate the severity of a situation in their mind: The pattern of their feedback and their choice of words. Unfortunately, neither indicator is picked up by the average immigrant employee because these indicators are specific to North America. Figure 2.7 illustrates the **first** indicator graphically.

Most North American managers use four different patterns, which we number from 1 to 4, where 1 means "here is something you need to change—don't worry, it is no big deal" and 4 means "this is really bad—if you do it again, you will be placed on a performance improvement plan."

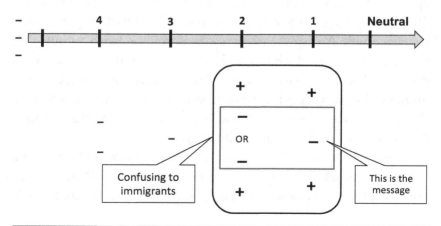

Figure 2.7 North American Negative Feedback Patterns

- In Position 1, North American managers give a feedback sandwich—a negative comment sandwiched between two positive comments. It sounds like "I like your report; it is full of mistakes, but you used a nice font." The meat of the sandwich is the negative comment.
- In Position 2, they give an open-faced sandwich (or the reverse)—there is only one slice of bread. This is more serious, but not a big deal yet.
- In Position 3, there is no bread left—there is only meat. This is serious; significant corrective action is expected on a short time scale at this point.
- In Position 4, they give two slices of meat for the price of one. It sounds like, "This behavior is inappropriate, and if you do not change quickly, something unpleasant will happen soon." In most cases, the time scale for swift change is measured in weeks at this point.

This approach confuses most immigrants because the first two patterns (Position 1 and 2—within the large square in Figure 2.7) are specific to North America. In much of the rest of the world, the feedback people receive is either good or bad, but it is never both in the same conversation. For example, the Chinese language does not have a word that means "feedback"—you get either praise or criticism, but not something that means both. As a result, people who did not grow up receiving feedback sandwiches are confused when they receive one. Those who are used to receiving more pointed feedback (e.g., Russians, Israelis, South Africans) interpret a feedback sandwich as implying they are doing a good job ("two pluses and one minus—overall, I am doing well") while those who are used to softer wording (e.g., Chinese, Filipinos, Koreans) take the message as much stronger than intended. The negative comment sounds much more negative to them than it does to the North American feedback giver.

Conversely, because they are not used to feedback sandwiches, the negative feedback given by most immigrants starts in Position 3. In the case of immigrants who come from countries where feedback is worded more pointedly than in North America, even a mild negative comment is likely to come across to their North American colleagues as harsh—much to the dismay of an immigrant who had no intention of triggering such a reaction.

Confusion also abounds when immigrant employees try to decode the **second** indicator used by Americans and Canadians, namely the choice of words. People here often tell you how bad the situation is in their mind through a careful choice of words. For example, if your manager tells you "this is a disaster," it is clear that the situation is worse than if he or she says "this is an issue." Table 2.1 shows how the severity of the situation is embedded in the choice of words.

In other words, Americans and Canadians have about fifteen different ways to tell you there is a problem, an error or a conflict. The word they choose gives you a good indication of how bad things are in their mind.

The trouble is that this message is not received by the average immigrant, particularly when English is not their first language. When people learn a second language, they are really happy when they have learned one English word for every word in their first language. It is easy to relate to this situation if English is your first language by

Table 2.1 North American Choice of Words

For the words *problem*, *error* and *conflict*, if the situation you are dealing with falls in position ___, the average north american manager calls it a ___.

POSITION	PROBLEM	ERROR	CONFLICT
1	Concern, challenge, situation, learning opportunity, development point	Omission, inaccuracy, oversight, discrepancy, typo, oops, boo-boo	Difference of opinion, misunderstanding, misinterpretation, miscommunication
2	Issue, trouble, difficulty	Error, glitch, hiccup, faux pas	Disagreement
3	Problem	Mistake	Conflict, argument, clash
4	Crisis, disaster, emergency, fiasco, debacle, train wreck, show stopper, catastrophe	Wrong, fault, failure, blunder, career-limiting move	War, fight, confrontation, battle, altercation, dispute, lawsuit, irreconcilable differences

flipping it around—when you try to learn Spanish or French, you are probably happy when you know one Spanish or French word for every English word in the sentence you are trying to make.

People who speak English as a second language end up in the situation where they know only one word—learning fifteen ways of saying "problem" is beyond their imagination. You can appreciate the challenges this creates by thinking of a situation where the only tool you have at your disposal is a hammer. In that case, you have two options: To hammer or not to hammer. You do not have a screwdriver, so that option is not available to you. As a result, many immigrants end up in the situation where they hammer a screw and unintentionally make a big mess in the wall because they used a word that was either much stronger or much milder than what they had in mind.

A good case in point is the word *problem*. In North America, a problem is quite bad, but it could be worse. Think of Apollo 13: "Houston, we have a problem"; that was a bad situation, but it could have been worse. Many European-based languages have a word that looks just like problem—in French, it is a *problème*; in Dutch or Afrikaan, it is a *probleem*; in German, it is a *Problem*; in Spanish, Italian or Portuguese, it is a *problema*. People who speak any of these first languages latch on to the word *problem* because it looks just like a word they know, and they use it as if it means the same thing, without realizing that a problem in North America (Position 3) is much worse than a Spanish *problema* or a French *problème* (Position 1). Again, the message received is different from the message that is meant to be sent.

We can have misunderstandings even with people who speak English as their first language. For example, the word *mistake* is stronger in North America than it is in the UK. In North America, *error* means "it happens," whereas *mistake* means "you should have known better." In the UK, it is the reverse—an error is worse than a mistake. We have seen British immigrants or expatriates tell their North American colleagues "you made a mistake" in front of peers or clients. While this comment falls in Position 2 by British standards, it falls in position 3.5 by North American standards (comments made in public are automatically worse than comments made in private). Similarly, the word *clash* has a stronger meaning in North America than in Australia. In one public accounting firm, a partner removed an Australian auditor from his project team (for fear of losing the client) because she characterized the difference of opinion between her and the client as a "clash."

Section 2.6: Bridging the Gap in Cross-Cultural Feedback

Many of the solutions we discussed in previous sections also apply when it comes to bridging the gap in cross-cultural feedback. The key is in two areas: building awareness and skills and providing tools (and training managers to use these tools).

People—Building Awareness and Skills

In our experience, most employees, managers and HR professionals are unaware of the cultural difference in cross-cultural feedback. For immigrants who are used to more pointed feedback, this issue surfaces when they receive their first written performance appraisal—the rating they often get is significantly lower than the rating they expected. By contrast, employees who are used to softer feedback may become very stressed if the feedback they receive sounds quite negative to them, when their manager and colleagues overall have a positive impression of their performance.

Therefore, building awareness is essential to bridging the gap. As discussed earlier, because people don't know what they don't know, building awareness requires some push, such as live training sessions and exercises. It gives people a chance to exchange their views and "clear the air." Cross-cultural coaching by an external coach also helps tremendously in our experience—by helping immigrants understand the feedback they get along the way, the coach can ensure that immigrants are not surprised when they get their first written performance appraisal.

The skills managers need to develop to give effective cross-cultural feedback are not that different from what managers need to give effective feedback to any employee. We all know that feedback needs to be timely and specific in order to be effective. The additional challenge is to make sure that immigrant employees pick up the negative feedback messages they are given as intended.

In particular, it is important for managers to dig into what may appear at first as inconsequential mismatches. When everything seems to match, except a little detail, don't let go of that detail. This detail may be just a detail; it may also be the tip of an iceberg of misunderstanding. For example, when Lionel worked in Italy, he discussed with his Italian colleagues the process they would follow to achieve a particular objective. Lionel described the process he was used to, which took about three months; his Italian counterparts described the process they were using, which was taking only three weeks. Since the outcomes seemed to be the same, they agreed to use the process recommended by his Italian colleagues. Two weeks later, it became clear that the outcomes were not the same and that they would not achieve their target. In this situation, Lionel needed to explore the mismatch (three weeks versus three months) to a much greater extent; by doing so, he would have realized that the outcomes were not the same.

Systems—Creating Tools and Training Managers

One of the most effective tools we have seen organizations use to ensure that feedback is received the way it was meant is for managers to create a scale for feedback and calibrate their employees on that scale. If you are a manager, calibrating the scale means that you and your employees sit down and agree on what each position on the scale means concretely. We typically suggest that people use a four-point scale, but the number of points is not critical—some people use a five-point scale or a ten-point scale. What matters is that you and your employees agree on what each position on the scale means. For example, in the case of a presentation, you and your employee will agree that feedback follows these guidelines:

- *Position 1* corresponds to minor changes that you want your employee to make, primarily cosmetic changes—for example, font type and size, background color or type.

- *Position 2* corresponds to more substantial changes that are still no big deal. Grammatical mistakes, reversing the order of two slides, putting a little more detail on one slide, splitting a busy slide into two, making a chart more to the point all fall in this category.
- *Position 3* corresponds to significant changes. Here, we are usually dealing with content problems. Feedback that falls in this position may include reshuffling the slide deck, adding more data, making the charts clearer, making the point of the presentation easier to grasp and so on.
- *Position 4* usually means "go back to the drawing board." A manager who gives feedback in this position is asking the employee to redo the entire presentation. This usually comes from a messaging problem—the message of the presentation may not be the message that the manager wanted to communicate, or the data does not agree with the message, or the data is clearly wrong and so on.

In our experience, a manager and the employee can create a common numerical scale for negative feedback in fifteen minutes. After that, they have a tool at their disposal—they can communicate the intensity of the negative feedback by using a number—and the manager can tell his or her employee, "This is a 3.5," or the employee can ask, "Based on what we have discussed, it sounds to me that we are at position 2—am I reading your feedback accurately?"

Having a scale for negative feedback can make a major difference:

I facilitated an off-site for the executive team of a joint venture between a French and an American company. During the off-site, one of the key issues the joint venture was facing came from one French team member's communication style—the way he was phrasing his comments and questions generated more problems than he solved. This French team member was considered "a little rough around the edges" by French standards, but his technical skills more than made up for this deficiency. By contrast, he came across as completely off the charts by American standards. The American team leader explained this point in four different ways to the leader of the French team using words; all she understood was that something was amiss. When I observed the difficulties they were going through, I turned to the leader of the American team and asked him: "On a scale of 1 to 4, where 1 is a concern, 2 is an issue, 3 is a problem and 4 is a catastrophe, where would you rate him?" The American team leader responded, "At least a 3." The French team leader realized the magnitude of the problem and took the corresponding action.

(Lionel)

Consistent delivery of feedback across the organization can be a challenge in culturally homogeneous organizations (managers do not all give feedback in a timely or consistent manner) and becomes even more of a challenge in multicultural organizations. Creating a common language (i.e., terms everyone understands) and tools (such as the four-point scale in Figure 2.7) to deliver feedback in a timely and consistent manner can significantly increase the productivity of the organization and employee engagement. In particular, we find that training managers on how to create and calibrate a negative feedback scale helps ensure that feedback is received by employees the way it was meant by their managers.

Notes

1. *How Canada Performs: A Report Card on Canada, April 2013*, The Conference Board of Canada. Retrieved from Conference Board of Canada website on May 10, 2013: http://www.conferenceboard.ca/hcp/details/society.aspx.
2. McLuhan, Marshall, Quentin Fiore, John Simon, and Jerome Agel: *The Medium Is the Message*. Columbia Stereo CS 9501, Mono CL 2701, ca. 1968. New York: Bantam Books, 1967.
3. Edward T. Hall: *Beyond Culture*. Knopf Doubleday Publishing Group, 1976. New York: Anchor Books/Doubleday, 1976, 1977, 1989.
4. To simplify Figure 2.6, we have placed Americans and Canadians together in the center. Note that Americans typically use stronger wording than Canadians do; as a result, Americans who work in Canadian organizations quickly gain the reputation of being "blunt" while Canadians who work in American organizations are often perceived as "beating around the bush."

Cultural Factors and Concepts—Part II

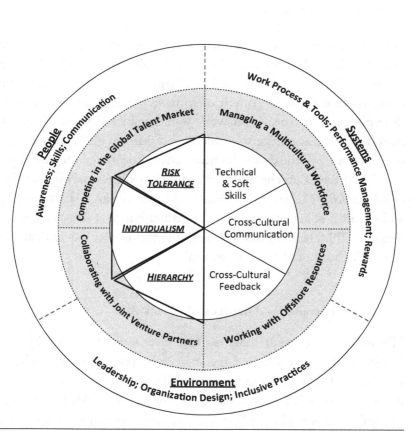

Figure 3.0 Roadmap of the Book

In this chapter, we discuss three additional cultural factors and concepts and analyze challenges brought by cultural differences in the context of immigrant employees in North American organizations:

- Hierarchy and its impact on work relationships and performance
- Individualism and its impact on teamwork
- Risk tolerance and its impact on problem solving, decision making and project management

This chapter examines each of these three concepts and discusses how to bridge the gap following the People–Systems–Environment solutions framework. As we did in Chapter 2, we look at these three concepts in the North American context, where people educated in different parts of the world work together in the same office. Our main focus is on solutions—readers who want to get a more detailed understanding of the dynamics involved are encouraged to read Chapters 7 and 8 of Laroche and Rutherford's book *Recruiting, Retaining and Promoting Culturally Different Employees*. We apply these concepts and the PSE solutions framework to other business situations in later chapters. This chapter ends by examining the answer to a critical question—"Who should adapt to whom?"

Section 3.1: Hierarchy and Impact in the Workplace

Hierarchy is a concept that was first extensively described by Geert Hofstede.[1] In the workplace, hierarchy corresponds to the psychological distance between an employee and his or her manager. There are vast differences when it comes to hierarchy around the world. The least hierarchical cultures tend to be Scandinavian countries, while African, Asian, Eastern European, Latin American and Middle Eastern countries tend to be significantly more hierarchical than the US or Canada. North America receives very few immigrants from Scandinavian countries (with the notable exception of some hockey players). Most immigrants come from cultures that are significantly more hierarchical than the US or Canada.

The fact that most immigrants come from countries that are more hierarchical than North America does not mean that every immigrant has a stronger sense of hierarchy than any of his or her North American colleagues. We need to be mindful and avoid stereotypes. We use the term *average* throughout this book to simplify the discussion.

Egalitarian people tend not to see hierarchy anywhere. By contrast, hierarchical people tend to see hierarchy everywhere. Here is a simple, yet telling, example:

Consider a case in which an egalitarian manager and his or her hierarchical report approach the front door of a building. Hierarchical employees make sure they get to the front door first so they can open it to let their manager go first. The trouble is that, in cold places like Canada or the Midwest, the building usually has a second door located a short distance from the first. Egalitarian managers get to the second door first, open it and suggest to their employee to go through. However, hierarchical employees feel that going through the door first conveys disrespect for their manager and insist on the manager going through the door first. Some North American managers find the ensuing standoff strange.

When egalitarian people work together, all have the opportunity to give their opinion and/or challenge others. When hierarchical people work together, they start by determining who is in the "one up" position and who is in the "one down" position. The person who is in the "one down" position phrases his or her suggestion or feedback softly, while the person in the "one up" position gives direction or feedback in a more pointed manner. The idea of challenging one's superior is completely unthinkable in many hierarchical countries.

In *Outliers: The Story of Success*, Malcolm Gladwell examines why airlines headquartered in hierarchical cultures (e.g., Korea, Colombia) experience plane crashes more frequently than airlines headquartered in egalitarian cultures. One of the key drivers of these crashes was the inability of copilots to challenge pilots or air-traffic controllers, even in circumstances where they knew the pilot's or air-traffic controller's direction was going to lead to the crash of the plane they were flying—and their own death.

This is a critical point: If hierarchical people feel they cannot challenge their superiors, even in a life or death situation, imagine how difficult it is for them to start challenging their managers when the stakes are not nearly as high. Korean Airlines did improve its flight safety record dramatically when it trained its flight crews to overcome their reluctance to challenge one another in the cockpit. In other words, it is definitely possible for immigrants from hierarchical cultures to adapt to the North American egalitarian perspective; however, keep in mind that this process takes a lot of time and effort for many people.

Hierarchy and Work Relationships

When hierarchical people and egalitarian people work together, they often feel disrespected, even in situations where their counterparts had no intention to be disrespectful. Here is a situation illustrating the impact of hierarchy on work relationship.

A young male engineer who came to North America a few years ago interacts with an experienced female administrative assistant (AA) who was born and raised in North America. The young male engineer obtained a university degree in his home country and joined the organization six months earlier. The female AA has been with the organization for twenty years but does not have a university degree. How do they see each other?

- The young male engineer sees himself in a much higher social position than this experienced female AA. Gender may be a factor, but it is often not the most important one. In his mind, the key is that he has a university degree and she does not—in his home country, education trumps experience.
- The experienced female AA sees herself in a slightly higher social position than this young male colleague because, in North America, experience trumps education. The gap is not as big in her mind as it is in his mind, but the order is clearly reversed.

The breakdown in communication takes only ten seconds: When he gives her a document and says, "Make me ten copies," she replies, "The photocopy machine is down the hall." At that moment, both people feel completely disrespected by the other:

- He feels his education is not valued adequately. He often interprets the situation as implying she does not value his degree the same as a North

American degree. He may interpret this as racism, if he belongs to a visible minority group—she would handle it differently if a white person made the request.

- She feels her experience is not recognized. She often interprets the situation as sexism—if he was dealing with a man, he would not handle the situation this way.

In our experience, nobody really understands the root cause of the problem, so the action steps they take rarely address the issue. The most frequent reaction of both is to stay away from the other until he or she learns to "show respect"—unfortunately, both have different definitions of that word.

Hierarchy and Performance

The most visible consequence of the strong sense of hierarchy of many immigrant employees is what their managers call a "lack of initiative." Figure 3.1 helps explain the root cause of this challenge. It graphically represents the normalized distribution of answers we have obtained when asking international assignees to choose the position that best represents their preference on the ten-point scale.[2] Figure 3.1 illustrates two key points:

I prefer working for managers who

give me enough freedom so that I can determine the best direction for myself.

give me clear directions so that I know what they want me to do.

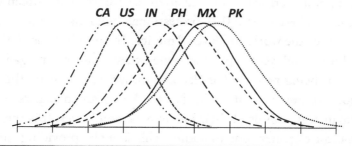

Figure 3.1 Normalized Distributions of Answers by Professionals in Different Countries

- First, you cannot judge a book by its cover. There is a wide range of preferences in each culture. As a result, we encourage readers to use this kind of information reactively rather than proactively since using this information proactively leads to stereotyping. In essence, using this information proactively is tantamount to saying, "Oh, my new employee is from Pakistan. Since Pakistanis like clear directions, I am going to give her very detailed instructions." As discussed in Chapter 1, this is not productive. We encourage readers to use this information to inform their observation of the behavior of their culturally different colleagues or employees and not assume every immigrant needs to have every instruction spelled out.

- At the same time, there are clear trends. The majority of North American employees want freedom to decide how to do their job, while the majority of Mexican, Pakistani and Filipino employees want clear directions. Because we manage the way we want to be managed, the average Mexican or Pakistani employee expects clearer direction from his or her North American manager than the average North American manager expects to give to his or her employees. When the manager is on the left of this chart and the employee on the right and they are not aware of this cultural difference, the manager usually considers that the employee "does not work independently" or "lacks initiative" while the employee considers that the manager "does not know his or her job" or "lacks leadership."

This last point is critical in our experience. Over the past fifteen years, we have coached over 2,000 professionals who have moved from other parts of the world to North America. The number one challenge hierarchical employees experience when they work for an egalitarian manager is being perceived as "lacking initiative." These are the most common comments written by North American managers on the performance appraisals of their hierarchical employees. It is therefore essential for organizations to address this issue by providing support to immigrant employees through orientation and on-boarding (see more on this point in Chapter 4).

Section 3.2: Bridging the Hierarchy Gap

Dealing with cultural differences is similar to dealing with personality differences. One of the four dimensions of the *Myers-Briggs Type Inventory* (MBTI) is one's preference toward introversion or extraversion. How do you apply your knowledge of this personality dimension? First, you determine whether your counterparts are introverted or extraverted by observing their behaviors in situations where differences are likely to become visible:

- Extraverted people tend to think things through by talking ("they think aloud") while introverted people prefer processing ideas on their own.
- On average, extraverted people participate actively and speak more in meetings and workshops than introverted people; they also tend to make more eye contact.
- When they are tired, extraverted people tend to draw energy by being with people while introverted people tend to recharge by being on their own. This point is readily visible at a conference—extraverted people head for the bar at the end of the day whereas introverted people go to their rooms.

If you have determined that your manager is significantly more extraverted or introverted than you are, how can you modify your behavior to work more effectively with him or her? This is a situation where being aware of the difference between introverted and extraverted people and adapting to your manager's preferred style can make a major difference for you. Think of a time when you want to describe to your manager a new program you want to implement:

- If you are introverted, your first reaction may be to send an e-mail to your manager and wait for him or her to bring it up. If your manager is extraverted, this approach is usually not as effective as presenting your idea verbally—your e-mail does not register as much in your manager's mind as a conversation. Presenting your program in person gives your extraverted manager a chance to process the information in the way that is most comfortable to him or her. This increases your chances of getting the support you want.

- Conversely, if you are extraverted, your first reaction may be to go and talk to your manager in person. While this may be comfortable to you, it does not give your introverted manager the time and space he or she needs to process information independently. Your initiative is more likely to be turned down in that case. Presenting your new idea to your introverted manager via e-mail or in a document gives him or her time to think things through alone. This increases your chances of getting his or her support.

We use a similar approach to bridge the hierarchy gap by first identifying whether your counterpart is more or less hierarchical than you and then determining how you can adapt your behavior to work with that person more effectively. Later in this chapter, we apply the same approach to bridging the individualism and the risk tolerance gaps.

People—Building Awareness and Skills

The first step is awareness—we need to understand the difference in people's sense of hierarchy and its impact on work relationship and performance. In our experience, most people in North American organizations have realized there is a cultural aspect. Whether they are born in North America or outside, most people sense that immigrants see hierarchy (and, in particular, their relationship with higher-ups) differently than do people who are born and raised in North America. However, we find that many misinterpret the behaviors they observe:

- A substantial number of immigrants interpret the situation from their hierarchical vantage point—they consider that Americans or Canadians lack respect for their superiors or elders.
- Similarly, many people born and raised in North America look at the situation from an egalitarian perspective—they tend to think that, if hierarchical people were given the opportunity, they would all want to live and operate in an egalitarian environment.

We recommend a two-step approach to build awareness and skills to bridge the gap:

- **Step 1: Observe the behavior** of your managers, employees or colleagues in order to determine whether they have a more or less hierarchical view of the world.
- **Step 2: Identify ways to modify your behavior** to work more effectively with these colleagues based on your observation.

To avoid stereotypes, we encourage readers to make this determination not based on people's country of origin or past experience (having served in the army does not imply automatically that one wants clear direction), but on observable behaviors. Table 3.1.1 lists some behavioral differences to look for in order to assess whether someone is hierarchical or egalitarian.

Step 1: Determine whether your counterpart is more or less hierarchical than you are by observing his or her behavior in the following areas:

Table 3.1.1 Hierarchical and Egalitarian Behaviors

	COMPARED WITH EGALITARIAN PEOPLE, HIERARCHICAL PEOPLE TEND TO	COMPARED WITH HIERARCHICAL PEOPLE, EGALITARIAN PEOPLE TEND TO
Titles and protocol	• Prefer formal forms of address ("Sir," "Your Excellency") • Use position title to address people ("Director," "Professor," etc.) • Pay more attention to protocol (where people sit, in which order they enter a room, who gets the bigger office or the newest computer, etc.)	• Prefer using first names, nicknames and informal forms of address • Not pay as much attention to protocol
Distribution list	• List people in decreasing order of title/position in the organization	• List people in alphabetical or random order
Interactions with others	• Show extensive deference to people they perceive as being above them • Show little concern for people they perceive as being below them • Delegate tasks that they are expected to do (photocopy documents, print reports, etc.) to people they perceive as being below them	• Show the same amount of deference and concern to everyone • Take care of small tasks themselves; when they ask for help with these tasks, recognize that this help is discretionary (as opposed to mandatory based on the relative positions of the people involved)

(Continued)

Table 3.1.1 (*Continued*)

	COMPARED WITH EGALITARIAN PEOPLE, HIERARCHICAL PEOPLE TEND TO	COMPARED WITH HIERARCHICAL PEOPLE, EGALITARIAN PEOPLE TEND TO
Decision making	• Provide frequent updates to their managers • Run every decision by their managers; in many cases, ask their managers to make the decision	• Provide less frequent updates to their managers • Make decisions on their own; occasionally run major decisions by their managers
Approach to tasks and responsibilities	• Prefer closed-ended assignments • Prioritize tasks and responsibilities based on the position and title of the delegating person • Report frequently to their managers and verify that their managers concur with the direction they are taking	• Prefer open-ended assignments • Prioritize tasks and responsibilities based on their importance and urgency for the organization • Take initiative; make decisions and implement them without checking with their managers first
Need for direction	• Ask more questions, look for more detailed guidance and request more specific instructions • Keep asking questions after egalitarian people consider that they have given sufficiently clear directions	• Ask fewer questions and request fewer specific instructions • Stop asking questions and are ready to leave before hierarchical people consider that they have given sufficient direction
Problem solving	• Focus more on analyzing the root cause than on solving it and preventing it from occurring again • Place significant importance on finding who created the problem (blame)	• Focus more on solving the problem and preventing it from occurring again than on the root cause analysis • Place limited importance on finding who created the problem; focus on learning from mistakes
Performance evaluation	• Avoid evaluating the performance of their managers • Avoid writing the first draft of their own performance evaluation	• Want to contribute to the performance evaluation of managers and peers (360 feedback) • Prefer writing the first draft of their performance evaluation
Career management	• Be motivated by the title of the next position and by the opportunity to have more people reporting to them	• Be motivated by the content of the position and by the opportunity to have access to more resources
Influencing others	• Quote famous people, articles or books • Mention the titles and/or positions of people when bringing them up in conversations	• Quote personal past experience • Give only the names of people when mentioning them in conversations

Just like people are more or less introverted, people are more or less hierarchical—people's sense of hierarchy can be placed on a scale or continuum. When you use Table 3.1.1 to determine whether one of your colleagues, managers or direct reports is more or less hierarchical than you are, you are likely to find that he or she displays only some of the behaviors associated with a hierarchical or egalitarian view of the world. Some people may even display several characteristics of hierarchical people and one characteristic of egalitarian people (or vice versa). For example, they may be on a first name basis with everyone while showing extensive deference to higher-ups and less consideration to people below them; on balance, the strong sense of hierarchy of this person is likely to create challenges in North American organizations. The key is therefore to use this table to get an overall picture of your counterpart's outlook on hierarchy before moving on to the next step.

Step 2: Adapt your behavior to bridge a hierarchy gap once you have identified who is more or less hierarchical based on their behavior.

1. Working with people who have a stronger sense of hierarchy than you do:

   • **Emphasize the principles and theoretical arguments that support your position and quote statistics.** Personal past experience does not weigh nearly as much in the minds of hierarchical people as statistics—they tend to see any specific example mentioned by egalitarian people as a potential outlier.

   • **Quote experts in the field.** Hierarchical people tend to respect the opinion of experts and follow their recommendations. A quote that supports your point from an expert whom your hierarchical counterparts respect is likely to have significant weight in their minds.

   • **Mention your title and your department.** This information helps them place you in their mental map of the world. Present your business card the same way they present theirs to you. For example, East Asians hand their business card with both hands. They consider people who do not bother to give them a business card back or who hand it over casually rude.

- **Mention the degree(s) you have obtained and the university(ies) where you studied.** Hierarchical people place a lot of emphasis on formal education and on obtaining degrees from universities that have good rankings. If you have obtained a postgraduate degree (master's, Ph.D., MBA) from a well-known university, mentioning it to your hierarchical counterparts helps establish your credibility in their minds.
- **Refrain from commenting negatively on their ideas in front of their managers or employees.** While egalitarian people may interpret such a discussion as neutral (we are discussing whether someone's idea works or not), hierarchical people may interpret this situation as decreasing the confidence that their manager or employees have in their technical skills. Using the four-point negative feedback scale discussed in Chapter 2, a situation like this may register as a 0 or 1 by egalitarian standards and as a 3, possibly 4, by hierarchical standards.

2. Working with people who are less hierarchical than you are:

- **Emphasize past relevant experience to support your position.** In egalitarian cultures, relevant past experience carries a lot more weight than principles, statistics or theoretical points. The key for hierarchical people is to learn to describe their past experience in a way that helps egalitarian people see the relevance of their points.
- **Use concrete examples to explain your perspective.** Egalitarian people tend to be more easily convinced by concrete examples than by quotes from experts or statistics.
- **Participate in meetings to a greater extent than you normally would.** Participation in meetings (asking questions, making comments or suggestions) is considered an important contribution by egalitarian people.

The sense of hierarchy plays a major role in the relationships between managers and their employees, so it is important to train both employees and managers so they can take their respective senses of hierarchy into consideration when their direct manager or reports are culturally different from themselves. Let's start with the relationship between employees and their managers (see Table 3.1.2).

Table 3.1.2 Working with a Manager Who Is More or Less Hierarchical

WHEN MANAGER IS MORE HIERARCHICAL	WHEN MANAGER IS LESS HIERARCHICAL
Get back to your manager more often to ensure alignment. Your manager expects more frequent reports than you may consider necessary—making sure that your manager continuously supports the direction you are taking will save you a lot of frustration down the road.	**Do your homework before asking questions.** Think of all the ways of achieving the objective you have been assigned and rate the various options according to their pros and cons. Then ask your manager whether you are on the right track.
Check with your manager before taking new initiatives. In particular, check with him or her before starting a new project.	**Take initiative.** Get involved in new task forces, new projects and new initiatives. Do not wait for your manager to suggest that you join.
When your manager has made a decision, implement it. Challenging the direction they have set is not viewed nearly as positively by hierarchical managers as it is viewed by egalitarian managers.	**Avoid asking open-ended questions.** Your manager expects you to take initiative and make suggestions. Asking your manager "What do you think?" "How would you like me to do it?" or "What approach should I take?" is likely to irritate him or her, since your manager expects you to look for and find the answer to these questions by yourself.
Request projects that are not on your manager's critical path. Your manager is more likely to allow you more latitude on such projects, particularly if they are exploratory in nature, than on projects that are critical to his or her success.	**Request projects that are really important to your manager.** He or she is likely to provide you with more direction on such projects than on others.

Let us now look at the reverse situation—where you are the manager and one of your employees is significantly more or less hierarchical than you are. This situation can also create significant challenges for you. Table 3.1.3 provides some suggestions.

Promoting Communication

As discussed, hierarchical people and egalitarian people have different perspectives on what respect means and who needs to "show respect" to whom. For example, let's go back to the situation of the young male engineer and the experienced female AA who each felt disrespected by the other. If they are aware of the root cause (i.e., cultural difference), then they can practice resolving the difference through communication.

Table 3.1.3 Working with an Employee Who Is More or Less Hierarchical

WHEN EMPLOYEE IS MORE HIERARCHICAL	WHEN EMPLOYEE IS LESS HIERARCHICAL
Meet more often to ensure alignment. Hierarchical employees expect to give their managers more frequent updates than you may consider necessary.	**Give them more leeway.** Allow them give you less frequent updates than you may consider necessary. Specify milestones and dates at which you want them to give you an overview of their progress.
Provide clear expectations and boundaries. When you delegate a task, specify clearly what is already set and what needs to be researched. This will save your hierarchical employees both time and stress.	**Explain your involvement to a greater extent.** Explaining why you want to keep your finger in their pie will help them accept your involvement more easily and welcome your input to a greater extent.
Teach them to take initiative. Ask them to do a complete analysis of the situation and come to you with recommendations. Explain that this is not a trick question— you are not testing them to determine whether they can come up with your answer. Hierarchical employees may interpret your request for recommendations as your attempt to assess whether they are capable of reaching the same conclusion you have already reached. You trust their judgment and want to see what conclusions they reach in this case and how.	**Let your employee do some exploratory work** before you specify all the parameters of their work. They would rather find the answer by themselves than be told.
Give them projects that are on your critical path. You will likely pay closer attention to their progress in that case.	**Give them projects that are not on your critical path,** that require significant initiative or that are fairly undefined at this stage. You will likely allow them more freedom in that case.

Applying a suggestion from Chapter 2, if the young male engineer noticed the tone of voice of the experienced female AA when she said "The photocopier is down the hall," he could **stop and clarify**, "It seems my request may not be appropriate, I hope I did not offend you in any way." Or if the experienced female AA caught herself thinking, "Who do you think you are?" she could **stop and ask**, "Is this something that AAs at your previous company usually did for you?" A lot of times, it just takes one person asking to defuse a contentious situation.

Systems—Reinforcing Desired Behavior through Processes

Work Processes and Tools

Differences in the sense of hierarchy often result in a gap or an overlap in decision making: Hierarchical people tend to expect a given

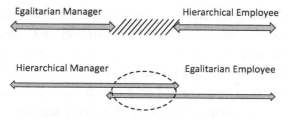

Figure 3.2 Decision-Making Gap or Overlap

Table 3.2 Decision-Making Tool

DECISIONS MADE BY
Manager
Manager with input from employee
Manager and employee jointly
Employee and check with manager
Employee

decision to be made at a higher level within the organization than egalitarian people do. As shown in Figure 3.2, the consequences are quite significant either way:

- When hierarchical employees report to egalitarian managers, both may expect the other to make a given decision—some decisions "fall through the cracks."
- When egalitarian employees report to hierarchical managers, both may want to make the same decision—they "step on each other's toes."

Therefore, to avoid the confusion or conflict, we recommend that organizations introduce the following decision-making tool to help managers and employees effectively bridge the gap. To do this, managers and their reports start by listing all the decisions they need to make on a regular basis and then classifying them in five categories, depending on who is making them, as shown in Table 3.2.

For example, a learning and development (L&D) manager and an L&D coordinator may agree on the following:

1. The L&D manager decides the organization's learning and development strategy based on discussion with business leaders and the budget.

2. The L&D manager determines any significant change to the scope of a workshop (making it significantly shorter or longer, turning it from a live workshop to an e-learning module, etc.) using the feedback gathered by the L&D coordinator.
3. The L&D manager and the L&D coordinator discuss and decide jointly the scheduling and logistics of a new program launch.
4. The L&D coordinator discusses dates of regularly scheduled workshops with the various offices, then runs the final list by the L&D manager.
5. The L&D coordinator makes decisions regarding routine L&D session logistics (room location and setup, food, equipment requirements, etc.) on his or her own.

This example is meant for illustration purposes. Each organization and each manager–employee pair may reach different conclusions as to who should make what decisions. According to the concept of situational leadership,[3] managers need to adapt their leadership style to the level of skills and motivation of their employees. We encourage managers to add a cultural dimension here and adapt their leadership style based on an employee's sense of hierarchy.

Performance Management
The performance management system is a great tool to help hierarchical employees understand that they need to treat everyone with respect. When it is clear that input is collected from the employee's coworkers or direct reports to form the final performance evaluation, hierarchical employees realize they need to interact with everyone in a more equal manner. This supports and reinforces the messages they are getting through coaching, mentoring and/or training.

Managers can also use the performance management system and tools provided by their organization in order to teach hierarchical employees how to take initiative adequately. For example, here is how one of Lionel's managers, Brian, taught him how to take initiative:

Starting from a concrete problem that needed to be solved at that point, Brian asked me what my plan was. My reaction was something along the lines of, "I will come and ask you what to do."

Brian then asked me to think about ways the problem could be solved. Through patient communication, the two of us created a list of possible action steps that could be taken to solve this problem.

The next step was to evaluate these action steps in order to come up with a specific recommendation.

Once we had agreed on a course of action, Brian tied this exercise back to the performance management system and told me:

- If you come to me with a problem and ask me "What should I do?" I will give you an "Unsatisfactory" rating.
- If you come to me with a problem and an analysis of the situation, but no suggested solutions, I will probably give you a "Needs Improvement."
- If you come to me with a problem and a list of possible solutions but no recommendation, I will probably rate you as "Meets Expectations."
- If you come to me with a problem and a specific recommendation as to what you are going to do, I will probably rate you as "Exceeds Expectations." Note that your plan may include some very specific action items for me—for example, you may need me to talk to someone in another department. That's fine, as long as your request is very specific and is clearly something you cannot do on your own at this point.

Note the employee may come with a recommendation that is on the wrong track due to the limitations of his or her technical skills. Then the managers need to provide technical training, which is not the focus of this book.

Rewards

Similarly, the reward system can be used to help immigrants understand the behaviors expected of them. Hierarchical employees come from cultures where the gap in income between those at the top and those at the bottom of the organization is much larger than in North America. By explaining how the North American reward system works and comparing it with the reward system of organizations in their home countries, HR professionals and managers can help immigrants see that North American organizations value different skills and behaviors.

For example, some very competent and qualified technicians may earn more (in some cases, significantly more) than junior engineers in North America, a situation that is highly unlikely in the home countries of many immigrants. This difference clearly demonstrates the value placed by North American organizations on the competencies, experience and ability to solve practical problems that senior technicians bring to the table.

Similarly, helping hierarchical employees realize that the opinions of people who are lower than they are in the organization carry a significant weight in their performance appraisal and therefore in their raises and/or other incentives drives the point home that they need to treat everyone with consideration—not just the people above them. Since many immigrants came to North America for a better life and have a strong desire to succeed, they are strongly motivated by a reward system that clearly shows what behaviors are preferred.

Learning to read the reward system can make a major difference to people's careers because not all rewards come in the form of compensation or promotion. For example, one of the organizations we have worked with is a research center that has a very egalitarian culture, which initially confused many of the hierarchical immigrant researchers working there. There were only five levels in the organizations—technicians, researchers, team leads, lab managers and research center manager. The largest group was researchers (60% of the people fell in this category) followed by technicians (another 30%). There were only a dozen team leads, four lab managers and one research center manager. In this respect, people's career prospects were limited in the sense that the number of open managerial positions was quite small every year (in some years, there were none). Yet the organization provided people with concrete rewards that clearly indicated whether they were doing well or not:

- As a researcher, everyone could go to one conference per year; however, the conference one could attend often reflected one's standing in the organization. Everyone could attend a conference in Minneapolis or Winnipeg, but going to a conference in Hawaii, Asia or Europe was clearly an indication of how well people thought the researcher was doing.

- Similarly, how quickly one's equipment purchase requisitions were approved and how much money one could spend on new equipment also reflected how well people thought one was doing.

When hierarchical employees learn to pick up these signals, they can get a sense for whether they are doing well or not and measure their progress over time.

Environment—Sustaining Organizational Effectiveness

Leadership

Leading by example is critical to promote a culture aligned with the organization's business model and values. One of the key features of hierarchical societies is that the rules are not applied the same way to people at the top of society or the organization as they are to people below. In this respect, one of the most effective ways egalitarian managers can teach hierarchical immigrants how to operate within North American organizations is to show that they abide by the same rules as everyone else in the organization.

Here is one every concrete situation that illustrates this point very well.

I am a pharmacist in Ontario; I own one pharmacy in a small town. Last year, I had an intern who came from the Middle East. I was his preceptor for four months. At the end of his internship, we sat down together to reflect on what he had learned during his internship. Mohamed told me that the situation that struck him the most happened on his second day. I was filling some paperwork and he could see me from where he stood. He described the situation like this: At one point, I tore a piece of paper, crumpled it and threw it in the paper recycling bin. The bin was full, so the paper fell on the floor. He said that I got up, put it back into the bin and carried on. When I threw another piece of paper into the bin, it also fell on the floor, so I got up and emptied the bin in the large paper recycling bin at the back of the pharmacy.

I listened to his description of that event and could not figure out what was so striking about it, so I asked him. What he answered floored me. He said that in his home country, my reaction would have been totally different. I would have snapped my fingers, called one of the employees and told him or her to empty the bin at the back of the store. He said that he discussed this situation with his wife that night—it made him realize that being a good pharmacist in Canada meant something different than in his home country and that he needed to learn what that meant.

(Canadian pharmacist)

Organization Design

Organization design also plays an important role in how people approach their work. For example, most North American organizations have flatter structures than their immigrant employees are used to. The flat organization structure requires employees to become experts in certain areas in which their manager may not necessarily specialize. As a result, employees are required to take more initiative and have more decision-making latitude.

Many North American organizations also use a matrix structure, which requires that employees balance the needs and requirements of several people—their functional leaders and their project leaders, for example. This organization design is quite counterintuitive for hierarchical employees. In their mind, this implies that they have two full-time jobs—they are working eight hours a day for their functional leader and another eight hours a day for their project leader. It is very challenging for hierarchical employees to ask their managers to discuss their expectations and agree on one common set of priorities when the expectations of both managers add up to more than what employees can do in a single day.

Concretely, this means that North American organizations need to provide training, coaching and/or mentoring to their hierarchical immigrant employees so that they can learn the key skills required to operate effectively in an environment of a flat or matrix organization structure. The following questions need to be addressed:

- What are you expected to do when your functional leader and your project leader set different priorities?
- How is work organized in such an environment?
- How do you manage the flow of information?
- How is your performance evaluated?

Section 3.3: Individualism and Impact on Teamwork

Individualism is another cultural dimension that came out from Geert Hofstede's research. It refers to the extent to which people see themselves as self-contained entities (individualistic) or members of groups (collective). On a world scale, the US is the most individualistic country in the world (this point is usually obvious to most people, whether they are American or not), while Canada is slightly more collective (compare the health care system of both countries) but still high on the individualistic end of the spectrum. By contrast, most immigrants come from cultures that are significantly more collective than North America. Again this does not imply that they personally are more collective than the average American or Canadian. We need to observe people's behavior and not make assumptions based on where they come from.

For example, as shown in Figure 3.3, we write an envelope in the following way in North America:

The individual Jane is at the top of the pyramid. She is Jane, before she is part of the Doe family, then the place she works, then the city, then the province and the country.

In China, the envelope is written in the following way (Figure 3.4):

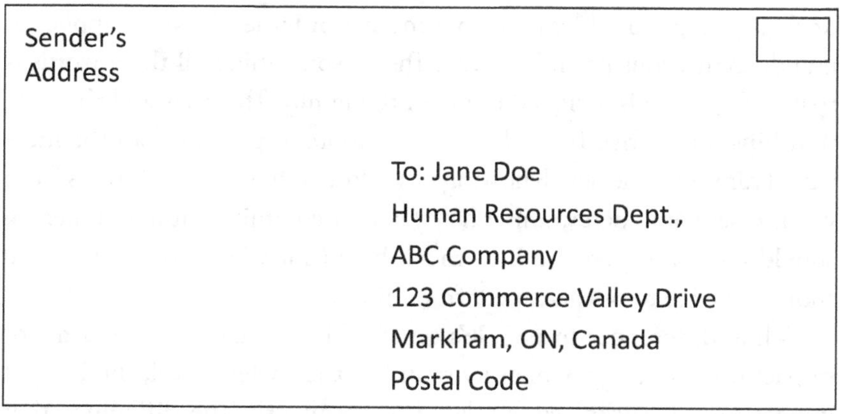

```
Sender's                                              ┌────┐
Address                                               │    │
                                                      └────┘


                        To: Jane Doe

                        Human Resources Dept.,

                        ABC Company

                        123 Commerce Valley Drive

                        Markham, ON, Canada

                        Postal Code
```

Figure 3.3 Envelope in North America

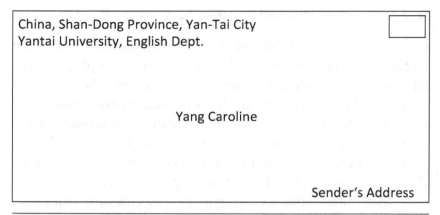

Figure 3.4 Envelope in China

The individual Caroline is at the bottom of the pyramid; she belongs to her country, then her province, then her city, then the place she works and her family before she is finally an individual.

The difference in the sense of individualism is embedded in the language. For example, Chinese people find it difficult to translate terms such as *brother, sister, aunt, uncle, grandfather* or *mother-in-law* into Chinese. The Chinese language has different words for brother or sister, depending on whether this sibling is older or younger than you are. It also has different words for aunt or uncle, depending whether this person is on your mother's side or on your father's side and whether this aunt or uncle is younger or older than your mother or father. This also applies to grandparents, cousins and in-laws. The reason behind all these words is that each person is assigned a role in the family. The roles and the relationships that derive from them are far more important than the individual himself or herself. Knowing how close or how far a relative is from you is essential to determining how far your commitment to that person should go—and therefore how much help (financial or otherwise) you should provide to or can expect from him or her.

While differences in people's sense of individualism have a major impact on people's personal lives and at the society level, the biggest impact in the workplace is related to teamwork. The difference that individualism makes in teamwork is clearly visible when you compare the way a Chinese restaurant operates with the way a North American restaurant operates:

- In a Chinese restaurant, all staff members are responsible collectively for all customers. When you raise your hand to ask for service, the person who comes to serve you is the person who is closest to your table at that moment. When you raise your hand the next time, a different person comes and serves you. Tips are pooled into a box and shared among all servers.
- In a North American restaurant, staff members have their assigned areas or tables. When you raise your hand to ask for service and the person who is closest to you at that moment is not your server, he or she says, "I will get your server." In other words, "I am not responsible for your table—I will get the person who is." Servers are rewarded by the tips from the tables they serve.

Picture the following situation: Let's take Chinese servers and put them in North American restaurants. How do other servers judge their performance if they operate the Chinese way? Chances are these Chinese servers are seen by their teammates as "meddling into everyone else's business" and "trying to steal my tips." If you ask them, "Are these Chinese servers good team players?" the overwhelming majority will answer "No way!" because they are judging the Chinese servers' performance by individualistic standards. By collective standards, these servers are great team players; unfortunately, they are playing different games.

The outcome is no better if we take American or Canadian servers and ask them to work in Chinese restaurants. If they operate the individualistic way, they are perceived as "lazy" and "selfish" (because they take care of only a few tables and keep tips from those tables). Again, if you ask their Chinese teammates whether they are good team players, the overwhelming answer is likely to be "No!" because they are using collective standards. By individualistic standards, these servers are great team players; unfortunately, they are playing different games.

Individualistic vs. Collective Teams

In our experience, this kind of dynamics is at play in many North American teams because many organizations have people who are at very different places on the individualism continuum. Figure 3.5 graphically represents the way individualistic people and collective people think of their teams (for simplicity, we are contrasting here the two ends of the spectrum).

In an individualistic team:

- Roles and responsibilities are clearly defined. As a matter of fact, individualistic teams cannot function without defining individual roles and responsibilities. This is the first order of business during the first team meeting. "Who is responsible for what?" and "Who is doing what?" are the key questions individualistic team members need to answer for themselves in order for the team to get started.
- Individualistic team members do not need to know one another well to get moving. Going around the table and stating your name, department and anticipated role in the team is usually sufficient.
- Information is shared within the team on a "need-to-know" basis. In practice, this means, "If you need the information I have to do your job, please ask and I will give it to you. I may also pass it on to

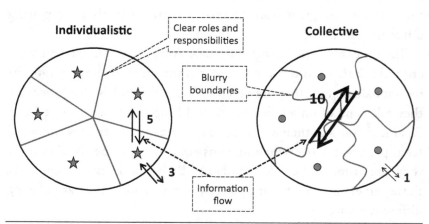

Figure 3.5 The Individualistic and Collective Mental Pictures of How a Team Operates

you without you asking because it seems to me that you may need this information to do your job."

- Information is shared with people outside the team also on a "need-to-know" basis. The difference between the flow rate of information within the team and the flow rate of information between the team and the rest of the organization is small—it is not difficult to obtain information about the progress of an individualistic team, even if you are not a member of that team.
- The motto of individualistic teams can be summarized as, "If I do my job and you do yours, we will reach our goal."

By contrast, in a collective team:

- Roles and responsibilities are not clearly defined. The boundaries between people's responsibilities are often blurred or simply do not exist (as in the case of Chinese restaurants). Everyone is responsible for reaching the common goal.
- For collective people, being on the same team generates significant responsibilities because teammates are expected to cover for one another. As a result, the key question during the first team meetings is, "Who is part of the team and who is not?" The thinking is that, "If you are part of my team, I need to cover for you; and I expect the same in return." People want to know how far their commitment goes.
- Information is shared extensively within the team. Every team member passes on every piece of information he or she obtains to every other team member. The logic is, "As soon as you become member of my team, you need to know all about what I am doing and I need to know all about what you are doing so that we can cover for each other effectively." The individualistic concept of "need to know" does not make sense to collective people—everyone needs to know everything.
- On the other hand, team members extensively discuss what information the team will share with people who are not part of the team. Collective teams want to avoid "airing their dirty laundry in public." Any information one team member considers communicating outside the team needs to be vetted by the rest of the team. Concretely,

this means it is often difficult to get information about the progress of a collective team if you are not a member of that team.

- The motto of collective teams can be summarized as "One for all, all for one!"

Mixed Teams

Most North American organizations have teams that include members from both individualistic and collective cultures, as shown in Figure 3.6. They each misinterpret the behavior of team members from the other culture and label them as "not a good team player." Collective team members may view individualistic team members as selfish and hoarding information, while the individualistic members' idea of good teamwork is to look after one's own responsibilities. Individualistic team members may view collective team members as meddling into other's affairs and wasting time, while the collective team members' idea of good teamwork is to help everyone else on the team.

One of the situations where the behavior expected of team members is quite different between an individualistic team and a collective team is when one team member (A) thinks another team member (B) is not taking care of a task properly:[4]

- In an individualistic team, A is expected to discuss this with B one on one, behind closed doors. If this does not work, A escalates the

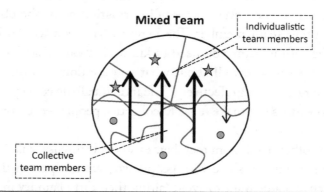

Figure 3.6 The Modus Operandi of a Mixed Team with Individualistic and Collective Members

issue to the manager, who then determines whether A has a point or B has everything under control and then decides to what extent he or she needs to get involved.

- In a collective team, A first brings this issue up during a team meeting. Everyone then tries to figure out whether A has a point or B has everything under control. If this does not yield the desired outcome, A jumps in and starts doing the task. A tells B something like, "I know you are really busy with [. . .], so I will get it started and you can take over when you are done with what you are currently doing."

Obviously, when teams include both individualistic and collective team members, everyone gets frustrated with their counterparts' way of managing their teammates' performance:

- Individualistic team members get quite irritated when collective team members mention an issue related to one of the tasks they are responsible for during a team meeting since they have not had a chance to discuss it privately before. Their reaction tends to be, "Let's take this off-line." Since collective team members do not get the reaction they are looking for, they go to the next step and start doing the tasks, thereby generating an even stronger negative reaction from their individualistic counterparts. To them, it means their collective teammates are telling them they are incompetent.
- Collective team members get quite confused when individualistic team members come and talk to them one on one about issues. Their reaction tends to be, "Let's discuss this during the next team meeting." When the manager comes and brings up the issue, many collective team members realize their individualistic teammate talked to the manager. To collective team members, this is tantamount to backstabbing.

Either way, people react quite negatively. To protect themselves, they stop giving information to their teammates. They also discuss the situation with like-minded teammates, and everyone agrees—we can't work with these people since they are not good team players. In many cases, the team breaks down completely, without anyone involved having any idea of what led to the breakdown.

Note that some collective employees may also be seen as poor team players because they show an unwillingness to help others. This is probably because they don't consider themselves part of the team. Immigrants often come from countries that are more densely populated than North America. Because one cannot help everyone, people must define the group they belong to; in most cases, this dictates how far they choose to go when it comes to helping others.

Section 3.4: Bridging the Individualism Gap

People—Building Awareness and Skills and Promoting Communication

Building Awareness and Skills

When we bring up individualism and its impact on teamwork during coaching or training sessions, it is clear that people have never realized the issues they observed were cultural in nature—they usually interpreted them as "performance problems" or "personality conflict." It is fascinating to see that individualistic people tend to interpret challenges from a personality perspective while collective people see far more cultural differences. In extreme cases, some very individualistic people have a hard time acknowledging the existence of culture itself. As a result, awareness is the key first step when trying to bridge the individualism gap.

As in the case of introversion and hierarchy, we bridge the individualism gap through a two-step process as shown in Tables 3.3.1 and 3.3.2:

Step 1: Determine, through observation of your colleagues' behavior, whether they are significantly more or less individualistic than you are.

Table 3.3.1 Individualistic and Collective Behaviors

	COMPARED WITH COLLECTIVE PEOPLE, INDIVIDUALISTIC PEOPLE TEND TO	COMPARED WITH INDIVIDUALISTIC PEOPLE, COLLECTIVE PEOPLE TEND TO
Language	• Use the word "I" extensively • Describe personal accomplishments	• Use the word "We" extensively • Describe group (department / company / team) accomplishments
Communication	• Have a narrow distribution of information (short cc list)	• Have wide distribution of information (long cc list)
Teamwork approach	• Follow the motto: "Let's each do our own job" • Focus on one's role and responsibilities • Not follow closely what other team members are doing • Provide help only upon request	• Follow the motto: "One for all, all for one" • Focus on relationships within the team • Keep track of what team members are doing • Provide help when they consider that help is needed (even when no help has been requested)
Decisions	• Make decisions based on the impact of these decisions on their own areas of responsibility • Expect people responsible for other areas to speak up if the decisions they make impact them aversely	• Make decisions based on the impact of these decisions on the whole group • Expect everyone to take into consideration the impact of their decisions on every other member of the team
Compensation	• Be motivated by individual incentives (as opposed to team or group incentives)	• Be motivated by team or group incentives (as opposed to individual incentives)
Networking	• Have their own, individual network that cannot be shared with others	• Share their network with other members of their group
Vacations	• Take their vacation alone or in a small group	• Take their vacation with others (family, organized tours, etc.)

As in the case of hierarchy/egalitarianism, individualism and collectivism are two sides of a continuum, not absolute or "black and white" concepts. Some people are more individualistic than others, and the country they come from is only one factor that drives their personal preference, so we need to look at everyone on an individual basis and observe them to understand their perspective.

Step 2: Once you have determined whether one of your colleagues is more or less individualistic than you are, you can modify your approach to this person to work more effectively with him or her.

Table 3.3.2 Working with Colleagues Who Are More or Less Individualistic

WHEN A COLLEAGUE IS MORE INDIVIDUALISTIC	WHEN A COLLEAGUE IS LESS INDIVIDUALISTIC
Focus on your own role and responsibilities and let your colleague take care of his or her own. Any attempt to influence or help is likely to be perceived as an intrusion. Wait until you are asked for help to provide it.	**Invest time to get to know your team members and build good working relationships.** Collective team members feel more comfortable working with people who they know and who have an interest in them.
Do not comment on other people's work unless you are asked. Help only when asked. If progress is not what you expect, talk to the manager and focus on how the lack of progress affects your area of responsibilities.	**Offer help more often than you normally would.** Many collective people's default answer is no when offered help because the assumption in their culture is that you will jump in to help. So ask a few times to make sure it is a true no.
Talk about your personal accomplishments. Learn to separate what the group did from what you did. Use the pronoun *I*.	**Talk about the team's accomplishments.** Learn to put forward what the group did rather than what you did. Beware of being perceived as taking credit for the work of the whole team. Avoid singling out individual accomplishments in public. Use the word *we* more frequently—at times, even if you did the work on your own.
Check whether you are providing too much information to your teammates. Ask yourself whether they really need to know what you are going to tell them. How will it help them do their job better? Don't hesitate to ask if you are not sure—you may get a response like, "Don't copy me on anything unless you expect me to take action."	**Check whether you are not providing enough information to your teammates.** Ask yourself whether they would like to have more information on what you do. What else would they like to know? Don't hesitate to ask—you may get a response like, "I don't mind being copied on everything—I will delete it if I think it is not relevant to me."
Speak up if your teammate's decisions have an impact on you. Do not expect your teammate to anticipate how these decisions affect your work. Tell your teammates how their decisions affect your work.	**Consider the impact of your actions and decisions on your teammates.** They expect that when you make a decision you balance the needs of the whole team and not focus only on your own area.

Promoting Communication

Everyone wants to be a good team player, but collective and individualistic team members have different ideas of what that means in practice. As a result, we find that the most important step team members can take to support their success as a team is to ensure there is good communication within the team (in particular, by applying the suggestions made in Section 2.4) and create opportunities for team members to discuss how team members interact with one another. Managers play a major role in helping multicultural teams become effective because managers often set the tone in their teams. From time to time, team members need to discuss how they operate as a team, either in team meetings or between individual members, and examine questions such as the following:

- Are we aligned on the team's priorities?
- Is the objective clear? Does everyone agree on the objective?
- Are there any unresolved issues?
- When we have issues, how do we resolve them?
- When two team members disagree or get into a conflict, how do we handle this?
- Is there any conflict we need to address?
- Is the workload well distributed within the team?
- Are some team members contributing more or less than their fair share?

Systems—Facilitating Collaboration through Processes

Work Processes and Tools

One effective work process to improve team effectiveness and resolve cultural differences in teamwork is the discussion around the roles and responsibilities of each team member. In our experience, because individualistic team members cannot operate without having gone through that discussion, it is rarely skipped. However, the important part here is to ensure that everyone understands what "being responsible" means. To individualistic people, this means, "I take care of it and nobody gets involved unless and until I ask for help or it is absolutely clear that I will fail (and make the team fail)."

A widely used tool in many North American organizations, the RACI (Responsible, Approve, Consult, Inform) matrix helps multicultural teams discuss roles and responsibilities. This tool aims at determining the level of involvement of the various team members when trying to achieve a specific objective. Mike Jacka and Paulette

Keller described RACI in their 2009 book, *Business Process Mapping: Improving Customer Satisfaction*, as follows (we apply it here to a document the team needs to create):

- **Responsible:** The person who is ultimately responsible for the outcome (here, the completion of the document), the doer
- **Approve:**[5] People who need to sign off on this document—they need to approve its content
- **Consult:** People whose opinion needs to be integrated in the document; note that the final version may not include all their suggestions
- **Inform:** People who need to be informed of the existence of the document but who do not need to be consulted

This tool is very helpful with multicultural teams for meeting management, project management or just managing the day-to-day interface. Applying this tool helps flush out key differences in perspectives:

- When individualistic and collective people work on a RACI matrix together, individualistic people tend to include fewer names compared to collective people because they focus on individual roles and responsibilities.
- By contrast, collective people include more names and tend to place them farther to the left on the RACI continuum than individualistic people. For example, collective people may think a person needs to approve a final draft when individualistic people think this person only needs to be consulted.
- A very telling difference usually appears when discussing who is responsible. In individualistic cultures, only one person can be responsible—a responsibility shared by several people is not owned by anyone, and nothing gets done. Collective people usually prefer to write down the name of a team or a department in the "R" column—not only is it not a problem to have several people responsible, but it is actually desirable in collective cultures.

We have seen organizations applying this tool so that the needs of individualistic team members for clarity of roles and responsibilities and the needs of collective team members for clarity of the connection between individual roles and responsibilities are both met.

Performance Management

In our experience, it is important for managers and HR professionals to understand the existence and impact of individualism differences so they can help employees understand the true nature of the issues they are facing. In particular, managers need to be trained to recognize the symptoms of situations when collective people are trying to be good team players but end up coming across as poor team players to their individualistic teammates:

- A collective team member keeps commenting on or getting involved in his or her teammates' areas of responsibilities
- A collective team member brings attention to the shortfalls of teammates during team meetings
- A collective team member makes another teammate feel incompetent by working on tasks that fall under this teammate's "jurisdiction"

For example, a manager told his HR business partner that while one of his employees was really helpful to everyone in the team, he had to rate her as "not meeting expectations" because she did not meet her own targets. While this rating sends a clear message to the employee, it is also important that the manager helps the employee understand exactly what behavior she needs to change:

- She needs to determine when she should focus on her own deliverables (as opposed to helping others) and how to do that in a way that does not come across as rude or selfish.
- She needs to learn to identify when to get involved in other people's work because they truly need help and how to renegotiate her deliverables with the manager in such a situation.

The manager can also build on this employee's strength and make training or mentoring junior team members part of her goals—in other words, including "helping others" in her responsibilities. It becomes a win–win situation for both the employee and the team.

Rewards

Coupled with the performance management system, the reward system clearly drives employees to behave the way the organization wants them to behave. The key question that HR professionals need to ask themselves is as follows: To what extent does the organization want to reward individual performance relative to collaboration? Too little reward for individual performance may dilute people's sense of responsibility and ownership while too much may create a competitive environment with little collaboration. In other words, do I get a bonus because I achieved my own targets, or do we get a bonus because we achieved our group target? Consider the following situation, which took place in one large North American consumer product company.

Its operations in the European Union (EU) were split on a country basis; each country was headed by a country manager, who had profit and loss responsibilities for this country and was rewarded accordingly. Salary increases and bonuses of country managers were tied to the profit made by the organization in their country. While it looked like this was the best way to maximize profit initially, people in the US corporate head office realized it actually led to significant duplication. In some cases, the organization had plants making the same products on two sides of a border. Some of these plants were less than fifty kilometers apart. All attempts at rationalizing production on an EU-wide basis failed until the reward system was changed to tie the country managers' bonuses to the profit made on the EU basis. To be specific, raises remained based on the country's performance while 50 percent of their bonus was tied to their country's performance and the other 50 percent was tied to the performance of the organization at the EU level.

In our experience, it is important for HR professionals and managers to communicate how the compensation system works and to describe what behaviors are expected to be rewarded by the organization. Because they are usually quite driven to succeed in North America, many immigrants adapt their behaviors to meet the expectations of their organization.

Environment—Building High Performance Teams

Leadership

One key responsibility of managers and HR professionals is to help the team move as quickly as possible from one stage of team development to the next. There are many team development models. One of the widely applied is the four-stage model created by Bruce Tuckman:[6]

- **Forming:** Team members get together and determine roles and responsibilities.
- **Storming:** Issues invariably arise since people have different ideas of how to get work done.
- **Norming:** Team members agree on how to work together.
- **Performing:** The team works effectively together and becomes a high performance team.

It usually takes longer for multicultural teams to get through the forming, storming and norming stages and reach the performing stage because the starting points of team members are farther apart. Homogeneous teams can quickly agree on default behaviors for the team because everyone has learned the same behaviors since childhood. Members of a multicultural team have to discuss and agree on more rules of engagement because what constitutes acceptable behavior depends on the cultural context. We have helped several organizations go through the following exercises:

- **Initiate discussions for the team to create a common vision and mission,** then develop long-term and short-term goals that all team members support. We have observed many occasions where managers think the goals are very clear even though different team members have very different understandings of the team goals.
- **Create a forum to review the results and revisit the goals** when new information becomes available.
- **Develop team rules of engagement** so all team members know how they are expected to behave, and provide an opportunity for team members to bring up issues when some members don't follow the rules of engagement.

Organization Design

Managers and HR professionals can help multicultural teams move more quickly from one stage to the next by keeping team composition constant over time. In our experience, many North American organizations change the composition of teams more frequently than multicultural team members can manage. Every time team members leave and are replaced by new people, the team has to circle back, at least to some extent, to the first stage (forming) and move forward from there. Since it takes much longer for multicultural teams to go through the four stages of team development, relative organization stability ensures the organization capitalizes on the investment it has made in teams that have reached the high performing stage.

Section 3.5: Risk Tolerance and Impact on Project Management

The last concept we cover in this chapter is risk tolerance. Risk tolerance is modeled after Hofstede's uncertainty avoidance—it measures how comfortable people are when handling uncertainty and risk.[7] Risk tolerance translates directly into the following question: How much information do you need to make a decision and feel comfortable that you have made the right decision? The more risk tolerant people are, the less information they need to make a given decision.

Based on Hofstede's study, the US and Canada are on the higher end of risk tolerance whereas most the regions from which immigrants come—Latin America, the Middle East and most of Europe and Asia—are less risk tolerant. Risk tolerance is an interesting dimension and requires even more observation on an individual basis to avoid stereotypes. For example, two developed economies in Asia, Japan and Hong Kong, are on the opposite side the continuum. People who have done business with the Japanese (very low risk tolerance) often find that the Japanese ask for a lot of information including information that is considered irrelevant by North American standards, and the negotiation takes much longer than expected. In Hong Kong (very high risk tolerance), people make multimillion dollar business decisions with much less information, and the stock market is the hottest chit-chat topic at dim sum on Sunday morning.

For North American organizations, risk tolerance has a major impact on the following:

- **The financial industry:** The kind of investments people buy, the extent to which they borrow money, the kind of loans they get when they do (e.g., fixed-rate vs. variable-rate mortgage) and how far into the future they plan are all significantly affected by the extent to which they can tolerate risk.
- **The accounting profession:** For example, risk tolerance determines the threshold above which a transaction becomes material and needs to be audited in detail. Risk tolerant audits use higher thresholds than risk averse audits do.
- **Scientific and technical professions:** Risk tolerance translates into the number of experiments you need to run, the number of samples you need to take or the number or variables you have to study in order to prove your point.

In our experience, differences in risk tolerance create extensive frustration within project teams (particularly technical teams) because risk tolerant people and risk averse people do not manage projects the same way. Since they often are not aware they are dealing with cultural differences, this often creates significant challenges because it leads people to question the competencies of their culturally different counterparts. At the same time, risk tolerance is one of the areas where cultural differences can generate the most benefits for organizations (see more on this point in Chapter 8).

Figure 3.7 looks at two teams, one risk tolerant team and one risk averse team, who are both trying to go from the same starting point to the same end point, and graphically contrasts the way these two teams progress:

- A risk tolerant team starts moving quickly—they do not spend much time planning the execution of their project up front. As they move, they keep adjusting the general direction based on the data they collect along the way. As long as they are getting closer to their goals, they consider themselves to be making progress, even if progress is not a straight line.

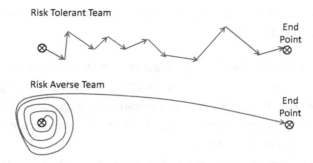

Figure 3.7 Risk Tolerant vs. Risk Averse Approach to Project Management

- A risk averse team starts by planning extensively. They collect data—usually more data than risk tolerant people think is necessary. In extreme cases, they collect data that risk tolerant people consider irrelevant. They also look at contingencies in order to be ready if and when events do not unfold as expected. When they feel they have a good overall plan that addresses both the base case and the necessary contingencies, they make a swift move.

Who reaches the goal first? In our experience, one approach is not inherently better than the other. The approach best suited to a particular situation depends on a number of factors, including the industry. The risk tolerant approach is not well-suited to the nuclear or airline industries, for example, whereas the risk averse approach is rarely applied in the software industry. In our experience, one of the important factors determining the effectiveness of a team is the level of skills of its members:

- A poorly skilled risk tolerant team may start moving in the wrong direction, and it takes time for them just to get back to the starting point. They may also be "oscillating"—they change direction so drastically at each step that their progress is very slow, which creates a lot of frustration in the team.
- A poorly skilled risk averse team may get stuck in a "do loop"— "analysis paralysis" sets in and they never move. The other potential downfall is that by the time they decide to make their move, market conditions have changed to the point that their original objective is no longer valid.

Section 3.6: Bridging the Risk Tolerance Gap

People—Building Awareness and Skills and Promoting Communication

Building Awareness and Skills

In our experience, the vast majority of managers and HR professionals have not realized there is a cultural difference here. Therefore, building awareness is the key first step when trying to bridge the risk tolerance gap. Helping people realize they are experiencing frustration because they were trained to approach problems in different ways generates an incredible amount of goodwill for the team to look for solutions together.

As in the case of hierarchy and individualism, we bridge the risk tolerance gap through a two-step process as shown in Tables 3.4.1 and 3.4.2:

Step 1: Determine, through observation of your counterparts' behavior, whether they are significantly more or less risk tolerant than you are.

Table 3.4.1 Risk Tolerant and Risk Averse Behaviors

	COMPARED WITH RISK AVERSE PEOPLE, RISK TOLERANT PEOPLE TEND TO	COMPARED WITH RISK TOLERANT PEOPLE, RISK AVERSE PEOPLE TEND TO
Planning	• Plan over a shorter period of time	• Plan over a longer period of time
Decisions	• Make decisions at a very early stage of the project • Ask that the team keeps moving • Want to avoid "collecting data for the sake of collecting data" or "analysis paralysis"	• Take a long time to make a decision • Ask for more data or information in order to have a "good grasp of the situation" and to ensure they are moving in the right direction
Problem solving	• Want to focus on variables most likely to have an impact on the problem • Focus more on practice, rules of thumb and empirical formula	• Want to do a thorough job and examine all possible variables • Focus more on theory and differential equations derived analytically
Presentations	• Use a limited amount of data to support their points • Focus on the implications of their work for the future and for their audience	• Use large amount of data to support their points • Focus on convincing their audience that they have looked at all possible aspects of the issue
Career management	• Prefer more entrepreneurial organizations (including start-ups)	• Prefer more established organizations (ideally government or Fortune 500 companies)

(Continued)

Table 3.4.1 (*Continued*)

	COMPARED WITH RISK AVERSE PEOPLE, RISK TOLERANT PEOPLE TEND TO	COMPARED WITH RISK TOLERANT PEOPLE, RISK AVERSE PEOPLE TEND TO
Compensation	• Be willing to take greater risk to get larger financial reward • Welcome compensation plans that have a higher upside based on performance such as commission	• Prefer job stability over higher income • Avoid variable compensation plans such as working on commission
Vacations	• Prefer spur-of-the-moment vacation plans	• Plan vacations well in advance

Like hierarchy and individualism, risk tolerance is a continuum, and people can be anywhere on the scale. People's risk tolerance is usually fairly visible to all team members. When we bring up this topic during workshops for intact teams, participants spontaneously point to the more risk tolerant and the more risk averse members of their teams. Identifying who is more or less risk tolerant than oneself is quite intuitive to most people.

Step 2: Once you have determined whether your counterpart is more or less risk tolerant than you are, you can modify your approach to work more effectively with this person.

Table 3.4.2 Working with People Who Are More or Less Risk Tolerant

WHEN A COUNTERPART IS MORE RISK TOLERANT	WHEN A COUNTERPART IS LESS RISK TOLERANT
Forego some data collection. The team may decide to move forward, even though you consider that there remains a large area of uncertainty and risk.	**Collect more data and information.** The team may decide that more data and information are needed than you think.
Demonstrate the value and necessity of the additional data you want to collect. If your colleague wants to move ahead, he or she is unlikely to accept the idea of stopping and waiting for the collection of additional information. You will need to build a case and demonstrate the need for this information. How much uncertainty is there without additional data? How much does this uncertainty affect the possible outcomes of the project?	**Demonstrate the value of moving ahead.** If your colleague thinks that more data are needed, he or she is unlikely to accept the idea of moving along. You will need to build a case for moving forward. How much will the project gain by moving forward? What is the cost of collecting this additional data? How can the team gather data as you go, rather than wait until the data are collected?

(*Continued*)

Table 3.4.2 (*Continued*)

WHEN A COUNTERPART IS MORE RISK TOLERANT	WHEN A COUNTERPART IS LESS RISK TOLERANT
Stay the course. Your risk tolerant colleague may change directions quickly. On some occasions, this may lead them to change course several times before coming back to the original course. Waiting for the high frequency noise to die down may limit the amount of "spinning" you experience. At the same time, when it is clear that the team has decided to change direction, adjust accordingly.	**Give him or her time to get used to a change in direction.** A risk averse colleague is likely to take more time than you do to adjust to a sudden change (such as a new project direction or a new manager).

Promoting Communication

Once you have identified whether your counterpart is more or less risk tolerant than you and some of the actions you could take to bridge the gap, communication becomes the key. Take the example of communicating commitment. If you know your risk averse colleague will never say, "Don't worry, I'll take care of everything. No problem," you will not press him or her to use these words to express his or her commitment. On the other hand, if you know your risk tolerant colleague will always say, "Don't worry. I'll take care of everything. No problem," you may want to probe and ask specific questions such as, "How confident are you in getting this done by Monday? 80 percent? 90 percent?"

Since the main challenge resulting from differences in risk tolerance among team members is the amount of data needed to make a given decision, it is important to discuss this point as a team. Team members need to feel they can challenge the team's decision to either collect more data or move forward without studying something further. They need a process they can leverage to discuss the pros and cons of collecting more information versus moving forward and to achieve the concrete outcome they want to see. Even if some members feel the team is moving too fast, or not moving fast enough, they at least understand the compromise they are making and why. Agreeing on key milestones, how and how often to check progress, meets the needs of both risk tolerant and risk averse team members.

Team members also need to discuss how far they need to plan into the future since "short term" and "long term" can mean different things to different people. Two years is long term for many North American organizations and short term for most Japanese organizations. Short term or long term is relative to people's sense of risk tolerance. People involved need to **communicate** and become very clear on the specifics. Don't stop at agreement in general because it will lead to nasty surprises down the road.

Systems—Converging through Processes

Work Processes and Tools

Many organizations have work processes set up that are consistent with their organization's risk tolerance level. For example, the public sector and the financial services industry usually have more rigorous approval processes for any spending, while the technology industry sets very aggressive time targets for new product development. One business leader we worked with said, "When an employee makes a serious mistake that costs the company money, customers or reputation, it's not the employee's fault. It's our fault. We need to set up systems to catch and prevent those kind of mistakes." So organizations need to do the following:

Explain these work processes to employees, especially those from different cultures. When the parameters of the process are not clear, have a process to discuss and clarify them. For example, allocate time at each project status or department meeting to discuss whether team members feel they are making progress or if anyone has any concerns.

Create checks and balances for tasks that are prone to human error. For example, when Caroline worked as a compensation specialist, her manager created a peer review process where not only the manager checked Caroline's work, but Caroline also checked her manager's work before sending it for approval or communicating to employees.

Performance Management and Rewards

It is very important for organizations to align the employees' behaviors with the organization's risk tolerance level though the performance management and rewards system. If the organization promotes innovation and risk taking, the managers need to encourage employees to learn from their mistakes rather than reprimand every small error.

Obviously, if an employee consistently fails to learn from his or her mistakes and exposes the organization to larger risks, that employee needs to understand that he or she needs to change behavior to be in line with the organization's risk taking level.

Environment—Leading by Example

Leading by example is key to teach employees the risk taking behaviors their organization wants to see. Here is a situation we witnessed (similar situations happen in many organizations on many occasions):

The team needed to make a decision in a situation it had never encountered before. They did not have all the information, but they needed to move forward. The manager said, "Let's give it a try. If it doesn't work, I will take the responsibility." Down the road, the team realized it was the wrong decision. The manager kept his word and encouraged the team to both learn from this mistake and look for new solutions. If in such a situation the manager had turned around and blamed others or, worse, blamed his or her employees for the mistake, the team would not have learned to take risks or make decisions.

* * *

Hierarchy, individualism and risk tolerance do not occur in isolation. Hofstede has analyzed the interactions between the different cultural dimensions. Managers and HR professionals may find them coming into play all at once in any given situation. Here is an example shared by an HR director that illustrates these cultural factors at play and how an HR team resolved the differences:

My team implemented a new salary band system after conducting market benchmarking and job evaluation. At the end of the annual performance review and salary increase process, the team decided we would give every employee a letter stating their performance rating and new salary as a way to improve communication, but the team ran into a disagreement. One of the four HR managers, Alice, wanted to include the salary range for each employee in the letter. She believed it would give the employees more information about the rewards program and motivate them to work hard to progress through the salary band. Another HR manager, Hiroshi, was not comfortable with sharing this information. He felt that the first year of implementing the salary band should be a pilot where we tested the effectiveness and improved it for the next year before communicating it to the whole organization.

I encouraged the whole team to discuss the pros and cons of sharing this information. Each team member expressed their thoughts one way or the other. In the end, I thought the best was to let each HR manager make the decision in partnership with the head of his or her business unit. Since the HR managers were accountable for supporting the respective management teams they knew well and worked closely with, I did not want to dictate the decision, and one of them should not be able to force his or her decision on others. As a result, two HR managers decided their employee communication letter would include the salary range information, while two other HR managers decided they would not include that information for the first year. The communication went well in all four business units, despite the minor difference.

It is clear that the two HR managers, Alice and Hiroshi, have very different risk tolerance. Their manager has a very egalitarian approach to decision making and facilitated a communication process for the team to express their views. In the end, each team member was given the latitude to make his or her decision and take ownership for implementing it. The result also shows that one approach is not inherently better than another. What is important is that the team becomes stronger through this collaborative problem-solving process.

Section 3.7: Who Should Adapt to Whom?

Before ending this chapter, we want to address the crucial question: Who should adapt to whom? We are asked this question at least once at every workshop, and there are two parts of this question:

- To what extent do immigrants need to adapt to North American culture in order to integrate into our organization?
- To what extent do organizations and employees born and educated in North America need to adapt to help immigrants integrate?

Figure 3.8 graphically represents our thoughts on this question. If the horizontal bar represents the gap between Canadians or Americans on one side and immigrants to Canada or the US on the other side, what

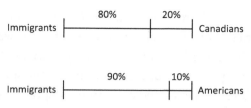

Figure 3.8 Splitting the Responsibility for Adaptation

percentage of the gap is each group expected to bridge? We find that the answer to this question is cultural in nature:

- In Canada, most people (whether they are Canadians or immigrants) answer 80/20. Most immigrants to Canada expect to make the bulk of the adaptation themselves because they chose to come to Canada. Coming from hierarchical cultures, where minorities are usually expected to adapt to the majority to a greater extent than in egalitarian cultures, making more than 50 percent of the adaptation is obvious to them. In turn, the average Canadian is fine with making 20 percent of the adaptation—going some of the way is okay, but meeting halfway does not seem fair to most Canadians. We do run into some immigrants who wish the split was 50/50 and some Canadians who wish it was 100/0 (meaning that immigrants make all the adaptation), but it is rare—most people in Canada agree that 80/20 is a fair split of responsibilities.
- In the US, the split tends to be 90/10. When Lionel described the split of responsibility as 80/20 there, American audience members stopped him and said "20% is too much—10% is okay." The difference is quite visible when it comes to the use of English language. In the US, there is a strong belief that everyone must speak English. Joe Wong, a Chinese who went to the US to study a Ph.D. in biochemistry but became a comedian, joked that he found a bumper sticker that said "Go home if you don't speak English" on the used car he bought only two years later. In Canada, people are more patient with colleagues or customers speaking English as a second language. Canadian banks and airlines actively advertise the diverse language capabilities of their staff as a competitive advantage.

- In many Western European countries (France, Germany, Italy, the UK), the situation is quite clear: "You adapt to us, we do not adapt to you." To integrate in France, Germany, Italy or the UK, immigrants need to make most of the adaptation—the split there is 99/1.
- In China, Korea or Japan, the concept of adaptation does not exist. You are either Japanese or you are not; you cannot become Japanese. Similarly, nobody can become Aboriginal in Canada or Native American in the US; you are or you are not. A good case in point is the announcement made by the Xinhua News Agency when Rewi Alley died. Rewi Alley was a New Zealander who went to China in 1927 to start an industrial cooperative. Because of the Japanese invasion, his efforts turned into rescuing orphans, raising them and providing them with an education in his industrial cooperative. He lived and worked in China all his life, a total of 60 years, through all the wars and revolutions. When he died in 1987, Xinhua News Agency announced his death by stating, "Today we lost a great friend of the Chinese people," and he was awarded a medal as one of "China's Ten Most Important Foreign Friends." If you think of the reverse situation—that is, someone who grew up in China and spent 60 years of his or her life in Canada or the US doing all sorts of good deeds for Canadians or Americans—chances are very high that when that person dies, Canadian or American newscasts will say, "Today we lost a great Canadian or American."

So the way we split the responsibility of adaptation depends on our culture. However, trying to find the "right split" is, in our experience, not the most productive use of people's time because agreeing on the split is not the real issue. In most situations, the real issue is that the gap is much bigger than everyone imagines. Figure 3.9 graphically represents the real situation: Because the gap is much bigger than everyone thinks, everybody responds at one point or another by saying or thinking, "I have done my part—now it is your turn to bridge the rest of the gap." The real challenge is therefore to bring the full extent of the gap into the open and to make it visible and conscious so we can work on it together. This is where the recommendations in this book become really useful—when people have made the conscious decision that they want to do their part in bridging the gap.

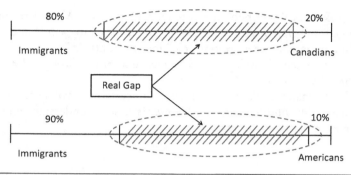

Figure 3.9 The Real Gap

We refer to this model in later chapters, as the split of responsibilities also depends on the business situation. A North American organization trying to sell its products and services overseas needs to adapt to a greater extent to the local culture and way of doing business (in this situation, the responsibility is likely to be split 20/80 the other way—the North American organization needs to make the bulk of the adaptation) than a North American organization that offshores work to an Indian or Chinese supplier, or two multinational corporations forming a joint venture (here, the responsibility of adaptation is probably split more equally between the two parties).

Notes

1. Hofstede uses the term *Power Distance* in *Cultures and Organizations: Software of the Mind.*
2. This is from a questionnaire that we use in our coaching program for international assignees. In this study, all respondents do similar work (audit) and have between three and ten years of experience. They are rated above average in their home countries (all are sent on international assignments). In other words, we are comparing professionals who do the same kind of work in different countries—we are not comparing the average person in each country.
3. Hersey, Paul, and Ken H. Blanchard: *Management of Organizational Behavior: Utilizing Human Resources*, 3rd ed. Englewood Cliffs New Jersey: Prentice Hall, 1977.
4. Chapter 8 of Laroche and Rutherford's *Recruiting, Retaining and Promoting Culturally Different Employees* contains a more detailed description of this situation—here we are presenting a summary in order to concentrate on solutions.

5. The Jacka and Keller book uses the term *Accountable*. Many later models changed it to *Approve* to make it easier to use, as many people find it hard to differentiate between "responsible" and "accountable."
6. Bruce Tuckman: "Developmental Sequence in Small Groups." *Psychological Bulletin* 63, no. 6 (1965): 384–99.
7. Hofstede made a distinction between uncertainty avoidance and risk avoidance. We find the term *risk tolerance* is easier to understand and apply in an everyday work context.

Managing a Multicultural Workforce

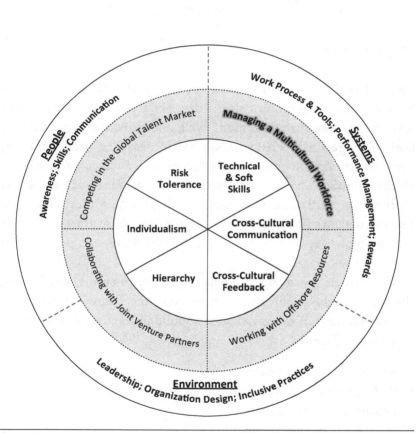

Figure 4.0 Roadmap of the Book

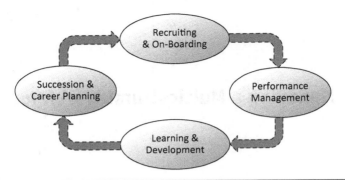

Figure 4.1 Talent Management Cycle

To further the discussions in Chapters 2 and 3, this chapter analyzes the challenges multicultural organizations experience at each stage of the talent management cycle and provides suggestions to both managers and HR professionals on how to bridge the gap between immigrants and North American educated professionals so that immigrants can contribute to the organization's success to their full potential. As discussed in Chapter 3, while immigrants need to make the majority of the adaptation, there are a number of action steps that North American organizations can take to help them.

While there are many different ways of segmenting and labeling the stages in the talent management cycle, the following four stages encompass most of the key elements found in the majority of models as shown in Figure 4.1:

- Recruiting and on-boarding
- Performing and performance management
- Learning and development
- Succession and career planning

Section 4.1: Recruiting and On-Boarding

Issues at the Résumé Screening Stage: Generalist vs. Specialist

Sarah is the recruiter of a large oil and gas company based in Alberta. She is recruiting for a process engineer position with the following key responsibilities: Work with lead engineer in the review of process engineering deliverables, including heat and material balances, process flow diagrams, piping and instrumentation diagram, equipment datasheets and design criteria.

She ran into a résumé with ten bullet points highlighting the candidate's qualifications, which started with the following:

- Over ten years of experience in project management, engineering and construction supervision in a broad range of industries (oil and gas and mining, manufacturing, utilities and services)
- Managed and coordinated projects from design to completion and ensured implementation according to specifications, time and budgets

The next eight bullet points emphasized the applicant's experience in management, business negotiation, construction schematics, quality control, entrepreneurial skills and various industries. After that, the employment history started, with the following position at the bottom of the first page:

- Business Development Coordinator, Global Educational and Consulting Services

Glancing through the second page, Sarah read that the candidate worked as an engineering manager and as an engineer in several engineering contracting companies; he put forward his experience in management and business development, but his résumé did not make the connection between any of the technical problems he had solved in the past and the job requirement. Sarah put the résumé in the "no" pile.

This situation illustrates what often happens at the résumé screening stage: The résumés of recent immigrants make them appear as if they can do anything and everything. Some of their experiences are related to the position for which they have applied, but the descriptions of these experiences are scattered all over the résumé and buried deep in the second and third page among words unrelated to the position's requirements.

The reason recent immigrants describe their qualifications in broad terms is because most immigrants come from countries where the percentage of people who have postsecondary education is much smaller than in North America. A university degree opens many doors in their home countries because it means they have demonstrated the ability to think and problem solve at a certain level and therefore can learn to function in many jobs. Because there are more positions than candidates at the college/university level, organizations tend to place people wherever the need is most pressing; as a result, the careers of many immigrants in their home countries span many professions and industries. For example, before immigrating to Canada, Caroline worked as the following:

- An English instructor at a university
- A translator/interpreter
- A contract administrator in the procurement department of an American oil company
- A human resources manager for the Chinese subsidiaries of two multinational corporations

As a result, when recent immigrants look for work, they present their broad knowledge in many professional areas and industries, hoping that it increases their chances of finding employment, as represented by the horizontal box in Figure 4.2.

This approach is often unsuccessful in North America because organizations value specialized knowledge and experience, as represented by the vertical box in Figure 4.2. Here, many people have college or university degrees, so organizations can choose among a slate of candidates who all have relevant experience.

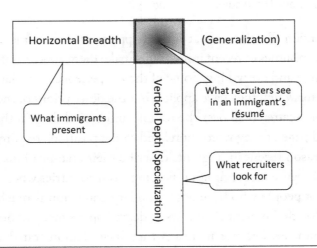

Figure 4.2 Generalist vs. Specialist Approach

This is particularly striking in Canada. Being located next to the largest economy in the world, Canadian organizations cannot compete with their US counterparts on size or price, so they compete through specialization—they focus on niche marketing. The Web sites of most Canadian organizations start with the words "We specialize in. . . ." Obviously, the specialization of organizations drives the specialization of employees—Canadian and American organizations are looking for depth of experience rather than breadth. As shown in Figure 4.2, because recruiters only have an average of thirty seconds to scan each résumé, they only see a very small portion of the candidate's qualification—that is, the shaded area. Many "diamond-in-the-rough" immigrants are overlooked as a result.

Issues at the Interview Stage: Lack of Fit or Canadian Experience

Janet is the HR manager of a nonprofit organization in a large US city. Today, she and a panel of colleagues are interviewing several candidates. The receptionist called her to let her know that the next one has arrived, so she goes to the reception area to meet him. The candidate does not look at her when greeting her; when she extends her hand, he keeps his at his side and does not shake hers. He follows her to the interview room, where he greets Janet's three male colleagues and shakes their hands. During the whole interview, he only looks at the male interviewers and never looks at Janet, even when the question comes from her.

When the interview panel debriefs the interview, they agree that this candidate has the right technical skills for the job but will not fit within the organization since about half of the staff and even more of the organization's clients are women. If this candidate cannot face a female HR manager during an interview, it will be very difficult for him to relate to female clients and interact productively with female colleagues. Since the organization values respect and diversity among all employees and clients, they do not want to risk their reputation.

This situation illustrates the next challenge, which usually comes up at the interview stage, where the soft skills of candidates are assessed. We discussed in Chapter 2 that there are many ways people can misunderstand each other when communicating across cultures. Recent immigrant candidates often come across as a little strange. For example, they may stand too close or too far when they first meet an interviewer. Some may refuse to shake hands with interviewers of the opposite gender, as in the previous example. Some may not make enough eye contact. Some candidates may answer the question "tell me about yourself" with a ten-minute account of their whole family history. In most cases, it is not one specific thing the candidate said or did poorly that leads recruiters to conclude that some immigrants are not the best candidates for the job, but rather a collection of small things, each trivial in isolation, that add up to a negative impression. When the candidate calls to ask why he or she is not going forward in the process, in the US, they often hear "you are not a good fit," whereas in Canada they often hear "you don't have Canadian experience."

We spoke with a number of HR professionals and hiring managers, asking them to define "fit" and "Canadian experience," because some of them did hire recent immigrants who had not worked in the US or Canada before. People mentioned words such as *attitude, initiative, enthusiasm, getting along with coworkers*—in other words, soft skills. One Canadian manager jokingly said that "having survived one Canadian winter" is part of what he calls "Canadian experience." Through such conversations, the people we spoke to came to the realization that Canadian experience is not the same as having worked in Canada, just like fit does not mean having worked in the US.

The HR professionals also realized they used similar responses for students and new college graduates. When new graduates do not demonstrate the soft skills required for a position, they are told after the interview that they "lack relevant work experience." However, it was clear from their résumés that they had not worked in the field yet (in other words, the recruiters did not need to bring them in for an interview to find that out). The manager of a health science laboratory said that she does not hire students who do not show respect for the lab environment, even if they have great GPAs. The challenge is that, in many cases, it is very difficult to articulate one's expectation of candidate behaviors; this lab manager tells unsuccessful candidates that they are not a good fit, which is an accurate description of the situation as far as she is concerned.

Bridging the Cultural Gap in the Hiring Process

Over the years, we have worked with many organizations that have developed approaches to expand their talent pool to new immigrants and/or look for candidates outside North America. Here is a summary of some best practices following our People–Systems–Environment solutions framework:

People—Building Awareness and Skills
and Improving Communication

Train the people involved in your recruitment and selection process. This training helps HR professionals and hiring decision makers understand the cultural differences immigrant applicants bring in their résumés and interviews. They can learn to adjust their communication style to culturally different candidates and find ways to obtain the information necessary to accurately assess the skills of these candidates.

For example, as mentioned in Chapter 2, people from East Asian cultures often leave a long silence during conversations, longer than many North American recruiters are comfortable with. Some interviewers interpret this pregnant pause as meaning the candidate either does not understand the question or does not know how to answer it, so they ask the same question again, rephrase it or start answering it as a way to prompt the candidate. In all cases, the candidate is likely to interpret the situation as if the recruiter simply took a breath, and the candidate is waiting patiently for a long enough silence to know it is his or her turn to speak. Here is a simple way interviewers can set the stage appropriately:

> I will ask you behavioral interview questions. I expect you to answer these questions by describing past examples. I know it is hard to come up with an appropriate answer on the spot. So if you are thinking and there is a silence, it's okay. I know you are thinking and will wait for you to speak up.

Give the benefit of the doubt to English as a second language (ESL) candidates during telephone interviews. Since there is no opportunity to observe nonverbal cues, phone interviews are very difficult for people who speak English as a second language and may not provide an accurate representation of the candidate's ability to communicate in the workplace. Obviously, if communicating by telephone is an important part of the job, this would be an important criterion in the selection process. For positions that do not require extensive telephone interactions, we suggest that HR professionals and hiring managers bring ESL candidates in for a face-to-face interview whenever possible. When we coach immigrants or international assignees, it is much easier to communicate face-to-face than over the phone.

Focus on transferrable skills. Overlook the mismatched job titles and industries and read between the lines of weird words or terms to look for common themes. For example, one of the immigrants we coached was a textile engineer who held several seemingly unrelated positions—he worked as a service center manager in a textile-manufacturing machinery company, as an inventory controller in a garment making factory and as a lecturer of textile engineering. His key skills were process and quality improvement; he was a certified Six Sigma Black Belt. Everywhere he went, he improved productivity significantly. One of the major Canadian banks hired him to spearhead the bank's process improvement initiatives, and he achieved significant cost savings for this organization.

Systems—Increasing Effectiveness through Work Processes
Create clear and specific position descriptions. Identifying, listing and clearly differentiating "must have" and "nice to have" skills helps candidates figure out whether they are qualified for the position or not. Many North American job postings contain a long list of characteristics the successful candidate needs to have. While these characteristics may appear to be equally weighted, the reality is often different. In most cases, a few of these characteristics are "must haves" while the others are "nice to haves." For example, how important is the ability to write English well (without spelling mistakes or typos) or to express oneself well for this position? This varies significantly from software

developer positions (where it does not matter much) to public relations positions (where this is a critical requirement).

While clear and accurate job descriptions can help all applicants, they can be especially helpful to people coming from different cultures. Think through the levels of skills required for the job. Use words that truly describe the job duties and qualifications. Caroline has helped hiring managers select the right words—for example, use *manage* and *lead* to describe a manager's duties and *coordinate* and *assist* to describe a coordinator's tasks.

Incorporate cultural competence in the job requirement when applicable, and develop assessment tools and criteria. Going back to Caroline's story at the beginning of Chapter 1, the hotel chain could include "cultural competence or cultural fluency" in all customer facing (or even back office) jobs, build behavioral interview questions to assess cultural competence and provide training during on-boarding to build these skills. It is important to think about the fit of the solution within the organization's existing system and practice. For example, people often ask whether there is a test or tool to assess cultural competency. Yes, there are a number of tools, such as surveys or questionnaires, to help measure people's cultural competence. They are mostly used for preparing and counseling expatriates going on international assignment. Some organizations may use these in combination with other tools to select international assignees. However, we are not aware of any organization that relies entirely on the result of a cultural competence assessment to determine whether or not an employee is suitable for an international assignment.

Similarly, if your organization already uses a tool (e.g., a psychometric test) as part of the recruiting and selection process, adding a cultural component is a feasible next step. If, however, you have relied on interviews as a main work process to select new employees, then it is more logical to build the cultural dimension into your existing interview process and train managers to identify both cultural competences and culturally driven behaviors that may come across as wrong but can be trained and adapted. For example, some organizations systematically use lunch meetings to interview candidates in order to observe the candidate's behavior in an informal setting. Behaviors such as chewing without closing one's mouth are probably considered rude in many cultures. However, HR professionals and manager need to ask two questions. First, how important is this behavior to the job? It may be very important for a sales manager but may not be important for a programmer. Second, is this a skill/behavior that can be changed through training?

Place people on the right level based on their job content and transferrable skills. The first job that many immigrants obtain in North America often does not fully reflect their capability. In addition, the titles of the jobs they held in their home country often imply something different in North American organizations (e.g., a "senior deputy manager" in India might be called a "senior process engineer" in the US). As a result, many immigrants are either rejected because their most recent position was at a much lower level than the position they applied for or are told they are overqualified because the titles of their positions back home made it sound like they had far more responsibilities. Don't reject candidates because their job titles seem too high or too low for the position for which you are hiring—take the time to understand what they did in the past and what transferable skills candidates may bring to the position.

When you have understood their ability and skills, place them at a level where they can apply their past skills and experience while learning how to get work done here. For example, many public accounting firms transfer a large number of auditors to their North American offices on temporary or permanent assignments. They usually place these transferees one level lower than where they were placed in their home country, or as if they had one less year of experience than they actually do; this practice has proven to be quite effective because it sets these new assignees up for success by giving them time to learn how to work with clients and colleagues who are very different from the colleagues and clients they worked with back home. Some of these assignees are able to move up the learning curve quickly and are subsequently promoted to the level they were in back home within a short time period. Others take longer to integrate but are able to be productive without feeling the pressure of having to sell a certain number of projects or complete certain tasks as soon as they arrive.

Here is another example. A high-tech company hires many immigrants already in North America and people overseas and brings them to North America on work permits. Over time, hiring managers at this company have developed the expertise to place these international new hires at levels in the organization that reflect their skills and experience. After that, their progress is reviewed regularly. Employees who quickly demonstrate the required technical and soft skills are given raises more often than the annual salary review cycle and are promoted to a higher level as soon as they demonstrate they can operate at that level.

Include culturally different people in your recruiting teams. Someone with international experience is able to explain to the rest of the recruiting team that the Indian Institute of Technology or the University of Science and Technology of China is the Indian or Chinese equivalent of MIT, or that a candidate who keeps saying *we* instead of *I* is trying to avoid taking credit for the work done by a team rather than trying to hide behind the team because he or she did not contribute much to its progress.

Post your organization's recruiting process on its Web site. An explanation of the steps involved in your recruitment and selection process, sample résumés outlining the preferred format and a description of the criteria used to evaluate candidates help all candidates, wherever they were educated. It gives candidates the opportunity to learn more about your organization and attracts candidates with skills and motivations that better align with your organization. For example, the Ontario Public Services Web site explains in detail how to answer behavioral interview questions, specifically to the point that "we want to hear what you did, therefore use 'I' not 'we' when answering questions."

Issues at the On-Boarding Stage: Unwritten Rules and Soft Skills

Many organizations invest significant time and money in creating a compelling employer brand to attract talent and a vigorous on-boarding program to ensure that new employees become productive as fast as possible and keep the branding promise communicated during the recruiting process. Strategies and programs include the following:

- A robust career Web site that communicates the organization's values and culture as well as various policies and programs
- Processes to ensure that all the IT setup is completed before the employee's first day
- Management accountability to have a good orientation program for new employees
- Assigning buddies to new employees

All these efforts contribute to the organization attracting top talent and engaging employees from the start. To take these best practices further, organizations need to understand the unique challenges many immigrants face. Recent immigrant employees are not only learning the new organization, they are learning a whole new system and its numerous unwritten rules. The reality is that many immigrants do not understand the organization's culture by reading the job description or the value proposition posted on the career Web site. They are new to this country and need a job to support themselves and their family. Once hired, they are very excited for the first few days or weeks and then become quite confused as to what to do and how to get the job done. Some may run into a conflict situation with their managers or colleagues. Consider the following situation:

Jorge was educated and worked for a large global engineering consulting firm in his native Venezuela. Four months after immigrating to Canada, he found a similar position in the Calgary office of the same engineering consulting firm. He was very excited and confident that his strong technical skills and his knowledge of the organization would result in a fast career progression. Five months into the job, he is quite confused.

- He was first assigned on a project that was already halfway through. He then worked on a few small projects that lasted a couple of weeks each. Now he is asked to help with a few specific tasks on a project or write proposals for new projects. In his home country, he used to be in charge of a significant portion of large projects that lasted more than a year.

- Since he does not have a lot of project work, he is able to go home at 5:30 p.m. every day, which he enjoys very much. His manager said during his interview, "We are very result oriented. I care more about getting the job done, less about how long you work at your desk." He figures that means there is no need for him to put in any overtime work.
- His colleagues seem to be only concerned about their small piece of the project and have no interest in the bigger picture. Each group has its own meeting about their portion of the project. He was accustomed to starting the project with the larger team and sitting on many project meetings. He asked to sit in on other groups' meetings. His manager reluctantly agreed to the first request. After that, his colleagues said no.
- Back home, he was always the best English speaker in his class or his company. Now, he finds that he has to pay extra attention to understand what is said by clients, managers or colleagues. One day, his manager said to him that he asked for permission too often and should "ask for forgiveness" instead. He didn't understand what that meant. When he asked, his manager and a colleague exchanged a look between them that he felt implied they had a poor opinion of him. He didn't ask again.

Here is what Jorge's manager, Sally, has to say about him:

- Jorge demonstrated very strong technical skills during the interview. He worked for our firm in Venezuela before and knew our methods, software and processes. I thought he would be a great fit. But five months into the job, Jorge is not coming up the learning curve.
- He asks a lot of questions. Every time I assign him to a project, he asks me numerous questions before doing any work. If I had all the answers to all those questions, I wouldn't need him. His colleagues run into the same problem. When they ask him a question, he asks three questions on why people asked him their original question. His colleagues feel that he wants information from others but never contributes to the team.
- Even though it seems like he worked at a very senior level in Venezuela, he just doesn't have the executive presence in front of clients. He does not appear confident or decisive about the solutions he puts forward.
- Right now, my biggest challenge is that his utilization is lower than average because project managers don't want him on their projects. Everyone is very busy, and many people on my team are working 60-hour weeks, while Jorge goes home every day at 5:30 p.m.

Many immigrant new hires run into situations like these in their first few months on the job. While their technical skills are clearly good, they are not integrating well into the organization. They appear to lack initiative and operate in ways that baffle their colleagues. Their soft skills are considered poor, and they do not follow the unwritten rules of the organization—because they do not understand what these rules are.

Many people, especially those working in technical professions, often think that, because the laws of physics work the same way everywhere in the world, the content of their job should be the same anywhere in the world. A pharmacist from Egypt said, "The drug going into a human body causes the same reaction everywhere in the world, whether you are white, black, yellow, red or brown." It is indeed true that in most professions about 80 percent of the work that people do is done in the same way around the world. However, the 20 percent that is different creates 80 percent of the challenge. One of Caroline's Canadian colleagues said after changing to a new job, "It's never the work that's challenging, it's the people." Understanding how people get work done is the biggest challenge for immigrant employees in their first two years with an organization.

The 20 percent that is different requires a lot of soft skills to pick up because there are so many unwritten rules. Every group, whether based on gender, generation, ethnicity, public or private sector, industry, small or large organization, has its own unwritten rules that are only known to its members. The trouble is that newcomers don't know what they don't know and existing members don't know what they need to explain. Think of football—the same word represents very different sports in the US, UK, Australia and Canada, and the rules are quite different. If an Australian football player tries to play American football following the rules of Australian football, he will quickly be sidelined by his teammates. In the workplace, some of the unwritten rules newcomers need to learn include the following:

- To whom do you communicate what?
- What medium do people use to communicate?
- How long should a report or presentation be?

- What should the executive summary/body/appendices of a report cover, respectively?
- Is working overtime considered positively or negatively?
- When people go for coffee together, who pays?
- How do we greet one another in the morning?

Organizations can help immigrant employees become productive right from the start by teaching them the soft skills they need to uncover the unwritten rules and navigate the system.

Bridging the Gap of Unwritten Rules and Soft Skills

Following the PSE framework, North American organizations can help bridge this gap in the following manner:

Improve communication and describe job expectations explicitly. Explain the unwritten rules and push the conversation upstream during the recruiting and on-boarding process. For example, one of our clients said that they explain the **technical skills and soft skills** model at the interview stage to help candidates understand the emphasis on soft skills; once hired, explain what soft skills are important to the organization and how employees can develop those skills.

Explain the organization's culture concretely, in plain and direct language. A statement such as "We are very result oriented. I care more about getting the job done, less about how long you work at your desk" may not carry the same meaning for immigrants. Instead, be honest and specific; say, "We are very result oriented. We work hard here. Many of us put in 60-hour weeks on a regular basis. We have set up systems that help employees get their job done remotely. I may leave at 5 p.m. to pick up my children, but I work two or three more hours in the evening after my kids go to bed." You would rather let candidates or employees choose to work for your organization because they identify with your culture than have them complain about overtime down the road.

Building Awareness and Skills

Become aware and accept that it takes immigrant employees longer to learn the job and the system. As described in Chapter 3, many immigrants come from cultures that are more risk averse than the US or Canada. They are likely to spend more time researching various solutions to a given problem or checking their work very carefully many times because they want to avoid mistakes. In their home countries, the same mistake has a much bigger negative impact on their career than it does in North America. In addition, operating in a second language takes longer. An e-mail message that takes 5 minutes for a native English speaker to draft may take 30 minutes for an ESL speaker to draft. As a result, both managers and immigrant employees should accept that new immigrant employees often need to work longer hours in the first year, just to be on par with new employees who are educated in North America.

Immigrant employees need to observe extensively and learn the unwritten rules of the organization by mirroring what their colleagues do. A French expatriate in the US realized that working overtime in his company was interpreted as being inefficient by his colleagues, so he took home work when he felt he needed to spend more time. The same applies the other way around. In Patricia Gercik's *On Track with the Japanese*, she described an American MIT intern who went to Japan and learned to stay as late as his Japanese colleagues, even when his manager told him to go home at 5:30 p.m. By staying late at work with his Japanese colleagues, he got an assignment where his expertise helped the team solve the problem at hand.

Most immigrant employees can learn the required soft skills and catch up with their locally educated colleagues. One manager Caroline worked with praised one of his engineers for having great communication skills, even though his English skills were limited. When asked why, the manager said this engineer knew how to supplement his lack of English skills with technical language. He drew diagrams or wrote equations when he discussed his design with colleagues or brainstormed solutions to a difficult technical problem. He was consistently rated as exceeding expectations in performance reviews and was highly respected by his colleagues.

Section 4.2: Performing and Performance Management

I conduct regular employee communication sessions to explain the performance management process. During one session, an employee questioned why he should write the first draft of his performance goals or the review before discussing it with his managers. He insisted that only managers can set goals or write reviews for employees because there is a conflict of interest if employees set their own goals or write their own reviews. (Canadian HR professional)

Performance management is the most important process to align employees' efforts and achieve the organization's goals. While most organizations have a performance management process, many managers and employees (including many educated in North America) do not make full use of this process to manage their work and career. Compounded with cultural differences, it is even harder for immigrant employees to apply this process. Caroline worked with a company that performed regular talent reviews. Because of a skills shortage in their industry, the company not only recruited many immigrants who were already in the US or Canada, it also actively recruited from all over the world and brought highly specialized talent to North America on work permits. The performance of immigrant employees ranged from top notch (several of the highest performers were recent immigrants) to very poor (many of the people put on performance improvement plans were recent immigrants). Behavioral issues (i.e., poor soft skills) were the number one reason these employees ended up on performance improvement plans.

The solution to bridge the gap is primarily around building skills for managers and employees—specifically teaching managers how to coach immigrant employees through the performance management process.

Taking Initiative and Working Independently

As discussed in Chapter 3, many recent immigrants are considered as lacking initiative by their North American managers. They find it difficult to decide what they should do and how to do their work without detailed instructions. As a result, many managers find themselves in the situation where they need to teach their immigrant employees both the importance of initiative and what taking initiative looks like in a North American context. Let's take Jorge's example, described at Stage 1 of the talent management cycle. The following is a coaching conversation when an HR manager (HRM) teaches Jorge what "taking initiative" and "working independently" mean in North America.

HRM: Jorge, I want to ask you a question. Imagine that I am your manager. This is Monday morning, 9 a.m. I have asked you to come into my office, and I describe a project I want you to take on. Let's assume that this project is going to take you approximately four weeks to complete. By the time I finish my description, let's say you do not feel you have enough information to know what you have to do. What do you do in this situation?

JORGE: Since you are my manager, I will ask you questions until I feel I have enough information and know what I have to do.

HRM: Okay. In a situation like this, I will probably answer the first couple of questions you ask me. After that, you are likely to see me become impatient. Do you know why?

JORGE: No, not really.

HRM: Because at that point, I expect you to go away and do some research on your own.

JORGE: What do you mean, do research on my own? I want to make sure that I do what my manager expects from me—how can I determine what my manager expects without asking?

HRM: This is what "working independently" is about. You are going to hear one phrase all the time—"Don't come to me with problems, come to me with solutions." This means that managers don't want their employees to come to them and say, "We have a problem— what do you want me to do?" They want their employees to come to them and say, "We have a problem; here are three possible solutions, and here is the one I recommend for this reason." This is called "working independently" or "taking initiative."

Going back to the situation where your manager has delegated to you a project, your manager expects you to ask him or her two, maybe three questions during the first meeting; after that, your manager expects you to go away and work on your own. When you are doing research, you can look things up on the Web, look up similar past projects in the department's shared folders, talk to your colleagues or consult with technical experts. You should avoid going back to ask questions to your manager until you have formulated a plan of action and are ready to present it.

JORGE: How much time should I spend doing research?

HRM: Good question. Typically, you want to allocate approximately 5 percent of the project time to planning. If your manager has told you that this project will take you approximately four weeks, that's about 20 business days, so 5 percent of that is one day. If your manager delegates this project to you on Monday morning 9 a.m., then you should create a preliminary plan of action on Monday and present it to your manager on Tuesday morning. Your presentation will sound like this: "You have asked me to do X. I have done some research, and I believe that the best way to reach that goal is to go through Steps 1, 2, 3 and 4. In Step 4, I am not 100 percent sure—I can think of a few ways of doing it—A, B and C; I think A is better for this reason, but I can see merit in B or C. What do you think?" The key is not to come to your manager with open-ended questions, like "What do you want me to do?" but with specific, closed-ended questions, like "I think I should do it this way—does that match your experience?"

This coaching conversation illustrates one of the most effective approaches in cross-cultural situations—the value of being specific. If you discuss "working independently" in principle, you will likely reach an agreement fairly quickly, but that agreement will likely be void of substance. As soon as you work on a concrete situation, you and your employee will realize that you have different perspectives on the situation and different interpretations of your agreement.

Once employees understand the importance of taking initiative, managers can help them apply this concept to drafting their performance objectives and coach them on how to set SMART (Specific, Measurable, Ambitious, Realistic and Time-bound) goals. Since each organization has its own approach to goal setting, we will not discuss goal setting in detail. The key message is that immigrant employees need more help to complete this exercise, especially for the first time, than the average North American employee. Note that it is equally important to help them understand that the approach they use to set goals for themselves and evaluate their own work is also evaluated as part of their performance, since self-awareness is an important soft skill in North American organizations.

Coaching to Improve Soft Skills

Clive came from South Africa, where he worked for several years before going to the US to obtain his master's degree; he is now working with a professional services firm. He and his manager, Alex, are preparing for his first performance review after his first six months at the company.

Clive's take on the situation: Alex is a good manager, and Clive likes working for Alex; in particular, Clive appreciates the fact that Alex knows her stuff technically; that's important to Clive, because he feels he can learn from her. However, Clive has several issues he wants to discuss with Alex:

- His colleagues are not strong technically. On several occasions, Clive had the chance to look at their reports or attend their presentations; they were often full of inconsistencies. For example, they have different numbers for the same variable on different slides. When Clive asked probing questions, he got some quick but vague answers that didn't really address his concerns.
- Clive's colleagues seem to take things far too personally—they really have "thin skins." When Clive asks questions during presentations or meetings, people become defensive and shoot back some nasty comments. Nobody seems to be ready to have a good debate, to really understand what is happening.
- Clive recently found out that there were team meetings to which he was not invited. Several of his team members met without him half an hour before an actual team meeting. Clive did not appreciate this behavior since it indicates they consider him a second-class member of the team.
- So far, Clive has worked on a large number of small projects; most of them lasted one to two weeks, and very few were related to the area of

expertise he wanted to develop. Clive wants to work on large projects in order to gain experience so he can be promoted.

Alex's take on the situation: Clive clearly has excellent technical skills. This point comes out loud and clear in any project Alex has assigned him— all his work is technically superb. However, without a change in attitude and approach on his part, the morale in her team will drop like a stone, and she may lose some key team members. Here are some specific situations of concern to Alex:

- On a few occasions, Clive raised his hand during meetings and said "I disagree" or "You are wrong." The people who made these presentations came to Alex afterward and said that this should not happen again.
- One colleague mentioned to Alex that Clive's questions made him uncomfortable: Clive asks pointed questions that focus on points that are really open to interpretation. This colleague said Clive's questions made him feel as though he were under attack, and he did not enjoy the experience.
- One team member came to Alex last week saying Clive told her that "her work was not good enough" after Clive reviewed one of her draft reports. This team member was clearly very unhappy about the situation since she had put a lot of effort into it. She asked Alex to make sure she would not work with Clive on future projects.

This is a situation we have run into frequently with immigrant employees. Coaching culturally diverse employees requires understanding the cultural differences involved in the situations. Going straight to the point and trying to have Clive change his approach rarely works because Clive will not understand the changes the manager is likely to recommend to him (such as "soften the way you make your comments in team meetings") because his approach worked well back home. You need to create a common foundation before going into exploring solutions.

We have developed a **six-step coaching process** and a tool to deal with these situations, which we have tested extensively in a number of organizations. Here are the six steps:

Step 1: Put all issues on the table—the manager's issues and the employee's issues.

Step 2: Ask the employee what the goal is and validate that you understand the goal; establish that you want to help the employee achieve that goal.

Step 3: Ask the employee to describe how he or she thinks his or her behavior or words are interpreted and how this will lead to achieving the set goals.

Step 4: Tell the employee how the behavior or words are actually interpreted and of the disconnect between the behaviors or words and goals.

Step 5: Brainstorm solutions that (a) will be acceptable to the employee and (b) will enable the employee to reach his or her goals within the context of your organization.

Step 6: Let the employee make the final decision—your goal is not to make the decision for him or her but to help the employee make an informed decision.

Now, let's look at each of these steps in sequence from Alex's perspective and apply them to Clive's situation.

Step 1: Put all issues on the table. This step is needed because in order to tackle such a problem together, we first need to agree on what the problem is. The situation described here is very typical of cross-cultural coaching—it is very common for the manager (you) and the employee (Clive) to have different issues on their radar. For example, Clive is not happy that his team members are meeting without him before the actual team meeting (they are doing this to ensure they reach consensus without Clive so he cannot derail the team through his pointed questions), whereas you may not be aware this is even happening.

When the same issue is on both radars, you and the employee often see it from different vantage points. For example, Clive feels his colleagues have "thin skins," while the main issue in your mind is the strong and forceful way in which he phrases his comments and feedback. We are dealing here with differences related to the way **feedback** is given (see Chapter 2). The two radar screens are quite different—in order to create an action plan that both Clive and you buy into, the two of you need to create a common radar screen and create an action plan that addresses all issues.

Step 2: Ask the employee about his or her goals. This step helps create a common foundation. When a manager gives advice to an employee who does not understand the rationale behind these recommendations because they are foreign to him or her, the employee often interprets the situation as "My manager has a hidden agenda—he or she wants me to go in a direction that may be good for him or her, but I don't see how it benefits me." To prevent this issue, we recommend that managers first ask what the employee's goals are. Some immigrant employees may not have thought about their goals consciously. Once you help the employee bring clarity to his or her goals, you can emphasize that your goal is to help the employee achieve those goals.

In Clive's case, his goal is to work on large projects and get promoted to a management position. You, as the manager, want Clive to understand that you are giving him advice to help him achieve his goal. As a manager, you can initiate this part of the conversation by asking, "If I am aware that something is holding back your professional progress, and I believe that you are not aware of it, would you want me to tell you?" Another useful question is, "What do you think my goal is in this conversation?"

Steps 3 and 4: Ask the employees how they think their behaviors are interpreted, and then tell them how they actually are interpreted. These steps complete the creation of the common foundation necessary for a productive brainstorming discussion. In most cross-cultural coaching situations, the employee is unaware of the impact he or she is having on other people. For example, Clive thinks the people around him have thin skins, while the people around him think of him as a bull in a china shop. The challenge here is that Clive analyzes his own behavior based on the impact it would have in his home country, without being aware that the impact he has in North America is quite different from the impact he wants to have. Questions you can ask include, "What impact do you think you are having on people when you [say . . . /do . . . /react like . . .]?" and "What was your intention at the time?" For example, in Clive's case, the question becomes, "What impact do you think you are having when you say 'You are wrong' during someone's presentation? What was your intention at the time?"

This is usually the point where the manager and the employee realize how much of a gap there is between the impact the employee wants to have and the impact he or she actually has. Managers may want to discuss why North American people interpret the situation in this way. For example, when Clive answers your previous question, "I want to make sure that any presentation coming out of our team is accurate—we will lose credibility in front of senior management otherwise," you can explain to Clive how his colleagues feel about his comments. To help bring the gap into the open, Table 4.1.1 is a tool we use in coaching conversations like this.

You and the employee list two to three technical and soft skills most important to the employee's job. Then you ask your employee to rate him- or herself on a scale of 0 to 100 for technical skills and for soft skills. Then you ask the employee to assign a relative weight to each set of skills based on the importance they have in his or her position. Once the employee has provided the answers, you provide yours as a way to help the employee see where the gap is.

Here is how it may sound in Clive's case as shown in Table 4.1.2:

Table 4.1.1 Technical and Soft Skills Rating Scale

	RATING (0–100)		RELATIVE WEIGHT (%)		WEIGHTED SCORE
Technical Skills		X		=	
Soft Skills		X		=	
Total Score	n/a		100%		

Table 4.1.2 The Employee's Rating

	RATING (0–100)		RELATIVE WEIGHT (%)		WEIGHTED SCORE
Technical Skills	90	X	80	=	72
Soft Skills	80	X	20	=	16
Total Score	n/a		100%		88

ALEX: Clive, I would like us to go through a short exercise that will help us understand what is happening. On a scale of 0 to 100, how do you rate your technical skills?

CLIVE: 90. (In real-life coaching sessions, people in Clive's situation usually give a number between 90 and 100.)

ALEX: What about your soft skills? On a scale of 0 to 100, what rating do you give yourself for your soft skills?

CLIVE: 80. (In real-life coaching sessions, people in Clive's situations usually respond with a number ranging between 80 and 100—keep in mind that they are measuring their soft skills by their home country's standards, not by North American standards.)

ALEX: Now think of the relative importance that technical skills and soft skills have in your position. If you think of it in terms of percentages that add up to 100 percent, what percentages do you allocate to technical skills and to soft skills in your job?

CLIVE: 80/20. (This is the most common answer in real-life coaching sessions.)

ALEX: All right. Let's do the math—we end up with an overall rating of 88.

ALEX: Now it is my turn. I agree with you that you have excellent technical skills and give you a rating of 90 for these as well. Your soft skills are not nearly as high as you think they are because I am measuring them by American standards—I rate you as 30. When you tell presenters that they are wrong in front of an audience, you alienate people to the point that they do not want to work with you—that matters a lot here. I also place significantly more importance on soft skills in your position than you do—I place equal weights on technical skills and soft skills in your job. So, overall, I am giving you a rating of 60. (See Table 4.1.3)

(We encourage managers to give employees the same rating for technical skills that employees give themselves in order to remove that variable from the table. If you give Clive an 85 when he gives himself 90, you will likely be discussing the difference between 85 and 90 for the next 30 minutes, and that is not the point of your discussion.

Table 4.1.3 The Manager's Rating

	RATING (0–100)		RELATIVE WEIGHT (%)		WEIGHTED SCORE
Technical Skills	90	X	50	=	45
Soft Skills	30	X	50	=	15
Total Score	n/a		100%		60

If you give Clive 95 when he gives himself 90, he will be flying high and the rest of the discussion about soft skills may not register with him.)

At this point, coaching sessions can go in two directions:

- Probably 80 to 90 percent of people we have coached in similar situations have reacted by saying something like, "Oh dear! I did not realize what impact I was having on others! What do I need to do to have the kind of impact I want to have?"
- A small number of people reacted by defending their ratings and weights—they are adamant that a rating of 30 is way too low and that they deserve 80. As coaches, our reaction at that point is to drop the soft skill rating mentally from 30 to 20 since this person is clearly lacking the ability to self-actualize. In this situation, the discussion will need to go back to Steps 2–4. The manager needs to ask the employee again, "What is your goal?" If the goal is to work on bigger projects in order to be promoted, then the employee needs to know the gap between his or her behaviors and the goal. Very few people like to receive negative feedback. That is why it is important to bring people's attention to their goals. If they have clarity and strong commitment to their goals, they are more likely to accept the fact that they need to change in order to achieve their goals. Sometimes, this circling back to Steps 2–4 takes a long time and perhaps several discussions.

Step 5: Brainstorm solutions with the employee. Once the employee is receptive to your coaching, the two of you can have a productive brainstorming discussion. Some employees come out of a coaching session like this one with a full year's worth of personal development action steps. The following are Clive's action steps:

- Observe how his team members express disagreement with one another during team meetings and mirror their behaviors.
- Work with colleagues one on one (as opposed to in teams) to improve the technical quality of their work.
- Become involved in some cross-functional committees as a way to practice his soft skills in an environment where his bluntness may not have as much negative impact on his career.
- Join Toastmasters as a way to practice his presentation skills.
- Read books on improving personal effectiveness and interpersonal skills.

As manager, it is important for you to recognize that, in a situation like this one, there are four action steps only you can take:

- You need to take the pulse of the team and get feedback from Clive's team members on a regular basis. If Clive asks his team members, "How am I doing?" they are likely to answer, "Fine." Clive's team members will not tell him what they really think of him if they see him as a bully. This point is particularly important in Canada—Canadians are reluctant to give negative feedback and even more reluctant to give it to someone they expect to fight back, so they will not do it unless they have to because of their position. You may want to gather feedback from Clive's team members and meet with Clive one on one more frequently as a way to ensure that some progress is quickly visible and that it is sustained over time—Clive's team members may say, "There he goes again!" otherwise.
- You can also help smooth things over between Clive and his team members by telling them, "I realize that Clive comes across like a bull in a china shop. I am working with him on it; when something happens that I should know about, please tell me. At the same time, please cut him some slack and encourage him when you see that he is trying to change his behavior in a constructive manner."

- You can role-play with Clive situations you have personally witnessed as a way to teach him more constructive behaviors. For example, if you saw him point out the discrepancy between two numbers representing the same variable on two different slides when that discrepancy was not important, you may have a conversation with him to brainstorm how he could handle the same situation in the future and role-play it with him as a way for him to practice in a safe environment.

- As manager, you are likely to have more influence on the kind of projects Clive works on than he does, so this is one action item you probably want to take on. At the same time, you can clearly tie the change of behavior you want to see (improved soft skills) to his goal—"Clive, I will talk to the project managers of the three projects you would like to be part of. At this point, I may get a cold shoulder if your reputation has reached them before I do. This is where you can help me to help you—if you improve your soft skills and your team members say you are contributing a lot to the team, it will become much easier for you to get the kind of projects you want." This again brings the employee's attention to the alignment between his or her goals and behavior.

Step 6: Let the employee make the final decision. In the end, the employee has to make the final decision; he or she needs to determine which behaviors to change and which behaviors to keep as is. As mentioned before, there are situations where employees are unable or unwilling to see the problem for what it is. In our experience, this usually has a huge negative consequence for their career—they will clearly never be promoted into managerial positions. If they have good enough technical skills to keep their job, they are likely to be oriented toward technical expert careers.

For example, Clive may decide that softening his approach by learning to use *feedback sandwiches* (see Chapter 2) does not work for him— that's just not like him. As a manager, you cannot force him to make that change; however, you can ensure that he makes an informed decision and recognizes that his current behavior will likely result in him working on smaller projects where technical expertise is critical—he will likely not be promoted into managerial positions. At this point, he has to decide which one is more important to him; in the North American context, he can have one or the other, but not both.

Performance Reviews and Challenging Behaviors

Late one afternoon, a manager came to see me. He looked quite beaten. He had just completed a very unpleasant performance review discussion with an employee. On a number of objectives he felt the employee barely met expectations; the employee insisted he put in a lot of effort and deserved an "exceeding expectations" rating. The major disconnect was that the employee worked long hours and did a thorough analysis of what he considered was the problem. However, in engineering research and design work, many variables change quickly. The employee did not take into consideration changes that happened and did not adjust his work focus accordingly. The manager tried to give the employee new direction to reflect these changes, but the employee did not realize the importance and continued on what he considered the right path. (Canadian HR professional)

The root cause of this problem is the level of directness or indirectness, as discussed in Chapter 2. Canadians are very indirect on the world scale. Even though they are close neighbors, Americans find that Canadians "beat around the bush" rather than "call a spade a spade." In this particular situation, when the manager said, "Thank you for putting in all the overtime. But please work on . . . instead of . . . . You will make progress even faster," the employee thought he was being praised for his hard work and had made progress. It took the two of them three rounds of difficult conversations to finally sort out the real issue.

Another challenge is that many new immigrants used to be star performers or straight A students when they were in their home country. They see a "meeting expectations" rating as being average, which does not match the expectations they have of themselves.

HR professionals and managers often have to deal with behaviors considered unacceptable by North American organizations. Here are some examples we have encountered over the years:

• A new immigrant employee accused anyone who disagreed with him of racial discrimination, including all his team members, the lawyer who helped him get his work permit and the real estate agent who helped him find an apartment.

• Another new immigrant employee had trouble working with his female colleagues. He was paired up to design a module with a female team member as part of his on-boarding training. This female team member had worked with the organization for five years and had extensive expertise in that area. While she was doing her best to show him the ropes, he tried every way he could to avoid taking directions from her.

• Another new immigrant employee made explicitly anti-Semitic comments during a casual conversation in the office.

These behaviors show that people from different cultures do not only look or sound different, they think differently. This is particularly true in Canada, where many immigrants join an organization after having studied and worked in their home country for a number of years. Helping adults changing behaviors takes time and a lot of conscious effort.

Bridging the Performance and Behavioral Gap

Following our PSE framework, building **awareness** and **skills** is the key to bridging the performance and behavioral gap.

Provide diversity and inclusion training to all new employees as part of the on-boarding process. Canada and the US are relatively progressive in a number of areas related to diversity and inclusion. Both countries have gone through a recent history of gradually accepting people from all ethnic backgrounds, religions and sexual orientations, to name a few dimensions of diversity. We have come a long way and are still on that journey. It is not long ago that women in the US and Canada had to fight hard for the right to vote. Same-sex marriage is only legal in a dozen states, while more states are taking this progressive step as time goes on. We need to remember that not everyone in the world has gone through the same journey.

In many homogeneous societies, people do not have the same experience of working with people from diverse ethnic groups. For example, in China, there are 1.3 billion people who look physically quite similar. Many immigrants probably do not know that the rainbow flag stands for LGBT pride in North America. For those who have seen it, it may mean different things in different parts of the world. In Italy, it means peace. In Peru, it represents the Inca culture. So the onus is on the organization to make its values and expected behaviors explicit right from the start. Explain what racist, sexist, anti-Semitic and homophobic comments or behaviors are—we have met immigrants who did not know the English words *anti-Semitic* or *homophobic*—and spell out that these comments and behaviors are not tolerated and explain the consequences of noncompliance using concrete examples.

Continuously reinforce the message. Remember that new immigrant employees are usually overwhelmed with information at the onboarding stage. Their focus during the first six months is most likely to be on learning the job. When people are provided information for which they do not have a mental file folder, the first reaction is to throw it in the mental garbage can.

In many cases, new immigrant employees easily see themselves as victims of discrimination because of their differences but are not aware that they could also behave in a discriminatory way. We coached an engineer from Eastern Europe. As a white man, he did not accuse others of racism or sexism, but he still claimed he was discriminated against when he could not make himself understood due to his limited English skills. It is important for the organization to teach its workforce that everyone is held accountable for demonstrating respect and inclusive behavior.

The most important person in this process is the manager. The manager can apply the six-step coaching process and have ongoing coaching conversations with the employee on what behavior is expected in delivering work, getting along with coworkers and assisting customers. The key here is to bring the employee's attention to his or her goals. If the employee sees the disconnect between the goals and the behaviors, he or she is more likely to accept the need to change. In all situations described previously, the employees need to understand that their soft skills (e.g., being self-aware, accepting feedback and developing the ability to work with people who are different from them) are evaluated as part of their performances.

In the example at the beginning of this section, once the employee and the manager are clear that the employee's goal is to obtain an "exceeds expectations" rating, the manager can use Table 4.1.1 as a tool to help the employee understand where he or she stands in terms of soft skills. From there, they can create a personal development plan the employee can implement to improve his or her soft skills.

When dealing with challenging behaviors (racist/anti-Semitic/sexist/homophobic comments or behaviors), managers need to make it very clear to employees that if they want to work in the organization, they must stop certain behaviors or comments. Using the negative feedback scale described in Chapter 2, make a statement such as, "This kind of comment or behavior falls at four on the four-point scale—if you do it again, you will lose your job." In extreme situations, HR and senior management need to be involved and take immediate action.

Section 4.3: Learning and Development

What Do Immigrant Employees Want to Learn?

I worked on a project with the faculty of engineering of a Canadian university to create soft skill courses. The faculty had identified that one of the soft skills immigrant engineers needed most (according to the engineering managers who were surveyed) was teamwork, so we decided to start our new program with a course on that topic. We designed a course titled "Increasing Your Effectiveness within a Multicultural Engineering Team" and started marketing it. The results were quite different from our expectations. Most of the engineers who signed up for the course were engineers who had obtained their degrees in Canada. We had very few internationally educated engineers—yet these were our target audience.

Upon reflection, we realized that trying to attract immigrants and enrolling them in soft skill courses could not work—we had to go back to the drawing board. We ended up creating an engineering design course; the twist was that all design work was done in teams. In essence, we embedded the soft skill training in a technical skill training course as a way to make it appealing to immigrants.

(Lionel)

In North America, most immigrants come from cultures that are significantly more hierarchical than those of the US or Canada. This has a major impact on the learning and development functions of North American organizations since hierarchical and egalitarian people have different ideas of what they need to learn and how they should learn it. As described in Chapter 2, hierarchical cultures place significantly more emphasis on technical skills than they do on soft skills. As a result, employees who come from hierarchical cultures tend to value technical skill training to a significantly greater extent than they value soft skill training.

Bridging the Learning-Needs Gap

Following our PSE solutions framework, organizations can manage this issue by combining several action items:

Leveraging the Performance Management and Rewards Systems
Set soft skills development goals. Once immigrant employees understand that they will be held accountable for improving their soft skills and rewarded for demonstrating behaviors in line with the organization's values, they are more motivated to invest in their own learning. We have seen many immigrant employees pay out of their own pocket for English classes because they realized how much benefit they derived from these courses. We have also seen many immigrants actively participate in Toastmasters to improve their public speaking skills.

Encourage immigrant employees to take soft skill courses even if they have taken similar courses in their home country because they need to understand the differences and similarities between their home culture and their host culture. For example, because what makes a good presentation in China, France or Mexico is quite different from what makes a good presentation in North America, immigrants will have to unlearn what they already know and relearn how to make good presentations by North American standards.

Embed soft skill training in technical skill training programs. For example, make group projects and presenting part of the technical training so that immigrant trainees learn these important soft skills while solving technical problems. When immigrant trainees go through the courses with their North American peers, they have a chance to learn from them by osmosis.

Create soft skills training for immigrants. In our experience, the design of many North American soft skill training programs assumes that trainees have an idea of what that soft skill is about and that they will deepen their knowledge by attending this program. Immigrants often follow the course without really understanding the assumptions and definitions involved—these need to be made explicit. One high potential immigrant employee said honestly after attending a leadership course, "All of these fly right over my head." While this comment is also a demonstration of her high self-awareness, the learning and development functions of North American organizations need to take this into consideration and offer a variety of learning activities for the concepts to gradually sink in and for the learners to practice the skills in a safe environment.

Section 4.4: Succession and Career Planning

Promotion Process in Egalitarian and Hierarchical Cultures

North American organizations need to take another important difference into consideration when supporting immigrants advancing their

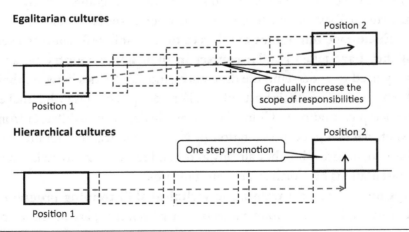

Figure 4.3 Promotion Process in Egalitarian and Hierarchical Cultures

careers: The steps employees need to take in order to be promoted are different in egalitarian and in hierarchical cultures, as Figure 4.3 demonstrates:

- In egalitarian cultures, people get promoted by gradually increasing the scope of their responsibilities and, in particular, taking on some of the responsibilities associated with operating at the next level. Egalitarian people often say that "you get promoted when you are able to do the job without the title"; when an opportunity arises, you are then the prime candidate for promotion.
- In hierarchical organizations, people get promoted by focusing on their current roles and responsibilities and making sure they do superior work. When Caroline worked for a Canadian company in China, the general managers enquired about her career goals during a performance review discussion. His question was, "What do you want to do five years down the road? Do you want my job? Do you want Jim's (vice president of HR) job?" Caroline was terrified at the question because coveting your manager's job is a career-limiting move in hierarchical cultures.

Because of these differences, the approaches some immigrants take to move ahead in an organization often work against them:

- They tell their manager they deserve a promotion or they want to be promoted in three months when their manager thinks they are at least two years away from getting to the next level.
- They may turn down opportunities to join special task forces or new initiatives because they want to make sure their current areas of responsibilities are well taken care of.
- Some ask for raises when their managers suggest an increased scope of responsibility, not realizing that raises come later in the process—they first have to prove they are capable of taking on these new responsibilities.
- When asked their career aspiration, they say they want to do a good job and downplay their strengths.

Bridging the Cultural Gap in Career Management

Using our PSE solutions framework, we encourage organizations to create open communication, provide tools and teach recent immigrants what leadership means in the North American context.

Foster open communication. Managers and HR professionals need to initiate the career management conversation, making it safe for employees to express their career aspirations. Again, the performance review process is the best opportunity to have this kind of conversation. When Caroline was an HR business partner, she had regular one-on-one meetings with high performers to discuss their work and their personal development activities. The next step is to help immigrant employees understand that they own their career and must actively seek opportunities to build their skills.

Provide support for employees to build their skills. Many organizations provide a career management Web site on their intranet, where employees can access self-assessment tools to understand their strengths and their interests in order to design their own development plan. However, since many immigrant employees focus their attention on technical skills, they may not take full advantage of these tools and learning opportunities. Again, the most important person who can help immigrant employees make the connection is the manager. Through ongoing conversations, the manager, with support from HR professionals, can provide opportunities for the employee to develop the skills critical to achieve his or her career goals. Here is a success story shared by an HR professional:

As an HR business partner, I had regular meetings with managers to discuss how their teams were doing and what support they might need. At one time, a theme emerged during these meetings: Two senior engineers, Nicole and Ivan, had very strong technical skills and were considered good candidates for promotions to manager or more senior technical positions that involved supervising and mentoring junior staff. However, their verbal English skills were not very strong; in particular, both had strong accent that made them difficult to understand. The manager and I decided to offer them one-on-one English tutoring.

When I broached the topic with them, Nicole took this offering negatively; she looked at it as management suggesting that her English was not good enough and felt quite offended. She attended a few classes, then stopped. As a result, she remained on the technical career track. Nicole's situation illustrates the need for immigrant employees to take ownership of their own career. While the organization can provide options and act as enablers, employees have to implement the change.

Ivan, on the other hand, was very excited because he went to a number of ESL classes but found them not very helpful because the class was too big for the instructor to give him individual attention. Ivan worked very hard with his tutor. In three months, he spoke much more confidently, and his colleagues noticed a significant difference. He was promoted to a manager position six months later, and he was still with the company twelve years later.

Develop leadership skills by North American standards. One issue related to differences in people's sense of hierarchy is that some immigrants behave in ways that are considered "dictatorial" or "arrogant" by their North American employees and colleagues when they are promoted. For example, one team member complained to HR that his manager, who used to be a coworker, said to him, "Now I am your manager. You do what I tell you to do." Some also come across as micromanaging to egalitarian employees. One Indian engineering manager said, "I want to make sure my employees don't run into the same problem I did with my manager—never knowing what he wants."

In this respect, training, coaching or mentoring for first-time managers can help smooth the transition. Newly promoted immigrants who have a strong sense of hierarchy can learn through these interventions that their managerial style may not serve them as well as they think; in particular, their innate managerial instincts may prevent them from moving higher in the organization. Again, the six-step coaching process is an effective tool HR professionals and managers can use to help recently promoted immigrants bring clarity to their goal (becoming an effective leader in North American organizations) and learn the leadership skills to achieve that goal.

* * *

Integrating immigrant employees can bring great benefits to the organization. Here is a story shared by an HR executive:

I was taking a walk on the shop floor. It was break time, and the production line was down. Most workers were resting with their heads in their arms. I noticed an Asian woman reading a thick book and went to talk with her. She showed me the book. Its title was *Engineering Design Principles*. I was amazed. "Wow, you are reading this—do you understand it?" She said, "Yes, I was an engineer before immigrating. I am now taking night courses to become an engineer again." I chatted with her a bit more and went back to my office. I called a meeting of my department and shared my conversation with this employee. I asked my team to come up with a program to recruit from our shop floor.

The program became a major success. Over the years we built a talent pipeline and recruited from our shop floor engineers, IT specialists and accountants. They all turned out to be great professional staff because we already knew them and could ask their supervisors for feedback on their work ethics and soft skills. We also saw a significant drop in our recruitment cost and an increase in morale on the shop floor. Production workers were now motivated to work hard and improve their education and skills with the goal to be promoted to work in the office.

5

Working with Offshore Resources

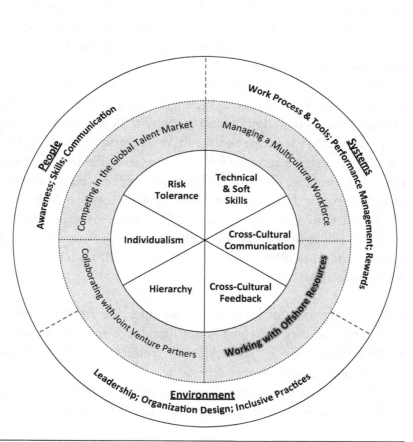

Figure 5.0 Roadmap of the Book

While offshoring has been controversial for as long as it has existed, this business practice will continue to exist and evolve. The Offshoring Research Network (ORN) points out that "companies are beginning to realize that offshoring is not an end goal, but an intermediary step toward evolving new global organizational capabilities."[1] The goal of this chapter is not to discuss the pros and cons of offshoring; we want to examine the challenges that North American organizations in general (and managers and HR professionals in particular) experience when working with offshore resources and discuss solutions to overcome these challenges.

We have worked on many projects with North American organizations that have offshored IT, engineering or accounting work to organizations in various countries. By far, the most common offshore destination is India; as a result, most of the examples used in this chapter involve Indian offshore resources. India is by no means the only offshoring destination. The top ten offshoring destinations according to the A.T. Kearney *Global Services Location Index 2011*[2] are India, China, Malaysia, Egypt, Indonesia, Mexico, Thailand, Vietnam, Philippines and Chile. Wherever North American organizations send work offshore, they have to deal with several challenges at the same time:

- Offshoring work to India or English-speaking African countries requires that they overcome both cultural and time differences.
- Offshoring work to Latin America requires that they overcome both cultural and language differences.
- Offshoring work to Eastern Europe or the rest of Asia requires that they overcome cultural, language and time differences.

In other words, wherever the offshore work goes, there will be challenges—the two teams/organizations usually experience some difficulties when communicating with one another.

Offshore resources may be internal, as is commonly the case in engineering consulting (e.g., firms such as SNC-Lavalin set up offices in India and have their Indian employees do the routine part of the engineering work for large projects), or they may be external, as is

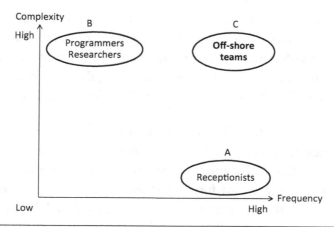

Figure 5.1 Two Dimensions of Human Interaction

more commonly the case in the IT sector (where IT consulting firms such as Infosys and Tata Consulting Services provide offshore services to many IT businesses and departments within large North American organizations).

Whether offshore resources are internal or external, the key challenging aspect of offshoring for North American organizations is that it involves interactions that are both frequent and complex between people who are quite culturally different and who usually never meet in person. Figure 5.1 describes the complexity and frequency when different groups of people interact with one another:

A. Most North American receptionists have frequent interactions with people who are culturally different from them, but these interactions are not complex. As a result, if one of these interactions goes awry, the impact on the organization is usually minimal.

B. Many programmers or researchers have complex but infrequent interactions with culturally different people. They may go to meetings from time to time, get the information they need and then come back to their work space and complete their work on their own. Again, if things go off track, the impact on the organization as a whole is small.

C. In the offshore situation, the interactions between culturally different people are both frequent and complex, the probability of misunderstandings increases and the impact they have on the organization as a whole becomes quite significant. Particularly, when North American organizations involve offshore resources in the delivery of services to their own clients, they may end up missing a deadline or not meeting their clients' expectations.

We explore in this chapter the interactions between a team in North America and an offshore team located in another part of the world. According to Tuckman's team development model, most teams go through four stages of forming, storming, norming and performing. When the team members have to manage cultural, language and time differences, the challenges at the forming and storming stage become much more frustrating and take much more effort to overcome. But it is possible to bridge the gap. We have been working with a number of organizations helping onshore and offshore teams work together. Comments we often hear include, "I wish I had learned this six months ago, when I started working with my [Indian/Filipino/Mexican/etc.] counterparts—it would have saved me so much time and frustration." We hope that reading this chapter will save you a lot of time and frustration.

Section 5.1: Forming the Offshore Team

Selecting Offshore Resources

As discussed in Chapters 2 and 3, hierarchical and egalitarian organizations measure performance in different ways—egalitarian organizations place more emphasis on soft skills than do hierarchical organizations. They also select employees for specific positions based on different criteria:

• North American organizations tend to emphasize specialization and experience. When screening résumés or interviewing candidates, North American HR professionals and managers typically look for candidates who have clearly demonstrated the skills their organization is looking for, and are familiar with their industrial sector.

- By contrast, the countries that perform offshore work are usually developing countries and often have proportionately fewer people who have postsecondary education. As a result, organizations in these countries usually emphasize education. Employees who hold graduate degrees are considered more qualified than those who hold undergraduate degrees, and those with bachelor's degrees are considered more qualified than those who have three-year diplomas. They are given opportunities to learn different jobs and gain broader experience. Consequently, breadth of experience is valued.

As a result, North American organizations and their offshore counterparts often identify different people as the best person for the job. This difference usually comes to a head in two circumstances: When selecting resources for a project and when deciding who should be promoted. We examine the selection of resources for a project here and look at promotion later in this chapter. Here is the challenge encountered by one organization:

The company experienced a burst of activity in Canada and needed to bring offshore resources from its facilities in India to meet tight deadlines. The Canadian HR manager, Sally, sent the job descriptions to the Indian HR manager, Indira, who made a first selection from her pool of candidates and sent a batch of résumés. Sally sorted these résumés and sent back two piles—the yes and the no. Since the yes pile was not sufficient to fill all the positions, Sally asked Indira to send more resumes. To Sally's surprise, the second pile of resumes included some of the people she had already rejected. She went through the same sorting process and sent back two piles, the yes and the no. Still not all the positions were filled, so Sally asked Indira to send more résumés. To her annoyance, the third pile contained résumés of people she had already rejected twice. At that point, Sally decided to call Indira in order to understand what was going on.

In the ensuing discussion, Sally and Indira realized they were using different criteria to evaluate qualifications for specific positions. Indira was focusing on education—in essence, she was looking at the highest degree obtained by candidates and the ranking of the university from which they obtained these degrees. For example, the pile of people who were rejected twice included several graduates of the Indian Institute of Technology (the best university in India). In Indira's mind, these were clearly the best candidates she could put forward. When Sally rejected these candidates, Indira reacted by reformatting the résumés of these top-notch candidates, thinking that, if she communicated their qualifications better, Sally would clearly see that these were top candidates.

By contrast, Sally was looking for specific experience. For example, have they programmed in these languages? Have they worked on these kind of applications before? Since the resumes of these top-notch candidates (by Indian standards) did not show this kind of experience, she rejected them, thinking they were unqualified for the position.

How can you bridge this gap? This kind of difference is likely to create challenges whenever people in North America and offshore resources are both involved in the selection process, so it is useful to discuss the criteria you will use to select candidates whenever you anticipate getting into such a situation:

Have this conversation as early in the process as possible. The longer you wait, the more likely frustration will build up on both sides.

Make this conversation as specific as possible. Take a real-life job description and some real-life résumés to ground your discussion with your offshore counterparts; if you have this discussion in principles, you are very likely to reach an agreement that will not withstand the first real-life test.

Ask your counterpart to rate or rank a set of résumés first, then tell them how you rate or rank them. If you go first, some offshore HR professionals react by telling you they would have rated these résumés the same way you did—they see your logic, but it is not the logic they would have used if you had given them a clean slate.

Establishing Credibility

When North American and offshore professionals get together for the first time, they introduce themselves to one another. In this situation, most people try to say something about themselves that will give others a measure of their capabilities—in other words, we all try to establish credibility. What we say about ourselves depends on what resonates with our peers; in most cases, this is culture specific. As a trainer who delivers workshops in several countries, Lionel is often in the situation where he introduces himself to a new audience; in this situation, he has two minutes to say things that resonate with the audience to make them feel that the workshop organizers found the right person and that they are going to learn something from him. Through experience, Lionel has found that he needed to adapt his approach to the cultural background of his audience:

- In Canada, the main driver for credibility is having similar experience with a similar organization. Saying that "I have delivered workshops on the same topic to organizations similar to yours" and giving specific examples of these workshop topics and organizations usually generates a positive response from a Canadian audience.
- In the US, Lionel has found that having a degree from a recognized American university helps a lot. When American workshop organizers introduce him, they usually mention the fact that he has a Ph.D. from Caltech and is a recognized expert in the field—this usually sets the right tone for the workshop.
- In France, Lionel emphasizes his undergraduate degree. Having graduated from the École Polytechnique means a lot to French people—it is like graduating from the Indian Institute of Technology in India, from the University of Tokyo in Japan or Qinghua University in China. To French people, it means you are a smart person, worth listening to, even though the subject Lionel studied there is engineering, not human resources.

In most countries where North American organizations offshore work, the important factors tend to be as follows:

- Education: From a hierarchical perspective, graduate degrees give you an edge over people who have a bachelor's degree—the idea that a Ph.D. provides theoretical expertise but not the technical skills to solve practical problems does not exist in developing countries.
- Ranking of the university/universities from which you obtained your degree(s): The higher the ranking, the better.

- Position title
- Number of people reporting to you: Higher numbers make you more important in hierarchical cultures.
- Names of organizations you have worked for: The better known they are, the more credibility you get.
- Business trips you have taken overseas: If people need you to go overseas to work on a specific problem, it means you bring a lot of value to the organization.

Our recommendation to North American professionals who work with offshore resources is to identify ahead of time the elements in your professional past and current situation that generate the most positive response from your offshore counterparts. In the case of people who have degrees or titles that are likely to generate a positive response, the solution is relatively simple.

In our experience, the people who run into the biggest challenge when trying to establish credibility with their offshore counterparts are those who have many years of experience but no college or university degree. For example, think of people who graduated from high school in the 1970s and found programming really cool; they got into IT and became the organization's guru in a very specific technical area (let's use online transaction security as an example). They might have only one intern student reporting to them, but the CIO includes them in any visioning discussion. These professionals score low on many of the criteria hierarchical people use to measure one another—no college or university degree, no reports. However, they can establish credibility in the minds of their offshore counterparts by mentioning three things: First, an important-sounding title, such as senior chief engineer; second, their close connection to someone who has a high position in the organization; and third, the articles/books they have published or presentations they have made at international conferences. While doing this usually feels quite uncomfortable to many North American professionals, remember that the goal here is to establish credibility—since people use different criteria, you might as well use an approach that resonates with them, even if this approach seems strange to you.

The Bridging Team

When a North American organization decides to offshore work, some positions may be eliminated in North America while others are created elsewhere. This is not a one-to-one process. Offshoring the work done by twenty professional staff in North America does not result in the elimination of twenty positions in North America and the creation of twenty positions in the offshore location. The experience of many organizations seems to indicate the following:

- There is often a need for more offshore resources than the prior resources in North America. The ratio is typically 1.5 to 2. Initially, organizations have to invest time and resources to train junior resources to become familiar with their domain. The productivity improves after a few years, but the cost goes up, as they have to pay for the experience of senior resources.
- On the North American side, organizations often need dedicated people who combine good technical skills with good soft skills to support the offshore resources and have the following:

  ○ The ability to translate the business requirements into specifications that "speak" to their offshore resources—in particular, deep technical breadth to answer questions knowledgably on a wide variety of topics and to be seen as a technical expert in those areas

  ○ The cultural dexterity to be able to influence their offshore counterparts with as little recourse to hierarchy as possible—in particular, flexibility to adapt to time and cultural differences

  ○ Good soft skills to interact with their North American peers and make them understand both the strengths and the limitations of the offshoring model

A number of our clients have jumped into offshoring with both feet and could have benefitted from a more gradual transition. In particular, it is important to recognize that there will be a learning curve when an organization goes from having Bob or Sally down the hall work on X to having Bhavesh or Iulia work on X halfway around the world. Many North American organizations find that their work processes need to change to adapt to the offshore model. Doing a pilot project with part of the organization and reapplying the lessons learned to the remainder of the offshoring project is an effective way to achieve the strategic cost-saving goals desired through offshoring.

To effectively connect two teams from different cultures and time zones, many organizations have created a group that acts as a bridge between the two organizations. This Bridging Team is a small group of people who do the following:

- Interact with one another very frequently (at least daily) and therefore get to know one another very well
- Shift their regular working hours in order to increase the overlap between their work days so they can communicate by phone or videoconference more frequently
- Meet face to face from time to time (maybe once a quarter) as a way to do status updates and clear the air of misunderstandings that may have accumulated over time

Different organizations have set up the Bridging Team in different ways:

- In some organizations (e.g., engineering consulting firms), the Bridging Team has members located in both countries. Its purpose is to be an internal resource for people who are experiencing difficulties with their colleagues in the other location. Members of this team provide advice on how to improve the quality of the relationship, increase communication effectiveness and bring projects back on track.
- In others (e.g., financial institutions), the Bridging Team is located in North America and includes people from the North American organization and onshore representatives of the offshore organization. They meet at the end of each North American business day. After that, the onshore representatives talk to their offshore colleagues and guide them (e.g., by providing either more detail or more context to the e-mail messages sent by the North American organization).

In our experience, this is an area where HR professionals can add significant value to the business. By becoming part of these Bridging Teams, you can get to know your offshore counterparts and become a source of advice for the technical teams in North America. You can augment the knowledge of cultural differences you acquire through firsthand interactions by providing coaching and training to help technical teams understand cultural differences and deal with interpersonal issues.

Section 5.2: Storming through Initial Challenges

Getting Honest Feedback

One of the most frequent frustrations egalitarian North American managers experience when working with their offshore resources is the absence of feedback. A typical situation in many organizations is when the offshore team is asked to perform certain tasks. Managers in North America hear "yes" all the time, which they interpret as "no issue" on the offshore side. When the deadline comes, they experience a nasty surprise. It turns out the offshore team did not have the resources, tools or expertise to complete the tasks. But no one wanted to tell their North American managers. They tried all kinds of things and worked extremely long hours hoping they could find a way to pull it off. But in the end, they could not.

The root cause of this problem is that offshore employees often grew up in more hierarchical cultures than those of the US or Canada. They view their North American counterparts as higher up than they are in general and observe a certain hierarchy within their own local team in particular. For example, this is what happens during the conference call on the other side of the line.

Tim is the IT director of an American organization. He is chairing a conference call with the offshore team in India. The two teams are working concurrently to implement a new application. They run into a problem that may delay the go-live schedule. Tim asks one offshore software architect, Deepa, "What do you think of this solution? Is this going to work?" Deepa looks to Ashok, her IT director. Ashok makes a gesture that clearly means,

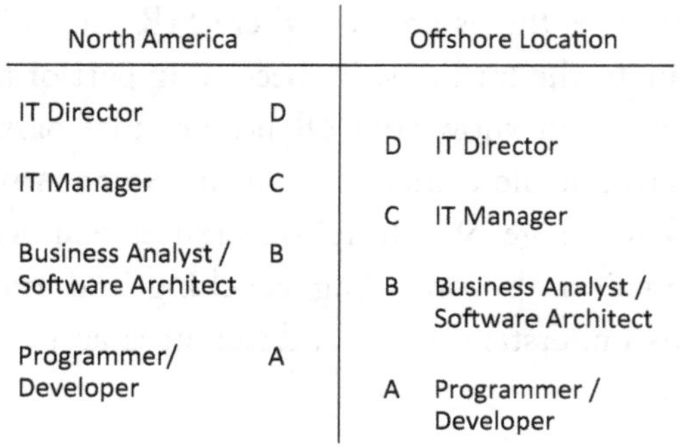

North America		Offshore Location	
IT Director	D		
		D	IT Director
IT Manager	C		
		C	IT Manager
Business Analyst / Software Architect	B		
		B	Business Analyst / Software Architect
Programmer/ Developer	A		
		A	Programmer / Developer

Figure 5.2 Offshore Resources' View of Hierarchy

"No problem, we will get it done." Deepa answers, "Yes." Since the communication between Deepa and Ashok is done nonverbally, all Tim can hear is a short silence and then "yes" from Deepa.

In this situation, Ashok views Tim as higher up than he is because, in the mind of the offshore team members, people in North America are slightly higher than their offshore counterparts because they are closer to the center of the organization. In other words, a North American IT director trumps an offshore IT director. Figure 5.2 represents this sense of hierarchy graphically (while different organizations may have different titles and levels, the concept remains the same). Being a good employee in hierarchical countries is to do what your manager tells you to do. Once Ashok said yes, Deepa has no chance to disagree, even though she is the technical expert and is closer to the problem than Ashok. Disagreeing with one's manager may often jeopardize one's career in ways inconceivable to egalitarian people.

Bridging the Hierarchy and Feedback Gap

North American managers need to probe one on one with the key offshore technical experts and handle very carefully the first few situations when an offshore employee gives them feedback. In the previous example, Tim could call Deepa after the team meeting to follow up. If Deepa finally gathers enough courage to tell Tim that she thinks the solution will not work, Tim should do the following:

- Praise her for giving him this feedback in private. Do not mention this during a team meeting since this will imply she has talked to Tim individually, and her managers will start wondering what else she has told him. They may go and ask her in that case, which will put her in an uncomfortable situation.
- Listen carefully to Deepa and take notes.
- Ask clarifying questions only when she has finished saying her piece because she may misinterpret clarifying questions as justifying his perspective.

More generally, managers can ensure getting feedback from offshore employees more often and reading the feedback they provide more accurately by combining the following action steps:

Consider using suggestions in Chapter 2 on how to deal with feedback intensity differences **and in Chapter 3** regarding hierarchy differences.

Keep the relative position of your offshore counterparts constantly in mind. In particular, get a copy of their organizational chart and learn to recognize who is above or below whom. Also learn to recognize who is above or below you since this will likely have an impact on how much weight they place on your suggestions.

Use higher bandwidth communication media whenever you have a choice. The higher the bandwidth, the more likely you are to pick up that someone is reacting negatively without expressing his or her thoughts verbally. For example, video conferencing can give you an idea of people's body language; you cannot get it by telephone. Obviously, there are practical limitations to this. Meeting face to face is usually best, but the economic benefits of offshoring will be quickly wiped out by travel expenses if your team meets in person regularly.

Include in your North American team one person who is familiar with the culture of your offshore resources. This is relatively easy in most cases if you are located in a large metropolitan center. You can find immigrants from India, the Philippines or Mexico who can help you "read between the lines" and understand the interpersonal dynamics on the offshore side. In the movie *Fail-Safe*,[3] the American president asks his interpreter to tell him of any nonverbal cues he can pick up while listening to what the Russian president says. This is one of the roles this team member can play. He or she can also translate a term or an expression into the first language of your offshore resources (if English is not their first language) to enhance their understanding of critical points.

Ask your offshore resources to write minutes of every conference call or meeting. This enables you to see what they took away from the conversation and whether there are gaps. When you find gaps (sooner or later, there will be), inquire about what is missing from the perspective of a misunderstanding or a difference of interpretation. They may be trying to tell you they disagree with a decision made during the call by leaving it out from the minutes.

Listen between the lines. Another approach offshore team members use to express disagreement is to ask what your manager thinks of a decision/solution. If you hear them asking, "What does the VP or CEO think?" you should probe further and ask what concerns the VP or CEO might have. This provides them an avenue to express their concerns without sounding like they disagree with you.

Create a personal relationship with your offshore resources. Many offshore resources feel their North American managers only care about the work they produce and do not care about them as people because they never get any personal questions from them. From a North American perspective, this implies "I respect your privacy" and "I want us to be efficient." However, long-term efficiency is usually improved through good working relationships, and some relationship building goes a long way in most offshoring situations. In most cultures, you get more of the real scoop if people feel you are connected with them on a personal level. Here are a few suggestions:

- **Pay attention to the topics they discuss and to what they say** when they chit-chat (e.g., either with you or among themselves when you are all waiting for a conference call to start). Asking them questions down the road about an event they mentioned in passing helps build rapport. For example, if offshore employees mentioned that their kids are taking exams on Friday, asking them on the following

Monday how their kids did on their exams shows you are interested in them above and beyond the work they produce.

- **Ask questions about them or their country.** In order to avoid bringing up a topic that may hurt their national pride, ask open-ended questions. For example, "If I were to watch one [Indian/Filipino/ Romanian/etc.] movie that would help me understand your country better, which one would you recommend?" Another safe topic is the educational system in your offshore resources' country. This topic is of interest to everyone around the world, and learning about the educational system in a country helps you understand better how people from that country think.

- **Go and visit your offshore resources if you can arrange it.** This will help you develop even more of a personal relationship with them. If you go there on business, make sure you spend some personal time there and visit somewhere meaningful to the local people. Most offshore resources react quite negatively to the North American approach to business trips—fly in on Monday, work until Friday and fly back as soon as the last business meeting is over. Most people interpret this behavior as implying a lack of interest in their country and culture. If you fly to India, make sure you visit one culturally meaningful site before leaving—your offshore resources will be more than happy to take you there.

- **Consider taking a vacation** there if your organization has a travel budget freeze and you cannot make it happen as a business trip. If you go there at your own expense, your offshore resources will probably go out their way to host you, help you find good deals and show you around. You are guaranteed to learn extensively about their culture and the way they think; you will obviously also enhance your work relationship.

Building a personal relationship with your key offshore counterparts can make a major difference; in most cases, they welcome the opportunity to do so. For example, the Canadian person who negotiated the offshoring of IT processes to India on behalf of his corporation said that in two weeks he learned more about his Indian counterparts than he had learned about some of his Canadian colleagues in ten years, and this really helped smooth things over during some of the tense negotiating moments.

Section 5.3: Establishing Team Norms

As teams overcome challenges in the forming and storming stage, they gradually start to establish some group norms and communication protocols. Let's look at a few situations where North American and offshoring teams need to establish how they want to work together.

Brainstorming Effectively with Offshore Resources

Tim's team includes people in the US and India; from a hierarchical perspective, the team is composed of people at four different levels (IT director, IT manager, business analyst or software architect and programmer or developer, in decreasing order of rank). Tim is holding a brainstorming session and wants ideas and suggestions from the whole team. However, he only gets participation from the American team members and from the Indian IT director, as represented graphically by Figure 5.3. The Indian IT manager contributes a word or two, mostly agreeing. The Indian software architects, business analysts, programmers and developers hardly say anything. Tim gets very frustrated and tells everyone at the beginning of the next brainstorming session, "Let's check the titles at the door—everyone here is expected to contribute equally to the discussion, no matter what your title is. I want to hear ideas from everyone."

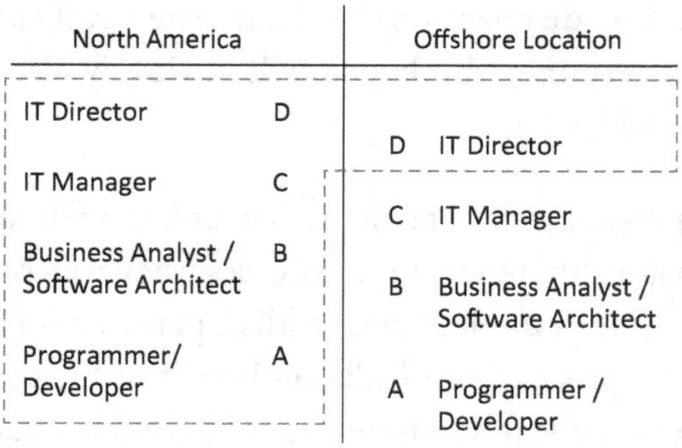

North America		Offshore Location	
IT Director	D		
		D	IT Director
IT Manager	C		
		C	IT Manager
Business Analyst / Software Architect	B		
		B	Business Analyst / Software Architect
Programmer/ Developer	A		
		A	Programmer / Developer

Figure 5.3 Participation in Joint Brainstorming Sessions

The Indian employees' behavior is completely in line with their cultural norm. They do not want to say anything that may be perceived somehow as wrong by their superiors, and they do not see themselves as being able to add much value in their superior's presence. In their mind, their primary purpose for attending the meeting is to listen and learn from their superiors so they can anticipate what to do down the road. The idea of "checking the titles at the door" makes complete sense in an egalitarian environment (it is possible to suspend hierarchy during a brainstorming discussion in North America). Such a statement makes no sense at all in hierarchical cultures. In most cases, asking people who have grown up in a hierarchical environment to remove hierarchy from the discussion is like asking North Americans to cut in line—it violates social rules that are deeply ingrained in them and simply cannot happen. Indians or Mexicans are just as likely to "check titles at the door" as Americans or Canadians are to cut in line; they will also be just as uncomfortable when trying to do it the first time.

This does not mean that people cannot learn to adjust their behavior. People can learn, particularly if the offshore resources have worked extensively with North American organizations or have studied in Western countries (meaning North America, Western Europe or Australia/New Zealand). However, it is important to recognize that brainstorming in groups where some people are higher than others is hard to do in a hierarchical culture; different approaches are needed.

One approach that works well is to break down the group into separate groups by level as shown in Figure 5.4. In other words, you ask the business analysts and software architects in both locations to brainstorm as one group and the programmers and developers to brainstorm as another group. If you have three or more IT directors, have them brainstorm as a group; if not, include them in the IT managers' brainstorming discussion, but ask your offshore IT director not to get involved in the brainstorming discussion until the IT managers seem to run out of ideas (his or her presence may otherwise skew the results of the discussion of that group). As the arrow in Figure 5.4 indicates, you also want to ask groups to present in reverse order of hierarchy; in other words, you first ask the programmers/developers

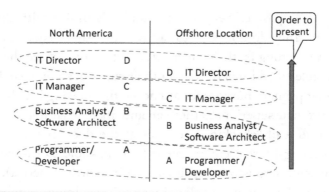

Figure 5.4 Separate Brainstorming Groups

group to present the result of their discussions, then you ask the software architects/business analysts group to present and you keep moving up the hierarchy. This approach prevents a group of junior people from saying, "We found the same conclusion as this group [of more senior people]" when they may have in fact come up with better ideas.

If you, as a North American manager, already have formulated ideas, but want to get honest feedback from everyone, there are a few approaches you can take:

Present your idea as "an idea" that was given to you by an unspecified person. By disconnecting your name from the idea, you have a better chance of getting everyone's thoughts. When you use this approach, remember to remain as noncommittal about this idea as you possibly can be. Hierarchical people are usually very good at reading the nonverbal cues of the people who are above them in the organization because being able to determine what their managers want without them having to explain it is an important skill there. (Hierarchical people practice that skill extensively with parents and teachers and are good at it by the time they get into the workplace.)

"Plant" your idea with one of the North American members of your team whose position will not become a factor in the discussion. For example, if you talk to one of your programmers or developers before the meeting and ask him or her to mention your idea as if it was his or hers, you can remove the hierarchy variable from the evaluation of this idea.

"Poll" people at each level. You present your idea at one meeting and then say you will discuss it at the next meeting. In between, North American programmers talk to their offshore counterparts to find out what they think, North American software architects talk to the offshore software architects to get their perspective and so on at each level. This process enables you to get the perspective of every team member.

Note that you can remove the hierarchy variable from the discussion to some extent, but not completely. Even if you remove the connection between you and your idea to make it safe for the offshore members of your team to comment on it freely, they will still be paying attention to the hierarchy on their side. For example, if one of the offshore IT managers says your idea is a great idea because of X, the offshore business analysts and programmers are now precluded from saying they think it may not work or providing suggestions to make it work better.

Changing the Scope of an Offshore Project

Tim has convened a meeting and is explaining to the offshore resources that he needs to change the scope of the project for a number of reasons. One of the meeting participants on the offshore side has a higher position than Tim does—she is a vice president (VP) while Tim is at the director level.

Here is what happens on the other side of the line: When Tim describes the change he wants the offshore team to make, they all immediately turn to the highest-ranked person on their side (the VP) and ask nonverbally, "What do you think?" Because the question is asked nonverbally, Tim does not notice anything if this is taking place during a conference call. The response of this VP is key: If she gestures something like, "Do what you are asked to do," everything is moving along swimmingly. However, if she gestures something like, "Ignore this—keep doing what you were asked to do before," then whatever Tim says during the remainder of this meeting will be dutifully ignored.

Again, this phenomenon is the result of differences in the sense of hierarchy within the offshore team. From their perspective, the VP is responsible to her superior in North America. They are responsible to the manager directly above each of them. If the highest person on their side has decided to move in a certain direction, there is a good reason for that, and it is not their role to question it. To handle such a complex situation, there are several things North American managers can do.

Schedule a call with this VP ahead of the team meeting to ensure alignment. This gives you a chance to gauge how supportive this VP is and better plan how to position the change.

Present the change as tentative, as something you are considering and want to get feedback on from your offshore resources, if this off-shore VP appears at the conference call unexpectedly and you are not sure of her position on the change. You may then call this VP afterward in order to understand her perspective. You also want to understand why she showed up at this particular meeting—her presence can be explained in many different ways, but if it is an unusual event, you want to understand what brought her there. One of the possible explanations may be that your offshore resources got wind you were planning such a change in project scope and wanted to tell you they disagreed but could not do it themselves.

Bring in reinforcements by asking your manager, a North American VP, to be part of the meeting if you anticipate resistance from the offshore VP. In that case, make sure your manager comments positively on the change you are proposing during the conference call so it is clear to your offshore resources that you have support from above.

When working with hierarchical offshore resources, you are likely to need to involve your manager in your work more frequently and to a greater extent than you usually do for several reasons:

- Hierarchical people copy their own managers on a higher percentage of their e-mail messages than egalitarian people do, so you end up at times having to copy your manager on messages you normally would not.
- There are times when the only way to break through some deadlock is to bring in your manager and have him or her give you support explicitly.

In our experience, one key consideration is whether your manager is looking at his or her additional involvement (above and beyond the level of involvement he or she would have if you were not working with offshore resources) as a limitation on your part. In this context, you and your manager need to agree that some additional involvement on his or her part is by no means a sign of ineffectiveness on your part—it is simply a reflection of the stronger sense of hierarchy of your offshore counterparts. As you can see, the offshore business model may have an unexpected influence on how North American managers and employees work together. Adjusting to the changing needs is the key to achieve the goals of offshoring.

Bringing an Offshore Technical Expert to North America

Here is a situation that many managers have encountered:

Tim's team has been working on a difficult technical problem for a little while now. One of the offshore software architects (Bipin) is clearly contributing extensively to the solution of this problem. Some of the North American team members asked Tim to bring Bipin onshore to speed up the team's progress. When Tim mentions this option to Bipin's direct manager, Jasbinder, he is clearly underwhelmed. Tim follows up with Jasbinder on several occasions. Every time Tim asks when Bipin can come to North America, Jasbinder responds, "Later—after X is completed. . . ." Tim is wondering what is going on here.

The key question here is whether Jasbinder has already been overseas or not. If the answer is no, then having one of his direct reports go to North America before he does upsets the apple cart—Bipin will see his social status boosted significantly by his stint in North America, to the point where Jasbinder may feel his position within the organization is threatened by Bipin's sudden rise. The easiest solution for him is to postpone Bipin's trip continuously until it becomes not useful anymore or until Tim realizes he needs to bring both to North America.

Many egalitarian managers have a difficult time with this last point, particularly when they are external clients. They react by saying, "You mean that I need to bring both Bipin and Jasbinder and pay for the time and travel expenses of both people, even though I only want Bipin?" In most cases, the answer ends up being, "Yes, you do—no matter how illogical or ineffective this may seem to you."

In a situation like this, you probably want to talk to the IT director (Ashok, in this case), before discussing it with either Bipin or Jasbinder, in order to understand the situation—within the chain of command, who has already traveled overseas and who has not? How do people feel about this idea? As you move up the hierarchy, the chances that people have traveled overseas increase, so you will probably not need to bring Jasbinder's manager as well—chances are he or she has traveled overseas sufficiently for his or her social status not to be affected by Bipin's trip. Once you have established that you need to bring Jasbinder in order to have Bipin, you can structure the trip so that you meet your objectives while they meet theirs. For example, you may bring Bipin to North America for three months so he can work closely with your onshore team, while you bring Jasbinder for two weeks and have him meet several high-level people in the North American organization (meeting these high-level people gives him extensive social status, which more than compensates for his shorter trip). This arrangement may incur more cost for the short term but can turn out to be a good long-term investment.

Section 5.4: Reaching High Performance

Promoting Offshore Resources

From an organizational perspective, the other area where differences in the sense of hierarchy make a difference is promotions among offshore resources (see Chapter 4 for more on promotions):

- The promotion process in hierarchical cultures is different from the promotion process in egalitarian cultures: In hierarchical cultures, a promotion is a step change, where the employee trades a set of responsibilities, title and compensation for another, while in egalitarian cultures promotions are gradual increases in responsibilities followed by a change in title and compensation.

- The criteria used to judge who is best positioned for a given promotion are different: In hierarchical cultures, more weight is given to technical skills (in particular, education) while egalitarian cultures place more emphasis on soft skills.

These differences create challenges for North American organizations when a managerial position needs to be filled and the person who gets this position needs to achieve objectives set by the North American organization through a team of offshore resources. If the two organizations (North American client and offshore service provider) make these decisions independently, they often end up in the following situation:

- From the offshore organization's perspective, the people who end up being promoted on the North American side are often considered as the wrong choices because they are not strong enough technically. Given the same slate of candidates, people in the offshore organization would have chosen someone else—usually someone with better technical skills, as demonstrated by the fact that this person has a higher degree or graduated from a better university than the person who got the position.
- From the North American organization's perspective, the people who end up being promoted on the offshore side are often considered the wrong choice because their soft skills are not as good as those of some of the other candidates. For example, people on the North American side will often place quite a bit of importance on the ability of the successful candidate to communicate well in English by e-mail and during conference calls. In most cases, people on the offshore side place much less weight on that skill when making the promotion decision.

In other words, we often end up with people on both sides scratching their heads and wondering why people on the other side decided to promote X when Y was clearly a better candidate. So how do we bridge this gap?

In our experience, the solution to this problem combines two action items:

Educate people involved on the cultural differences that exist between the two organizations. This helps them see the rationale of their counterparts—the difference in outcome comes from a difference in performance evaluation criteria. This step helps remove some of the frustration experienced by many in this kind of situation.

Discuss the criteria used to assess people's qualifications for a promotion and the relative weights placed on each criterion. The conversation is similar to the conversations managers and HR professionals have when jointly selecting people for specific positions—the suggestions made earlier in this chapter apply here as well.

Note that the second action item assumes each organization has some input in the other's promotion process. This is more likely to be the case when the offshore organization is a subsidiary of the North American organization than when the offshore organization is an independent service organization that provides offshoring services to a large number of multinational organizations.

Retaining Offshore Resources

Most of the destination countries of offshore work are going through rapid economic growth. As a result, while there is a large labor pool available, there is also a skills shortage in the sectors and professions to which North American organizations offshore work. One North American organization mentioned that they had a total of ten positions to fill in India one summer. Eight candidates accepted their job offers; only one showed up on the first day of work.

When the labor market in which they operate becomes an employee's market (think of the IT sector in the late 1990s, the audit sector when Sarbanes-Oxley was being implemented or Alberta or Texas between 2005 and 2008), organizations usually experience significant retention challenges. Employees who are in any way dissatisfied with their situation can find other positions very quickly and often get raises in the process. From the organization's perspective, the biggest casualty in this environment is project continuity. Experienced people leave and are replaced by people who are new to the project, meaning that they need to be introduced to the objectives, work methods and people, sending the team going through the forming, storming and norming stages again.

Retention has become a major issue in a number of offshore organizations. It is important for North American organizations to both understand what that situation means for their offshore counterparts and to recognize that hierarchical and egalitarian organizations deal with these issues differently. The following are the most powerful tools hierarchical offshore organizations have to retain their employees in a boom period:

- **Titles and promotions:** By giving their employees rapid promotions, they can entice people to stay, since obtaining a high-level title is a common career goal in hierarchical cultures.
- **The opportunity to go overseas:** Trips overseas increase employees' social status and make them more valuable.

When offshore resources interact with their North American counterparts, this can create tension between people:

- Some of the people in the North American organization may not understand (or may even become envious of) the rapid promotions their offshore counterparts receive. Some of the people we coached one on one said they felt "left behind" by their offshore counterparts who got three promotions while they got only one, if any.
- "Title inflation" may result in some young offshore resources having titles that could not be obtained in North America without significantly more years of experience; this may translate into significant gaps between expected and actual levels of skills. If it takes twenty-five years to obtain a title such as "principal architect" in North America and someone in India has obtained it in nine years, the North American counterparts of this person are likely to expect a level of performance in line with what the title means in North America, whereas it may mean something different in India.

- Bringing people to North America can be a significant financial burden that reduces the economic benefits of offshoring for the North American organization.

Continuous communication between offshore and North American managers and HR professionals is critical in order to help alleviate this kind of issue. For example, through such conversations, one of our clients found a creative way to balance the need of the offshore organization to promote people frequently while keeping titles consistent across geographies. They divided each of their North American levels into three levels. Where no differentiation was made between software programmers in North America, their Indian subsidiary had junior software programmers, intermediate software programmers and senior software programmers. The key success factor in this communication process was a strong desire on both sides to look for solutions that met the key needs of everyone.

Providing Cross-Cultural Training

In the experience of our clients, providing cross-cultural training to the people involved in offshore work helps the teams move through the first three stages faster. It provides everyone with a framework to analyze their experiences. In particular, understanding the interactions between hierarchy and cross-cultural feedback helps explain many situations people have experienced. When training people who have already worked with offshore resources for a while, we frequently hear, "Now I understand what happened when [. . .]!" It also provides them a forum to discuss and identify new approaches they can implement when they experience similar situations in the future.

Organizations that decide to provide cross-cultural training to their North American employees involved in offshore projects may want to keep the following two points in mind:

- It is important to consider when is the best time to provide this kind of training. Because many people react by saying, "I wish I had known this before I started interacting with my offshore resources," it is logical to conclude that this kind of training should be offered before people start working on offshore projects. In our experience, this kind of training is best scheduled a few weeks or months after people have started working with their offshore counterparts. We find that participants need to have experienced some of the frustrations involved in offshoring in order to make them feel that the problem is real and that they need to adapt. We also find it is best to provide this kind of training before people have developed an "us versus them" mind-set.

- The same training should be provided to the offshore employees. In every workshop we have delivered in North America, participants ask, "What kind of training do my offshore counterparts get?" Implicit in this question is the expectation that "they should get the same training and make at least as much effort to adapt as I am required to make." It is an investment that can increase the overall success of the offshore project and a valuable retention tool for the offshore organization.

Continuing the Relationship Building

Coming back to our question of who should adapt to whom, while people on both sides agree that offshore resources need to make more effort to adapt to the North American organization's way of doing business, there are many things North American organizations can do to make their share of the adaptation. Here are a few suggestions:

Lead by example: For example, change "meeting" times so the inconvenience does not always fall on the offshore resources. An expatriate to the Philippines realized the local people were getting up at 2 a.m. to take conference calls, but no one wanted to tell their North American counterparts to schedule calls at a different time. One manager in Hong Kong said she has conference calls every day of the week at 9 p.m., including Friday evening. What kind of work–life balance does she have?

Because we are dealing with people who have a very high sense of hierarchy, people on the North American side of the line need to initiate the conversation and offer to make an effort to accommodate their offshore counterparts' needs. This simple action demonstrates to hierarchical employees the egalitarian culture in a concrete way and helps build a collaborative work culture among the project team.

Be a good host: Take good care of the offshore resources when they come to North America for training or temporary work. When North American colleagues leave the office on Friday afternoons with a short "Have a good weekend!" the visiting offshore employees find it very strange. They do not know the place well and often do not have access to a car, which can be very inconvenient if your office and/or their hotel are in the suburbs. But they are too shy to ask for help. As we discussed in Chapter 3, collective people wait for help to be offered.

When Caroline came to Canada for training in 1992, two Nortel HR managers, who had nothing to do with her visit, came from another office to take her out for lunch at the CN Tower because when they visited China, the local people treated them with overwhelming hospitality. So go the extra mile, arrange for your team members to take the offshore employees out for meals or sightseeing or shopping (even just for groceries). Do this in turn so it is not too much for any one person, and everyone benefits from the relationship building. Caroline once took a colleague from Taiwan along for the ride when she went to pick up her son from a Scout camp. The colleague said seeing the Canadian countryside was the highlight of her trip. It is a small thing but can generate tremendous goodwill.

* * *

The offshoring business model requires that people from different cultures, in different time zones and speaking different languages work closely together. It requires a lot of conscious effort and hard work from team members on both sides. Building cultural awareness, developing cross-cultural communication skills, providing commitment to ongoing communication, creating clear work processes and demonstrating leadership are key success factors to help the team move through the forming, storming and norming stages and achieve sustainable high performance over time.

Notes

1. Couto, Vinay et al.: *Offshoring 2.0: Contracting Knowledge and Innovation to Expand Global Capabilities*. Durham, NC: Center for International Business Education and Research, Duke University, 2007.
2. Peterson, Erik et al.: *Offshoring Opportunities amid Economic Turbulence—The A. T. Kearney Global Services Location Index 2011*. Chicago, IL: A.T. Kearney, 2011.
3. *Fail-Safe*. 1964. Columbia Pictures, California. Director: Sidney Lumet.

6

Collaborating with Joint Ventures Partners

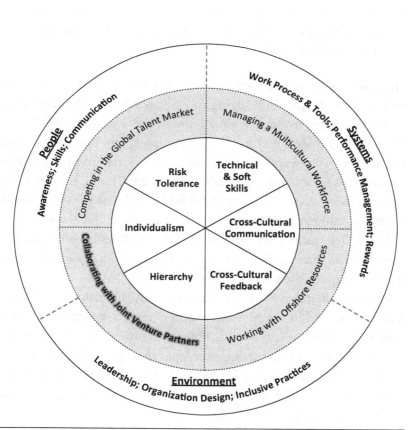

Figure 6.0 Roadmap of the Book

So far, we have examined cross-cultural interactions (immigrants coming to North America in Chapter 2, 3 and 4, offshoring in Chapter 5) where the onus of adaptation was clearly more on one group than on the other:

- Immigrants need to adapt more than North American professionals do because they chose to come to North America.
- Offshore resources need to adapt to a greater extent than their North American clients because they are on the supplier side of the client–supplier relationship.

Obviously, adaptation efforts on the part of North Americans are both welcome and helpful in bridging the gap, as we have discussed so far.

This chapter examines situations where the responsibility for adaptation is distributed more equally among the various stakeholders, namely joint ventures (JVs) of international companies. What happens when a company headquartered in China and a company headquartered in the US form a 50/50 JV in Canada? What about a Canadian company creating a joint venture with a Japanese company in Peru? Determining who needs to adapt to whom becomes harder in this case—in our experience, everyone has a good a reason why others need to adapt to them!

Because all stakeholders are important in this situation, the challenges described in the previous chapters tend to be combined in the case of joint ventures; as a result, managing multicultural JVs can be at times quite difficult. In particular, we find that hierarchy, individualism and risk tolerance can play havoc on JV team members because each team member answers the question "Who makes what decision based on what information?" in a different way.

Section 6.1: The Impact of Hierarchy, Individualism and Risk Tolerance

Who Makes What Decision?

In Chapter 3, we examined the impact of differences in people's sense of hierarchy, and Table 3.1.1 shows the observable differences between hierarchical and egalitarian people at the **individual** level. Here, we are looking at differences between hierarchical and egalitarian **organizations,** which are highlighted in Table 6.1.

For example, when an American organization partners with a Japanese organization to create a JV in Canada, the overall go/no-go decision may be made by the head of the Canadian subsidiary of the American company, while it is likely to be made in Tokyo in the case of the Japanese organization. Similarly, the signing authority may be quite different—the CEO of the Canadian subsidiary of the American company may have ten times the signing authority of the CEO of the Canadian subsidiary of the Japanese company.

In Chapter 3, we examined the impact of differences in people's sense of individualism, and Table 3.3.1 shows the observable

Table 6.1 Differences between Hierarchical and Egalitarian Organizations

	COMPARED WITH EGALITARIAN ORGANIZATIONS, HIERARCHICAL ORGANIZATIONS TEND TO HAVE THE FOLLOWING ATTRIBUTES	COMPARED WITH HIERARCHICAL ORGANIZATIONS, EGALITARIAN ORGANIZATIONS TEND TO HAVE THE FOLLOWING ATTRIBUTES
Decision making	• A given decision is made at a higher level of the organization. • Only the top leaders have the authority to commit the organization.	• A given decision is made at a lower level of the organization. • Managers at lower levels are delegated the authority to commit the organization.
Control from headquarters	• Review meetings by the parent company/head office and visits by head office representatives are more frequent.	• Review meetings by the parent company/head office and visits by head office representatives are less frequent.
Organization leaders	• Most emphasis on degrees from the "best" universities.	• More emphasis on business experience and practical knowledge.
Organization design	• Organization structure is tall with many layers between the first line of workers and the highest executive. • There are more salary bands and wider salary gaps between the bottom and the top.	• Organization structure is flat with fewer layers between the first line of workers and the highest executive. • There are fewer salary bands and smaller salary gaps between the bottom and the top positions.

differences between individualistic and collective people at the *individual* level. Here, we are looking at differences between individualistic and collective *organizations*, which are highlighted in Table 6.2.

For example, when American and Japanese organizations create a JV, more Japanese than Americans attend meetings —even though many of the junior Japanese team members do not say a word during the meeting.

Table 6.2 Differences between Individualistic and Collective Organizations

	COMPARED WITH COLLECTIVE ORGANIZATIONS, INDIVIDUALISTIC ORGANIZATIONS TEND TO HAVE THE FOLLOWING ATTRIBUTES	COMPARED WITH INDIVIDUALISTIC ORGANIZATIONS, COLLECTIVE ORGANIZATIONS TEND TO HAVE THE FOLLOWING ATTRIBUTES
Decision making	• Fewer people are involved in making a particular decision ("too many cooks spoil the broth").	• More people are involved in making a particular decision ("two heads are better than one").
Number of people attending meetings	• Fewer participants attend meetings.	• More participants attend meetings.
Allocation of responsibilities	• One person is accountable for a specific project.	• One group (team/task force/department/etc.) is responsible for a specific project.
Rewards	• Who is the owner of a particular idea is defined more clearly; credit goes to the individual. • Incentives are individual based.	• Who is the owner of a particular idea is not as important; credit goes to the team. • Incentives are team based.
Getting to work	• Very little introduction is needed before getting started.	• There is a strong need to get to know their new colleagues extensively before getting started.
On-boarding of new hires	• New Employee Orientation Program (NEOP) is short, usually half a day to two days. • On-the-job training is provided to help new hires learn the content of their new position.	• NEOP is long and may last up to two years. • On-the-job training is provided to help new hires see the connections between the various departments of the organization and learn the unwritten rules.
Organization leaders	• Leaders tend to be people who have outstanding accomplishment in the key area(s) that drive the financial results of the organization.	• Leaders tend to be people who work well with various stakeholders.

We discussed in Chapter 3 the RACI matrix (Responsible, Approve, Consult, Inform), a tool many organizations use to discuss roles and responsibilities. In the case of a JV between a collective and an individualistic organization, joint project teams often experience difficulties identifying who falls into what category. Collective people tend to think of groups as being responsible, while individualistic people tend to want to identify specific individuals as being responsible. This can create misunderstandings and tension in JV meetings since publicly singling out the responsibility of one person in collective cultures is often interpreted by that person as setting him or her up for failure (the equivalent of publicly putting the person on a performance improvement plan in North America). As a result, when individualistic JV members push to have the name of only one person listed under "Responsible" as opposed to the name of a department, this often generates significant tension on the collective side. Conversely, having the name of a group listed as "Responsible," as collective people like to do, generates significant stress on the individualistic side—as the North American saying goes, "When everyone is responsible, nobody is responsible." In addition, collective people tend to place the same names more to the left on the RACI continuum than individualistic people do; for example, individualistic people may think a particular person needs to be informed, while collective people see the need to consult this person.

In the case of joint ventures, differences in hierarchy and individualism combine to yield very different answers to the question "Who makes what decision?" In hierarchical and collective organizations, the decision is made by a group of high-level people (in many cases, these people are physically located in the organization's head office), whereas it is made by a lower-ranked person by him- or herself in an egalitarian and individualistic organization. The differences tend to show up almost right from the start. In most situations, these differences become visible even before the deal is signed because the way the teams representing each JV partner approach the negotiation of the JV agreement already reflects these differences.

How and When Are Decisions Made?

Chapter 3 examines the impact of differences in risk tolerance at the **individual** level in Table 3.4.1. Table 6.3 highlights differences between risk tolerant and risk averse **organizations**.

Table 6.3 Differences between Risk Tolerant and Risk Averse Organizations

	COMPARED WITH RISK AVERSE ORGANIZATIONS, RISK TOLERANT ORGANIZATIONS TEND TO HAVE THE FOLLOWING ATTRIBUTES	COMPARED WITH RISK TOLERANT ORGANIZATIONS, RISK AVERSE ORGANIZATIONS TEND TO HAVE THE FOLLOWING ATTRIBUTES
Project planning	• Plan in detail only the first few steps of the project and examine only the most likely and/or most potentially damaging contingency scenarios • "We will cross that bridge when we come to it"	• Plan over the entire life of the project and examine many contingencies ("What if?") • "Leave no stone unturned"/"An ounce of prevention is worth a pound of cure"
Rules, regulations and policies	• Create few rules and regulations, often in response to a past problem in an effort to prevent it from happening again • Create rules that describe the "spirit of the law," leaving the "letter of the law" up to the people who implement and regulate the rules	• Create rules in algorithmic manner ("If this happens, then . . .") • Create many rules and regulations—so many that, in extreme cases, some rules contradict one another
Theory and practice	• Use past experience, practical approaches, "rules of thumb" and simulations to resolve complex problems • Final product tests are considered as overall demonstrations of the know-how of the organization and are given top priority; the best technical people are assigned to running these tests	• Use theory, principles, mathematical models and simulations to resolve complex problems • Final product tests are considered as validations of the theoretical models used to create the product and are given limited importance; relatively junior people are assigned to running these tests
Approvals	• Have a simple approval process; a verbal okay is often enough • Require less data, analysis and documentation	• Have an elaborate approval system and often require more signatures for any given decision • Require more data, thorough analysis and documentation

For example, the difference related to risk tolerance became striking when a joint venture between an American company and a French company asked their respective IT suppliers to submit proposals to merge their separate IT systems into one cohesive whole. The French proposal was a 200-page document that tried to anticipate many potential challenges, while the American proposal was a 20-page document where the solution to many issues was "to be determined through discussions with all parties involved."

The main impact of risk tolerance differences is felt on the management of projects at the JV level. As described in Chapter 3, risk tolerant JV team members see their risk averse counterparts as "overly conservative" and interpret their frequent requests for additional data as "analysis paralysis," while risk averse JV team members see their risk tolerant members as "reckless," "cowboys/cowgirls who constantly shoot from the hip" and fundamentally unprofessional. Differences between risk averse and risk tolerant people create major issues when decisions need to be made by the JV as projects progress because the two approaches to decision making tend to be quite different.

Figure 6.1 illustrates the following:

• Risk tolerant teams tend to make incremental decisions; each decision builds on the previous one, and decisions already made are

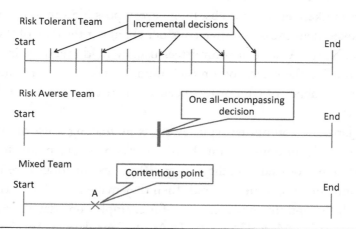

Figure 6.1 Decision Making by Risk Tolerant, Risk Averse and Mixed Teams

rarely revisited unless there seems to be absolutely no other way of going further.

- Risk averse teams tend to make one single, all-encompassing decision that examines all relevant variables at the same time and takes all relevant contingencies/risks into consideration.

For example, let's compare the way a North American team and a Japanese team organize an off-site. Both teams create a committee, often a subset of the team scheduled to attend the actual off-site, and task them with organizing this off-site. How do the organizing committees tackle this task?

- A North American organizing committee typically starts by deciding the date of the off-site (March or April?), then its duration (one or two days?), then the list of participants (who needs to be there?), then the location (in a hotel downtown or a resort out of town?), then the topics of each segment, then the team building activities and so on. While the exact order varies from committee to committee, decisions are usually made sequentially, and each decision builds on the previous one. In this example, once the date is set and blocked in everyone's calendar, the committee is unlikely to revisit it. If their top venue pick is not available on the desired date, they will look for an alternate location available on that date rather than reopen the date discussion. Only in the unlikely event that absolutely every possible venue is already booked does the committee consider changing the date of the off-site. North American committees usually hold meetings in order to finalize their decision on each item; in most cases, the number and frequency of committee meetings increase as the event draws nearer.

- A Japanese committee typically starts by making a list of criteria to rank the options it wants to consider and assigns points to each criterion. For example, they assign 10 points for total price and 5 points for travel time required. Then they make a combinatorial list of all the options they consider—for example, "one day in March," "two days in March," "one day in April," "two days in April" and so on. The committee then rates each option on each criterion. After that, they add the points of each option, and the option that gets the highest number of points is clearly the best choice for everyone. At that point, everyone knows what they need to do—no further meeting is needed.

When you mix the two, as multicultural JV teams usually do, you often end up with extensive frustration on both sides, as illustrated by Figure 6.1:

- If no decisions have been made by the time they have reached Point A, risk tolerant team members feel decisions are not being made quickly enough. They often react by saying things such as, "We are going to be here until the cows come home." In their minds, the lack of decision making means the competition is going to pass them by. This usually generates a tremendous amount of stress.
- Conversely, if decisions are made in the risk tolerant way, risk averse team members feel decisions are being made too quickly and not studied in enough detail, thereby resulting in suboptimal solutions. In their minds, reaching consensus on the "best" solution enables everyone to move forward with a very clear picture of what they need to do once the all-encompassing decision has been made. They will save time down the road.

It is important to keep in mind that one approach is not inherently better than the other; if we look at risk tolerance at the country level, there is no correlation between risk tolerance and development— some developed nations have low risk tolerance (Japan is a good example) while other developed nations have high risk tolerance (like the US and UK). While it is quite tempting to try and convince your JV partners that your approach is better by showcasing the accomplishments of your organization, keep in mind that their organization is also quite successful and can point to accomplishments of their own. Your organization would not have chosen them as a JV partner otherwise.

So how do we deal with cross-cultural issues stemming from risk tolerance differences in the context of JV teams? Here are some practical suggestions:

Conduct an analysis of the costs and benefits of moving forward versus collecting more data. Everyone can challenge their own assumptions. Risk tolerant team members may see the value of collecting one specific set of data but may not go as far as risk averse team members would like to. Similarly, risk tolerant team members may see the benefits of moving forward without collecting specific pieces of data because the risk created by not collecting that data is small or can be readily mitigated down the road.

Introduce additional milestones in the project plan. This helps bridge the gap between the two approaches—the closer the goal is, the more similar the two approaches become.

Avoid discussions at the principle level, and focus any discussion on concrete examples. Look at each situation on its own merit; ask your counterparts how they handle it within their organization, then describe how you handle it within your organization and look for ways that meet every organization's key requirements (not all requirements can be key).

Section 6.2: Forming the JV Team

Like offshore teams, as discussed in Chapter 5, the JV team also goes through the stages of team building—forming, storming, norming, performing. In our experience, the challenges all teams face when going through the first three stages on their way to the performing stage are magnified by cultural differences.

Selecting the Members of a JV Team

Right from the beginning, when selecting team members for the JV, each organization uses its own criteria to determine who is best qualified for the positions. As discussed in Chapter 2, the relative importance each organization assigns to technical skills and soft skills causes major friction. When the joint venture is between a hierarchical and an egalitarian organization, the hierarchical organization is likely to emphasize technical skills (in particular, they may select potential team members based on their degrees and the universities they graduated from) while the egalitarian organization emphasizes soft skills when selecting JV team members. They may also define transferable skills in a different way:

- Hierarchical people see project management experience as more transferable than egalitarian people. In many hierarchical cultures, the key variables are related to the size of the projects people have managed. If you have managed a $200 million project that involved 1,000 people before, you are probably capable of managing a $400 million project with 1,500 people, but you cannot jump to a $5 billion project involving 5,000 people from there. You need some intermediate stepping stones. On the other hand, if you have managed an organization with sales of $500 million and 5,000 employees in the transportation sector, you can probably manage an organization of a similar size in the energy sector.
- Egalitarian people focus more on the industry in which you have gathered your work experience. A move from the transportation sector to the energy sector does not make much sense in egalitarian cultures. They would rather select someone who has managed smaller projects in the same industry than someone who has managed similar-sized projects in other industries. For example, oil sands are unique to Canada. As a result, the only people with oil sands experience are likely those who have worked in Canada.

JV teams often end up with people selected independently by each organization based on different criteria—as a result, when everyone first sits down around the table at the kick-off meeting, some JV team members wonder why the other organization selected these people.

Getting to Know Each Other and Building Trust

During the forming stage, team members need to get to know one another. The challenge in the case of multicultural JV teams is that different people want different pieces of information about their counterparts in order to feel that they "know" them.

When the members of a new multicultural JV team get together for the first time, what should they do? Individualistic team members usually want to introduce themselves in about three sentences, then move on to defining the goal of the team and who is responsible for what. By contrast, collective team members want to get to know their teammates way more extensively (quite often, they would like to get information about their teammates that individualistic team members consider private, such as whether they are married, have kids, have siblings, etc.). Getting through the forming stage usually takes a lot longer in collective cultures than it does in individualistic cultures—entire days may be allocated to having people introduce themselves. In addition, the forming stage in hierarchical cultures includes extensive meals with carefully crafted seating plans so that people who are expected to become each other's counterparts in the JV are seated next to each other. Tables are formed by levels—the "first come, first serve" approach of egalitarian team building meals does not work for hierarchical people.

As many team leaders learn over time, building trust at the forming stage is one critical element that sees teams and their members through the storming and norming stages. JV team members need to develop trust among themselves. While trust can be defined as "demonstrated performance over time" everywhere, there are significant differences between cultures as to what constitutes performance and how much time is necessary to build trust.

Figure 6.2 graphically illustrates how people from different cultures approach trust over time when there is no connection between the two people involved. In this diagram, trust is represented as a variable

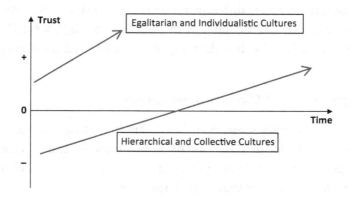

Figure 6.2 Trust as a Function of Time in Different Cultures

that can be either positive or negative (a negative value implies that we distrust the other person). Trust increases as we work more and more with the other person.

- As a rule of thumb, people in hierarchical and collective cultures tend not to trust people who do not belong to their group. When someone approaches strangers at random in the streets of Paris, Moscow, São Paulo or Shenzhen, these strangers are likely to react defensively. They are more likely to assume this person may be trying to take advantage of them in some way than to assume this person has positive intentions. As a result, it takes hierarchical and collective people more time to "warm up" to strangers. In other words, they take more time to build trust with people they do not know. This is represented graphically by the solid line that starts from negative at time zero.
- In egalitarian and individualistic cultures, people tend to be more trusting initially. They tend to trust other people until and unless these other people do something that leads them to not trust these people. They start from a positive point at time zero, as opposed to negative. They also build trust more quickly.
- It is possible to speed up the trust building phase in hierarchical and collective cultures by asking people who are respected and trusted by both parties to introduce them to each other. In this situation, this go-between "lends" the trust he or she has accumulated with each party to their relationship, thereby enabling the two parties to start from a positive point. This is why in countries such as Japan or the Middle East, business involves intermediaries to a much greater extent than in North America.

This difference in the speed of trust building has a very significant impact when the team composition is changed. When a team member is replaced by a new one, most teams end up being slowed down to some extent; the new team member needs to get to know the existing members of the team and to learn the mission, vision and rules of engagement of the team. The team as a whole may have to regroup in order to storm and norm again, to some extent. Because trust takes more time to establish in hierarchical and collective cultures than in egalitarian and individualistic cultures, it is important for the leaders of JV organizations to try and keep the composition of JV teams relatively stable over time.

Creating a JV Team Spirit

Becoming aware of cultural differences and their impact on JV teams is a good starting point to create a JV team spirit. Here are some solutions many organizations have applied to speed up the "get-to-know" phase:

Create opportunities for team members to exchange information about themselves in both formal and informal ways. For example, right from the start of the JV partnership, each partner can provide a formal biography of their team members to the other organization. Encourage one-on-one informal meetings over lunch, dinner or coffee.

Leverage social media. Encourage all team members to create a LinkedIn profile and connect with one another. This is a very effective way to convey a fair amount of information in a short amount of time. Remember that collective people want more information about their counterparts.

Be prepared for the "business card exchange ceremony." Americans and Canadians who have done business with Japanese and Chinese are always amazed by the way they hand over their business cards. They hold it with both hands and present it with a bow as if "they are holding a piece of their lives in their hands" (as one manager put it). When people in North America do not give them a card in return or hand over the card with two fingers, it is considered rude. The business card is like a formal introduction that gives them a chance to tell you their positions and to know your position so that everyone involved knows the appropriate amount of respect and deference to show.

As they go through the forming stage, team members need to start defining how they are going to work as a team—in particular, they need to define the communication protocols to be used within the team. In order to be effective, they will need to examine questions that are important to everyone but that individualistic and/or egalitarian people often answer differently from collective and/or hierarchical people:

- Who is part of the team and who is not?
- Who is responsible for what?
- Who makes what decision?
- What information is each team member expected to share automatically or upon request?
- What constitutes a proper request for information?
- What do we do when someone feels he or she was "left out of the loop"?

A frequently used approach to set a JV team on the right path is to organize an off-site for the whole team; this is most commonly done for the project kick-off meeting. In our experience, an off-site kick-off meeting is a double-edged sword; we have had the opportunity to witness both effective and counterproductive versions. In extreme cases, an off-site that goes awry is worse than doing nothing, as the following examples illustrate:

In one American–French JV, the first off-site was organized by the French with no input from the American JV team members. The informal team building activity was a seven-course, five-hour dinner in a five-star restaurant in Paris. The American team members felt uncomfortable during the whole dinner since they showed up in slacks and golf shirts when everyone else in the restaurant was in suit and tie (and the restaurant staff in tuxedos or long gowns). When their turn came, the American JV team members followed the same approach—they organized an off-site without any input from their French counterparts. The informal team building activity they selected was to split the JV team into two—each team built a go-kart and raced each other on a closed track—and then they closed the event with a casual barbeque. The French team members felt just as uncomfortable during this event as the Americans did in the five-star Parisian restaurant. Building the go-kart did not appeal to them (hierarchical people tend to shun manual tasks), and the barbeque did not qualify as a proper meal in their minds. Needless to say, the JV was not making much progress. The two sides were working independently of each other, each expecting the other to eventually accept what they had done as "the right thing to do."

In one American–Indian JV, the American JV team members decided to bring their Indian counterparts to the best restaurant in town—a steakhouse. They did not anticipate that half of their Indian counterparts were vegetarian. The only vegetarian option offered by the steakhouse they selected was a Caesar salad. Again, the off-site failure highlighted the disconnect within the JV—people did not know one another, the team had not "formed" yet and people were working in parallel rather than together.

How do you make sure an off-site kick-off meeting is effective? Fundamentally, the preparation and delivery of the off-site needs to reflect the approach JV partners want to use in their work interactions. Organizing an off-site gives JV team members the opportunity to resolve, on a small scale, the challenges they are likely to experience together on an ever-increasing scale as the JV progresses. In the case of a 50/50 joint venture, where the two partners are equal, the preparation and delivery of the off-site needs to reflect the equal weight given to members of both organizations and balance the needs of people on both sides:

Gather input from both JV teams to design both the agenda and the format of the off-site. The extent to which the opinion of each JV team member is taken into consideration often reflects the hierarchy of each organization—in hierarchical organizations, only the opinions of the top leaders of the JV team are sought, whereas the opinions of everyone are sought in the case of egalitarian organizations.

Organize team building activities (both formal and informal) that appeal to both groups. This can be quite tricky in the case of joint ventures between egalitarian and hierarchical organizations since egalitarian people want to do things together with their hands while hierarchical people prefer more intellectual activities. The word *intellectual* has a negative connotation in North America, while it tends to have a positive connotation in hierarchical cultures. In one Mexican–American joint venture, the American team members wanted to meet in resorts, preferably near a golf course, while the Mexican team members wanted to meet downtown in a big city and tour art museums or galleries together.

Arrange food that accommodates the preferences and restrictions of both groups. What is good food in one culture can be considered off-limits in another culture (e.g., sea slugs, a Chinese delicacy, do not appeal to most Westerners). This also requires some discussion on both sides to find a win–win solution. In joint ventures between Americans and Western Europeans, you often need to serve some drinks at room temperature while others are served ice cold.

While some of these points may appear trivial to many people, this is precisely the point. Working with JV partners from different cultures requires people to pay attention to little details we can all take for granted when working with people from the same culture. With high context cultures, much is communicated through little things (such as food, location, activities, people involved) that form the context. With careful planning that takes into consideration the cultural backgrounds of the two JV partners, the off-site and ongoing meetings can help the people involved in the joint venture create their own "JV culture." They come out of the off-site or kick-off meeting with mission and vision statements combined with rules of engagement for team members that give everyone a sense of the behaviors the team wants to encourage or discourage and the likely consequences for not following these rules.

Section 6.3: Resolving Conflict within a JV

While all teams go through the storming stage, getting through this stage successfully tends to be more challenging for multicultural teams than for culturally homogeneous teams because team members often have different ways of resolving conflict and reaching agreements. Different cultures resolve conflicts in different ways. In East Asian cultures, conflicts are resolved through go-betweens who are carefully selected by both parties, while in the US and Northern European countries (among others), conflicts are dealt with directly. We do not have to go very far to see differences in conflict-resolution approaches: Canadians and Americans do not resolve conflicts in the same manner. Here is how this difference plays out when resolving conflicts within joint venture teams.

The American Approach to Conflict Resolution

In the US, when two people get into a conflict (meaning they have a disagreement over something substantially meaningful to both of them), they first attempt to find agreement right on the spot. They each explain their perspective; if the disagreement surfaces during a meeting, the other meeting participants usually stay quiet until the two people in conflict reach an agreement.

If they reach an impasse, the next step consists of having the two of them go into an office, close the door and "hash things out." The tone of such conversations can be quite heated—some turn into shouting matches. The key is that if they reach an agreement during this conversation, both are expected to keep what transpired during that conversation to themselves—nobody should know how they reached that agreement.

If they are not able to reach an agreement during that one-on-one conversation, the conflict rises within the organization: Both people in conflict start to "lobby" the people above them. Eventually, the conflict reaches the level of someone who has authority over both of them; this person hears the two parties out and then makes a decision. When the person who has authority over both conflicting parties has called it, the conflict is considered resolved—the decision is usually not revisited, and everyone is expected to implement the logical consequences of this decision.

Americans have a strong need or desire to resolve important issues within a given amount of time. The more important the issue, the stronger the need to find a resolution by the deadline—also, the more likely the resolution will come at the eleventh hour. Leaving it hanging makes no sense in the US—that behavior is interpreted as a lack of leadership. While looking for win–win solutions is important to Americans, dealing with the issue within the given time frame is more important. In many cases, they would choose to break the deadlock by forcing one party to accept an unpalatable solution—because they have reached the deadline they have assigned to that issue—rather than postponing the resolution of the issue or agreeing to a compromise. The word *compromise*, in the US, has a negative connotation—it means "no one gets what he or she wanted."

The Canadian Approach to Conflict Resolution

In Canada, the process is quite different because Canadians want to avoid conflict at all costs; much of Canadian culture can be explained by the overriding desire to prevent conflict—and resolve it without loss of life when it happens. When a conflict between two people surfaces during a meeting and the tone rises, Canadians quickly sort out what they agree on from what they do not agree on. This sorting process takes a minute or two at the most. People then focus on the part where there is agreement and implement the action items related to this part, leaving the points where they disagree aside for the time being.

During meetings, this translates into statements such as "Let's revisit this point after lunch," "Let's sleep on this issue," "Let's work some more on this issue on Monday." Fundamentally, these statements mean, "When we discuss this point, there is too much conflict in the room—let's think about it separately and see where we can find a compromise." In Canada, a compromise is positive—it means "we have found something we can all live with."

Meanwhile, the "bones of contention" are put in a mental box, which is then put on a mental shelf and stays there for a prescribed amount of time. During that period of time, each side is expected to rethink his or her position and look for areas where he or she can give a little so the whole team can reach consensus. Involving people above you in the conflict ("escalating") tends to be viewed negatively in Canadian organizations—it implies you do not have good enough soft skills to prevent and/or resolve conflicts on your own.

After awhile, Canadians take the box from the mental shelf, open it up and separate again what they agree on from what they do not agree on. The parts that are agreed upon are implemented immediately, while the parts that are not agreed upon are put back in the box. Canadians then iterate until there is nothing left in the box. There is no expectation in Canada that a conflict needs to be resolved within a given amount of time. The best example of this behavior is constitutional issues, where Canadians have been iterating since 1760. Canadians do not expect to find a solution that resolves the French Canada–English Canada issue once and for all any time soon—they just want to find a solution that French Canadians and English Canadians can live with for the next few years.

Resolving Conflict in a JV Team

Conflict resolution is a key step to get through the storming stage. When all JV team members belong to the same cultural group, they all apply the same conflict resolution algorithm; when they belong to different groups, people often run into secondary conflicts when trying to resolve their primary conflicts. For example, when Americans and Canadians work together in JV teams we find the following:

- Americans judge the postponement of issues by Canadians as unprofessional. They often express it in the following manner: "Just as we were about to start having a frank discussion, Canadians punt—you can never get to the bottom of an issue with these guys." Americans often feel like boxers who want to engage in a fight with an opponent who is constantly retreating.
- Canadians usually find the American approach of discussing the issue right there and then as generating too much antagonism by their standards, and retreat; this is even more true of the one-on-one discussion behind closed doors (the second step in the American conflict resolution algorithm). By looking for areas where they can give a little on their side, but not getting the same in return from their American counterparts, they feel short-changed; this often leads to extensive resentment.

Since most people are unaware that conflict resolution algorithms are different in different cultures, we find it is often essential to bring in someone who understands the conflict resolution processes used by both organizations when JV teams get stuck in the storming stage. The goal of such interventions is to help JV team members do the following:

Separate substance from style: Is this a disagreement in terms of project direction/timing/resources/etc.? Or is this a disagreement in terms of communication style/conflict resolution approach/time management/etc.?

Enforce ground rules: In essence, the goal is to help the team get through both the storming and the norming stages by helping the team commit to its mission and vision statements and its rules of engagement so it can reach the performing stage more quickly by reaffirming how these rules are applied within the JV team.

Stay focused on the common goal: To be successful, JV team members need to be convinced they are better off together than they would be separately. Emphasizing the elements each party brings to the table, rather than focusing on the challenges of working together, is critical to the joint success of the team. In this respect, a facilitated discussion can help create an atmosphere where discussing differences becomes the norm and can teach JV team members how to do that constructively.

Section 6.4: Managing Time within a JV Team

One challenge most cross-cultural JV teams have to overcome when establishing the team norm is the fact that people use time differently in different cultures. It is striking to compare the day of the average Latin American or Latin European professional with the day of the average North American professional. (Here, the word Latin refers to Latin American countries and/or Latin European countries [Mexico, Italy, Spain, Portugal, France, etc.]. This description is meant to show the main trends that are common to all Latin countries; we focus on the differences and describe them as black and white rather than as shades of gray. Please keep in mind that each country and each individual has its own way of managing time—use this information in a reactive rather than proactive way.)

The North American Way of Managing Time

The day of most North American professionals typically starts between 8 a.m. and 9 a.m. They usually ramp up fairly quickly—when they arrive in the building where they work, they drop their coat at their desk, turn on their computer, walk to the coffee station and get a cup of coffee or tea. Once they have that cup in hand, they are ready. If you talk to them before that, they hear you, but they are not really listening—once they have that cup in hand, they turn to you and ask "What were you saying?" meaning that they are now "ready for input."

Their efficiency remains high throughout the morning. Lunch time is often short (15 to 30 minutes), somewhere between 11:30 a.m. and 12:30 p.m. Many North American professionals eat a sandwich at their desks so they can finish their work earlier. There is a drop in efficiency in the early afternoon—people do not participate as much in meetings at 1 p.m. as they do at 10 a.m. The day usually ends around 5 p.m.; while some people work later, you are likely to experience quite a bit of pushback if you try to schedule team meetings after that time.

In North America, it is much easier to ask people to come in early and have a breakfast meeting than to ask them to stay late and schedule a dinner meeting. Quebec is a notable exception in this case—time is managed in a more Latin way there than in the rest of North America.

If we look at how professionals manage time on a weekly or yearly basis, we find the following:

- On a weekly basis, the most productive days tend to be Tuesdays, Wednesdays and Thursdays. For example, people avoid scheduling training sessions on Mondays (people may forget they have signed up for it) and Fridays (people are ramping down in preparation for the upcoming weekend). Similarly, mornings are considered better than afternoons.
- On a yearly basis, the Friday before any long weekend is considered a write-off (many people leave early in the afternoon that day—if you want to convince yourself of this point, try scheduling a meeting at 3 p.m. on the Friday just before Memorial Day in the US or before Victoria Day in Canada). The low-activity periods tend to be the first week in July and the last week of August as well as the period between Thanksgiving and New Year in the US or between the end of the first full week in December and New Year in Canada.

The Latin Way of Managing Time

The day of most Latin professionals starts between 9 a.m. and 10 a.m. They usually ramp up more slowly than their North American counterparts because they start the day by going around the office to greet everyone, shaking hands with (in the case of men) or kissing on the cheeks of (in the case of women) all their colleagues. They also have a quick chit-chat about what everyone did the evening or the weekend before—all this reaffirms the relationships they have with their colleagues. If you miss someone, the person you miss feels snubbed and interprets your behavior as implying you are somehow cross with him or her.

Their efficiency remains high throughout the remainder of the morning until lunch. Lunchtime is longer (often one hour) and starts later (somewhere between 1 and 2 p.m.). Lunch usually involves eating with your colleagues in Latin countries—having lunch by yourself implies nobody wants to have lunch with you or you do not want to have lunch with anyone. The drop in efficiency after lunch is more pronounced than in North America—to the point where some people may have a nap (though this is fairly rare nowadays in the case of professionals).

In Latin countries, professionals end their days significantly later than in North America, and the most important meetings are often scheduled at the end of the day, when interruptions are less likely. Also, since senior professionals have support staff at home, they do not have to rush out the door to pick up their kids at day care—someone does it for them. If you really want to get to know someone in order to do business with them, you invite them for dinner—a breakfast meeting makes no sense in most Latin countries.

In Latin countries, we find the following:

- On a weekly basis, Mondays and particularly Fridays are good options for training sessions; Lionel once delivered a half-day workshop in Mexico from 3 p.m. to 7 p.m. on a Friday afternoon where all 25 people registered attended the session. Similarly, afternoons are preferred to mornings.

- On a yearly basis, the slow periods are different—in Mexico, the periods around Easter and Mother's Day are quite slow, whereas in France, May and August tend to be on the slow side (most French expatriates take their vacation in August). By contrast, they do not ramp down for the year-end holiday season nearly as early as North Americans do—people in Latin countries schedule meetings all the way to December 20 (there are far fewer year-end office parties in Latin countries than in North America).

Managing Time in a JV

When you put two different ways of managing time and different definitions of what being on time means together, you often end up with misunderstandings and frustration on all sides. Here are some concrete examples we have witnessed:

- In a JV between a French and an American organization, one challenge was agreeing to the start time of meetings—Americans team members wanted to start JV team meetings at 8 a.m. while French team members wanted to start at 9:30 or even 10 a.m. They tried various options and settled on 9 a.m.
- In a JV between a Chinese and a Canadian organization, Chinese expatriates initially proposed to schedule meetings on weekends. This generated extensive pushback and ill-will among their Canadian JV partners.
- In a JV between an American and Norwegian company, Americans considered their Norwegian counterparts unprofessional because they left the office at 3 p.m. on the dot, whereas their Norwegian colleagues saw the Americans as ineffective since the Americans needed to work much longer hours than they did.

In most JVs, everyone sees oneself as working harder than one's JV colleagues. The reason is straightforward, but many people fail to appreciate where it comes from: They see themselves working at times when their JV partners are not working and reach the conclusion that the others are not hard working or committed to their work. They often fail to value the times when their JV partners are working and they are not.

How do we bridge the gap? Can people change their sense of time and behavior? Our experience is that it is possible, even on a large scale, but it takes a very large amount of sustained effort. For example, China went from having a very approximate sense of time to paying strict attention to time in the last thirty years. Two anecdotes illustrate this radical change:

Caroline attended a village school when her parents were sent to the country during the Cultural Revolution. The village school had only one clock, located in the principal's office—only the principal knew what time it was. The village kids had chores to complete in the morning before going to school; these chores varied with the season and took more or less time, depending on the weather. The kids went to school when their chores were completed. The principal decided when class would start based on the number of kids present—when there were enough kids, she rang the bell and school started.

Yuan Geng (Chinese put family name first), the founder of the Shekou Industrial Park (located in Shenzhen, near the border with Hong Kong), is quoted as having realized the importance of time when he was doing business with a Hong Kong businessman in the early 1980s. The two of them had signed a deal, and the Hong Kong businessman came to Mr. Yuan's office to pick up the payment on a Friday afternoon. When he invited the Hong Kong businessman to sit down, relax and enjoy a cup of tea with him, the Hong Kong businessman responded that he did not have time—his limo driver was waiting for him downstairs so they could get to the bank before it closed. He wanted to deposit the check and earn interest over the weekend rather than wait until Monday to make the deposit. This had a major impact on Mr. Yuan, who decided to emphasize time to a much greater extent throughout his organization. A sign was erected in Shekou to remind people that "time is money; efficiency is life" (see Figure 6.3). Through Deng Xiao Ping's visit to Shenzhen and his visible support, this emphasis on time spread throughout the country.

As these anecdotes demonstrate, it is possible to change people's sense of time and behavior. Several hundred million Chinese people

Figure 6.3 "Time is Money" Sign in Shekou

changed behavior in the last thirty years. Action items JV teams can implement include the following:

Agree on what being on time means to the team and on the core business hours for the team so that team meetings can run without extensive coordination of different schedules.

Develop SMART goals for the team and individual team members. As long as the team members deliver the expected result, team members should give each other the benefit of the doubt.

Be patient with each other and with yourself. When people are late or have a more casual attitude toward time than we do, we often interpret the behavior as disrespectful. Withhold that judgment and allow people time to change behavior.

Section 6.5: Making a Multicultural JV Team "Gel"

As the JV team reaches the performing stage, there are a few key ingredients to help the team "gel" and sustain productivity over time.

Giving Feedback to Your JV Counterparts

One key ingredient is to find ways to ensure that feedback provided by members of one organization is understood by members of the other organization the way it is meant. In one JV team we worked with, one employee joked that she often had to take a deep breath and repeat a mantra before opening e-mail messages from her JV counterparts because their messages were worded so strongly they often created intense negative feelings in her. Another JV team member had to take a day off because he felt so offended by one e-mail message he received from his JV counterpart.

Helping JV team members see the impact of these differences and learn how to overcome them makes a major difference to the overall effectiveness of multicultural JV teams. This goal can be reached by combining several action items:

Provide cross-cultural training and/or coaching to JV team members so they understand the true nature of the issues they are facing.

Organize cross-posting assignments by having people from one organization embedded in the other. This enables people to become familiar with one another outside the formal JV meetings; the people who are seconded to the other organization can then act as translators of the feedback provided by employees of the organization that seconded them.

Run e-mail and communication messages by people who are familiar with the cultural backgrounds of JV partners in order to try and anticipate how they might interpret them and ensure that they interpret them the way they are meant.

Committing to the JV Culture

Another key ingredient is to create a forum where people can bring up issues, particularly those resulting from cultural differences, in a constructive manner. When JV teams run into cultural differences, many team members respond by trying to impose their own approach on the whole JV. In other words, they want their JV partners to adopt their way of doing things and usually find a good reason for that to be the "best" approach for everyone. Here are some of the reasons we often hear from JV team members:

- We brought more money/capital/expertise to the JV than they did.
- Our organization is more successful than their organization is—our stock price/sales/profits are increasing faster than theirs.
- They do not know the place/government regulations/local culture/ etc.
- They do not have as much experience dealing with joint ventures as we do.

In our experience, any of these statements, which frame the discussion in terms of "We know better than they do," is both a *symptom* and a *cause* of joint venture difficulties. When JV managers and HR professionals hear words like these, we encourage them to interpret this as a sign that some form of intervention is required to bring people back to their common goal—namely, the success of the joint venture as a whole—and go back to the elements each party brings to the table.

One of these forums is regular progress review meetings during which the team discusses not just the business/project progress, but also how the team operates as a whole. Here are a few suggestions to ensure these progress review meetings bring the team together:

Poll team members ahead of the meeting through one-on-one interviews by an internal HR professional or an external consultant or an online survey; these polls can speed up the identification of unresolved team issues and help the team zero in on the areas where additional attention is required.

Revisit the team's modus operandi on a regular basis in order to answer questions such as the following:

- Are team members following the rules of engagement?
- Are the consequences for breaching the rules of engagement implemented?
- Do team members demonstrate disruptive behaviors that were not discussed when the JV rules of engagement were created? If so, how do we want JV team members to behave in this situation?

Sharing and following the JV rules of engagement by every team member does not happen overnight. People need to rub shoulders on a regular basis in order to identify where the differences are between the two organizations and then come up with solutions that bridge the corresponding gaps.

Agree on who should adapt to whom. It is very important that JV team members have ongoing discussions and agree on who should adapt to whom. This is an important first step. We often find that each JV partner expects the other side to make 80 percent of the adaptation. They are constantly frustrated because they don't understand why the other side does not see their point. Agreeing on where to meet—say, 50/50—sets a clear expectation. Some people may not like it, but if it is the decision of the joint team, at least there is no ambiguity about the expectation.

Determine what constitutes the 50 percent. This is the next step and an ongoing challenge. The teams need to have good ongoing communication to discuss what adaptation is needed on both sides. There is no teamwork without storming. The teams may have to circle back to the various stages of forming, storming and norming to reinforce behaviors critical to sustained high performance.

* * *

Working in a joint venture is never easy; the degree of complexity is significantly increased when the people involved come from culturally different backgrounds and have different ways of making decisions, communicating, resolving conflicts and working in teams. Our experience working with multicultural joint venture teams around the world indicates that the key success factor is clarity and commitment to their common goal. This common goal helps people at all levels of the joint venture overcome the cross-cultural challenges they are bound to experience and stay focused when they run into difficulties.

7

Competing in the Global Talent Market

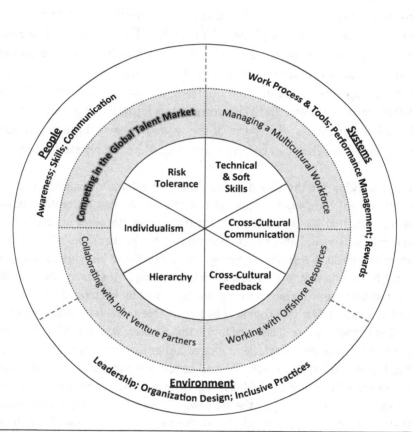

Figure 7.0 Roadmap of the Book

Many business travelers comment that they find the HSBC advertisement in airport boarding bridges inspiring. For example, "In the future, there will be no markets left waiting to emerge." The advertisements provide a unique perspective on today's economy, which is becoming more and more global. Many North American companies have expanded their operations to many different parts of the world; some have experienced more success than others. In this chapter, we use a case study approach to discuss cultural considerations that arise when organizations compete in the global talent market. The cases come from our years of experience working in subsidiaries of multinational companies (MNCs), or at the headquarters of MNCs[1] providing support to international operations, on international assignment or consulting MNCs. While most managers and HR professionals know that business is done in different ways in other parts of the world, the way these differences manifest themselves can be very surprising. Here is a revealing story.

I was working for the Canadian subsidiary of a large consumer products multinational company headquartered in the US. We had a sizeable market share in most of Western Europe except Italy; no matter what we did in that country, we were not able to get even close to the market share of a comparatively much smaller Italian company. So we decided to buy this company in order to acquire their expertise and understanding of the Italian market. We wanted them to integrate into our operations while keeping the creativity and innovation that this company had been able to achieve over the years.

One of the ways we decided to tackle this problem was to send a Canadian team to manage the integration process, rather than an American team. We had found that, when we bought small companies and sent American teams to integrate them into the fold, the American approach came across to many locals as "Let us teach you the right way." Since these people considered that they were doing a good job in the first place (we would not have bought them otherwise), we lost many key people through the integration process. This was particularly important in this case, because we had to get the approval from the European Union authorities to complete this acquisition; in other words, several months would go by between the moment we signed the agreement (and sent people to their operations) and the moment the deal was finalized. The business leaders driving this acquisition agreed that a team of Canadians would not come across as strongly as would a team of Americans and that we would therefore retain more of the key personnel of that Italian organization.

When the deal was signed, my team and I went to Italy and started to work with our Italian colleagues on the development of a new product. At the same time, we were trying to introduce a number of practices that were standard in our operations around the world but that were clearly foreign to this Italian company. When we performed an audit to certify their operations under ISO 9000, we found that there were a lot of what we perceived as gaps—our Italian counterparts clearly saw us as being overly rigid and structured.

When looking at it from afar, it looked like everything was fine and that they were following our processes and procedures; when we started delving into the details, it felt like they were breaking a lot of rules that we considered as essential. One event took place on the day the deal finally went through that summarized for me our challenges in Italy. Their operations included a cafeteria, complete with an espresso bar. After lunch, our Italian colleagues all lined up to get an espresso or a cappuccino; the bar also served grappa, a strong Italian alcohol that many locals enjoyed after a good cup of coffee. Obviously, having alcohol on company premises was completely unthinkable for an American company, so the bottle of grappa disappeared from the bar the day the announcement was made—it looked like they were adopting our ways of doing business. But looks can be deceiving. One day, I stood longer at the bar than usual because I was engaged in a passionate discussion with one of my Italian colleagues; over time, I started to realize that the bottle of grappa had simply moved from the shelf to the cupboard and that, if you asked in Italian, you could get some; if you asked in English, the response was that there was no grappa. (Canadian executive heading the Italian subsidiary)

The question of "who should adapt to whom" (see Section 3.7) in this context clearly underpins the approach that North American organizations use when expanding globally. We see a continuum from a highly centralized model to a highly decentralized model:

- On the highly centralized end, organizations send a large number of expatriates holding all key management positions to ensure that the systems and processes set up in the subsidiary duplicate as closely as possible those at headquarters.

- On the highly decentralized end, organizations try to stay out of the daily operations of their subsidiaries and adapt their business model to local market conditions. They run these subsidiaries entirely from a profit-and-loss perspective.

Where a specific organization chooses to be on this continuum depends on many variables. The key factor is the products and services of the organization, which drive their business model and the organization structure. For example, a technology company's organization is structured by product lines. Teams around the world work on different parts of a new product at the same time. Time zone differences play in their favor. When the team in Europe finishes work, the North American team takes over. When the North American team finishes work, teams in Asia-Pacific take over. The centralized approach makes a lot of sense for this kind of organizations. On the other hand, a mine in Mauritania may be using the same technology and work processes as its parent company, but its daily operations are intrinsically local (local workforce, suppliers, etc.). An insurance company may use the same processes, procedures and systems everywhere in the world, but the products and services they sell have to be adapted to their local customers' needs. The decentralized approach makes more sense for this kind of organizations.

The challenge is that organizations often do not make this decision consciously when they go global, and underestimate cultural factors and their impact on the organization's global expansion strategy, especially on the people side. The first few global operations often happen as a result of necessity, for example, cost saving, testing a new market, following a key client's expansion, a new partnership opportunity or filling a labor shortage. Managers in charge of the project do their best to make things happen while local employees struggle to understand the parent organization's business model and culture. As problems arise, people become confused and frustrated. Productivity and relationships suffer when people do not know how to resolve their differences and create a common ground to move forward.

Many North American organizations go through a cycle; they start with a decentralized approach, then centralize when things do not work out well and then decentralize again when their systems and processes are aligned and stabilized. In other words, the "who should adapt to whom" question is answered based on the progress made in the new location. Sometimes, local offices make a higher percentage of the adaptation to meet the requirements of the corporate office; at other times, the corporate office adapts more to meet local needs. The famous line "think globally and act locally" is a very valuable guideline in these situations.

Section 7.1: Talent Acquisition

We discussed in Chapters 2, 3 and 4 how immigrant employees bring their cultural assumptions with them and behave based on those assumptions. North American organizations also bring their own cultural assumptions with them when going global and manage their workforce based on those assumptions. Here is an example at the talent acquisition stage.

Case Study #1: Human Resources Project Manager in China

The following is an excerpt from a job posting of a Canadian company for an HR project manager in China:

Key Responsibilities:

- *Develop core HR programs including recruiting, retention, employee relations and compensation/benefits, etc.*
- *Identify local resources needed to implement plan and recruit a local HR director*
- *Design organization chart and staffing needs by department*
- *Set up recruitment plans to attract management, technical and factory staff*
- *Work with parent company to establish training needs and organize programs at each level*
- *Oversee delivery of training geared to plant opening date*
- *Transfer knowledge and programs responsibility to the local HR director*
- *Establish ongoing reporting and quality checkpoints for head office.*

Requirements:

- *15–20 years in human resources in manufacturing environment*
- *Extensive experience in collective bargaining and the unionized environment*
- *Specific experience in green field plant setups, preferably in Asia*
- *Prior experience in/knowledge of China preferred*
- *Some fluency in Mandarin a definite asset but not essential*

This is a typical example showing how unprepared some organizations may be when venturing into the global marketplace. This job posting prioritizes collective bargaining experience over knowledge of China and speaking Chinese. While experience in collective bargaining and the unionized environment is essential to any human resources management role in the manufacturing environment in North America, there is no real collective bargaining in China because unions are closer to employee councils or recreation committees than they are collective bargaining units. Many foreign investment enterprises in China, including Walmart, have unions in their establishments.

This example shows that organizations going global need to invest in building **awareness** of cultural differences and gain an appreciation of their impact on the business. In this particular case, the organization first needs to accept that setting up a plant and dealing with unions in China is a completely different ball game. For this they need to look for people with the right experience and knowledge to help them navigate through, what is for them, uncharted territory.

Education, Experience and Cultural Fit

Once the HR project manager in our case study is on the ground, the questions he or she needs to answer are as follows: Where do I find employees? How do I pay them? What is the regulatory environment around employment? To answer these questions, we need to start from another question: What kind of people are we looking for? When we recruit in North America, we consider the job requirements in three major areas: education, experience and fit to the organization's culture. It is the same in the global talent market; the difference is that we need to understand the local context.

We use China as an example to illustrate concretely the type of cultural considerations organizations should take into account when they move from talent acquisition to retention and development in an unfamiliar environment. We will use situations and examples from other countries throughout this chapter. Readers will see a common theme, as emerging markets share many of the same challenges.

Education

China has a long tradition of valuing learning and education. The modern Chinese education system was founded with heavy Soviet influence and used to have a strong focus on science and technology. Since the reform and opening in the late 1970s, disciplines focusing on business in a market economy have gained popularity. Educational institutions have created programs for business administration, marketing and human resources and are continuing the trend. The past three decades saw a fast increase in the number of educational institutions and university graduates. In 2011, China had over 2,400 universities and colleges, with 426,000 graduates receiving master's and Ph.D. degrees, 2.7 million graduates receiving bachelor's degrees and 3.3 million college graduates.[2] Adult education institutions and online courses also graduated over 3 million students. So there is a big talent pool of candidates with postsecondary education. The question is how to assess the quality of the graduates to meet your organization's talent needs. This is where local knowledge becomes critical when trying to get the right kind of talent.

Experience

In a mature labor market like North America, companies often scope out jobs with a certain experience level. Depending on your industry, your experience may be very different overseas, particularly in emerging markets. A woman named Shi-Hong Wu wrote a book about her experience of working with IBM for twelve years; she rose from a support staff to regional general manager, then became the general manager of Microsoft China (the first Chinese national holding that job). It is a real-life example of the stages of human resources development as part of China's transformation to a market economy. In the 1980s and early 1990s, the first MNCs that went into China were basically using the "import and train" model. They brought in many expatriates and hired only entry-level positions; they trained these people and promoted from within. Ms. Wu went through a thorough on-the-job training program and learned the IBM products and processes. By the late 1990s, Microsoft was able to hire a Chinese national who had experience in technology, sales and management to run its operations in China. By then the new human resources model became one of "localization"; by reducing the number of expatriates, MNCs could decrease their human capital costs and ensure that their Chinese operations were more in tune with the evolution of the local market.

There are limits to this approach. For example, if an insurance company is looking for an actuary who has experience in sales and management and speaks English, it is hard to find candidates who meet these requirements. China's insurance industry only started in the early 1980s and opened to foreign investors in the late 1990s in preparation for China's entry in the World Trade Organization (WTO). The first university insurance program was set up as the result of a Sino-British cooperation agreement in 1994. The China Association of Actuaries was founded in 2007 and had 516 members and 345 associate members in 2013,[3] in a country of 1.3 billion people.

Cultural Fit

During Caroline's ten years with MNCs in China, she saw many people come and go. Some people thrive in a Western business environment; others find themselves doing a lot better in a local business environment. Why do people choose to work for a local or a multinational company? Looking at it from the North American organization's perspective, how can HR professionals and managers predict the success of their local employees? We can apply the three cultural concepts based on Hofstede's research, discussed in Chapter 3, to analyze the talent pool for MNCs in the global talent market:

- As Hofstede's research indicates, many parts of the world (e.g., Asia, Latin America, Africa and Eastern Europe) are much more hierarchical than North America, meaning that workers accept and even expect their managers to have significant power over them. Employees who find the Western management style appealing are often looking for empowerment, which they are more likely to find in MNCs than in local organizations.

- In countries that score low on individualism, people see themselves more as members of a group than as individuals. Employees who thrive in North American organizations are probably more individualistic than the average in their country because they like the room for personal growth and individual expression provided by MNCs.
- Similarly, employees who leave the comfort of a familiar environment have more tolerance to risk and see risk as an opportunity. Therefore, they are more likely to be successful in a fast paced and challenging environment.

Another key component of the cultural fit required for local employees to operate successfully in the subsidiary of a North American organization is their ability and desire to work in English. While learning English is popular in China, many people cannot handle the requirement to operate continuously in English in the workplace. There are notable exceptions: Caroline had a colleague who quit graduate school, something very rare in China because of the tight competition to get in, in order to work for Nortel, just because he would be reporting to a Canadian manager and therefore would have the opportunity to speak English on a daily basis. He has subsequently studied and worked in the UK and Canada and is currently the regional vice president of an MNC in Hong Kong.

Bridging the Education, Experience and Cultural Fit Gap

Building Awareness and Skills

When venturing into a new country, HR professionals and managers need to understand and assess the local labor market conditions and design their people strategy accordingly. If the market does not have a sufficient pool of the particular kind of talent the organization is looking for, entering into a bidding war for the few candidates locally available may not be a good strategy in the long run. Instead, organizations need to take a long-term view of their global business strategies and commit to growing the talent they need. Some best practices include the following:

- **Send expatriates with a clear mandate** to build local capability.
- **Bring local hires to North America for training,** again with a clear mandate of going back to their home country to transfer the knowledge to other local employees.
- **Partner with local universities and colleges** to recruit the best graduates and to influence the curriculum.
- **Set up an internal development program** to build a talent pipeline for sustained growth.

Implementing a Process to Assess Cultural Fit

Once we have identified that people who are looking for empowerment, individual expression and personal growth opportunities have a better chance of succeeding in North American organizations, we can incorporate initiative, individual accountability, risk tolerance and adaptability into the selection process and look explicitly for these personality traits. Here are some suggestions:

- **Incorporate the company's values and performance requirement into explicit requirements in job descriptions.**
- **Train HR professionals and managers to look for those attributes.** This may be as simple as incorporating these cultural competencies into the behavioral interview questions; it can also involve implementing more sophisticated assessment tools (see more detail in Chapter 4).

Setting Up a Competitive Reward System

In many emerging markets, the first challenge is lack of credible market data and market positioning—how do you determine your comparator group? In North America, the factors often used to position an organization are industry and size of the organization. When operating in other countries, the factors that need to be taken into consideration to create a comparator group may be different. For example, in China, organizations need to consider one other factor, namely the type of organization, which cuts across industries and sizes. There are roughly four types of organizations in China; each category offers very different compensation and benefits structure:

- **Foreign investment enterprises** are usually the talent pool many North American organizations want to draw from; therefore, they represent a good benchmark. They usually have a compensation and benefit structure similar to that in North America, which combines base salary, short-term incentive and benefits, including the mandatory social insurance contribution and private extended health benefits. Long-term incentive and some perquisites may be offered to senior positions.

- **Private enterprises** usually offer a much lower base salary; they attract and keep people with promises of lucrative bonuses and IPOs (initial public offerings), which may or may not materialize. In the past thirty years, the Chinese stock market has grown exponentially, and there are numerous success and failure stories associated with IPOs. Sometimes, a dream is enough to keep people going. Over the years, some very successful private enterprises have grown and become multinational. A good case in point is Lenovo, which bought IBM's PC business in 2004. The company was founded by the Computer Technology Institute of Chinese Academy of Science in 1984. By 2002, prior to the many frequent changes in share ownership, employees (mostly senior management staff) held 35 percent of Lenovo's shares.

- **State owned enterprises** have gone through tremendous changes in the last thirty years and have taken hundreds of thousands of workers "off the post," another term for unemployment. The remaining workers are all in key industries such as railway, airlines, telecommunication, banking and energy and are in strengthened financial positions. They provide a good base salary, a bonus, many benefits and job security. Since China's population is aging, job security is becoming increasingly valuable to potential candidates.

- **Government, universities and research institutions** still have a more socialist structure, where people are paid by rank and tenure. Their base salary is very good, and they usually have better benefits and job security than anyone else once they are in the system.

Situations in many other developing countries may be very similar where there is a distinct difference between how local and foreign companies pay their employees. Understanding this context is important both when considering the overall compensation and benefit plan and when creating individual pay packages:

- At the overall compensation and benefit plan level, organizations must be clear about what types of organizations are included in the market analysis in order to determine the competitive positioning in the market.
- At the individual level, there can be big gaps when companies hire people from the four different types of organizations. For example, a candidate switching from the government to a foreign company may conclude that the salary increase does not compensate for his or her benefits and job security.

Flexibility, creativity and communication are critical to finding the right balance between making attractive offers, managing expectations and maintaining internal equity. Communicating the total value proposition and investing in understanding candidates' real motivations is critical to recruiting and retaining the right kind of talent.

Section 7.2: Talent Retention

In a competitive labor market, retention is always a key concern for HR professionals and managers. The following case study illustrates several best practices following our People–Systems–Environment (PSE) solutions framework.

Case Study #2: Total Rewards Program Design and Communication

A North American technology company was a market leader in a high-tech market segment and had built its research and development capability by acquiring small design firms in emerging markets such as India and China. It was in the process of acquiring a Chinese company that had a young and educated workforce. Most employees had engineering degrees; approximately a quarter had a bachelor's, half had a master's and a quarter had Ph.D. degrees. The local market was very competitive, and these highly educated employees were the targets of many competitors and search firms. Under these circumstances, there was a very pressing need to present a fair and competitive total rewards package to the employees as soon as the acquisition was announced to ensure that the company would retain the key talent, thereby protecting the value of the acquisition.

Aligning with the Corporate Culture and Organization Design

In Case Study #2, the Chinese company had a very hierarchical structure (see Table 7.1). There were fourteen levels of positions that depended on a combination of factors:

- Level of education (bachelor's, master's or Ph.D.)
- Alma mater (Tier 1 or Tier 2 university)
- Program (engineer, science or other)
- Work experience

On the other hand, the North American parent company had a much flatter organization design and career path to support its business model, which required product execution through teamwork across geographies (see Table 7.2).

While the difference in organization design and job levels created a major challenge for merging the acquired employees into the parent company's organization and total rewards structure, the company

Table 7.1 Chinese Company's Technical Career Path

LEVEL	TECHNICAL CAREER PATH
14	Sr. chief engineer
13	Chief engineer
12	Sr. fellow engineer
11	Fellow principal engineer
10	Sr. principal engineer
9	Principal engineer
8	Sr. staff engineer
7	Staff engineer
6	Sr. engineer
5	Engineer 2
4	Engineer 1
3	Associate engineer
2	Assistant engineer
1	Technical assistant

Table 7.2 North American Company's Technical Career Path

LEVEL	MANAGEMENT	PROFESSIONAL	SUPPORT
6	Director		
5	Senior manager	Principal engineer	
4	Manager	Staff engineer	
3		Senior engineer	
2		Engineer	Senior technician
1			Technician

decided to introduce the change from the beginning and to integrate the acquired employees into the parent company's egalitarian culture, which was essential to innovation and teamwork.

The project team reviewed the job descriptions, gathered input from technical managers who were going to lead the Chinese team after the acquisition and performed an initial mapping of all positions into the parent company's career path. When the project team arrived in Shanghai, the team members interviewed every Chinese engineer to understand his or her technical expertise and level of responsibility. The information was then used to validate and adjust the job-level mapping. The result was that some managers were moved to the same level as some of their former direct reports and some senior level engineers were placed at the same level as people who were at a lower level before. The project team implemented a comprehensive communication strategy to make sure the change was received positively. This is described in detail later in this section.

Driving Results and Retention through the Rewards System

While incentives are key features of total rewards in North America, the Chinese company did not have a true incentive program. Rather, it had a technical training program that sent employees to work in its US subsidiary for one to six months on a regular basis. This became a primary incentive as many young local professionals embraced the opportunity to be trained or to work overseas. The company had a very complicated retention program that paid bonuses to returning employees for completing a certain length of service after the training and a penalty system for anyone who left the company prior to completing the service commitment.

The North American company had always used an annual incentive program to reward accomplishment of certain product development and financial goals. It also had a broad-based, long-term incentive program with restricted stock units (RSUs) and stock options to align the employees' efforts with the interests of its shareholders.

To support the parent company's one global team business strategy and pay-for-performance philosophy, the finalized total rewards program for the new Chinese operation had the same components as the parent company's global total rewards program. This integrated design with the following components ensured global alignment at the program level with local benchmark data and recognized local practice:

- **Base salary** was benchmarked locally.
- **Annual incentive** was expressed as a percentage of base salary and differentiated by career level. The performance measurements for determining annual incentive payment were a combination of company performance, business unit performance and individual performance, all of which drove the message of pay for performance and succeeding by working together.
- **Long-term incentive** was delivered by RSUs with grant size for various positions set as a blend of the company's global guidelines and data gathered from local market.
- **Benefits program** consisted of three basic parts: various social security premiums required by law, extended health benefits and paid time off, which was based on prevailing market practice and aligned with the parent company's benefit strategy.

This practice matched the local employees' expectations as they were mostly in the early stage of their careers and therefore had a stronger focus on cash rewards than on benefits. When it came to benefits, their key concern was vacation as the Chinese company had a very stringent vacation policy and complicated administrative procedures. The new vacation policy was more relaxed and easy to administer, which emphasized the importance placed by the new parent company on results as opposed to face time and reinforced the company's culture of innovation, initiative and trust.

Communicating the Value Proposition

The success of any total rewards program depends on communicating its value to employees. This is even truer in an acquisition. The project team communicated the overall value proposition face to face with the local employees in various formats within a tight time frame. After the Chinese company's management announced the acquisition, the new parent company's senior business leaders presented the company's overall business results and strategy to employees in a town hall session to get across the message that they were becoming part of a successful global company and that they would have the opportunity to work on new, cutting-edge technologies.

Following the senior business leader's presentation, the HR manager presented the various elements of the total rewards package offered by the new parent organization:

- A culture of innovation and performance
- Learning and development opportunities
- Monetary rewards
- Benefits, including vacation policy

After the town hall meeting, each employee was presented with an individual offer confirming his or her base salary, annual and long-term incentive target, benefits and vacation eligibility. The HR manager then met with key employees one on one to help them understand their individual offer and answer their questions. Special attention was given to employees who ended up at the same level as others who were at lower levels before. The focus on communication was instrumental in building trust. Over a short time, many employees had internalized and accepted the change. They responded very positively and started to discuss their future within the company. They were particularly impressed with the overall message of fairness, commitment and trust this process conveyed.

The investment in building trust yielded very positive results: 95 percent of the acquired company's employees stayed beyond the first year of the acquisition. Furthermore, the new Chinese team designed a new product, which was successfully launched in the first year.

While the overall program design and communication was a success, one of the lessons learned was that rewards must match the recipients' past experience to have perceived value. For example, even with the comprehensive communication strategy and an HR manager who spoke Chinese, some local employees had trouble accepting the value of RSUs for two reasons:

• Many employees did not have and did not know anyone who had experience with any North American long-term incentive vehicle, such as stock options or RSUs, let alone any positive experience of benefiting from them. People cannot see value in something they do not understand.
• The employees lived in a very fast paced market. With their short work experience, it was very hard for them to see beyond one year. Therefore, RSUs that would have value in three years were significantly discounted.

Alternatively, in this case, the long-term incentive program could be designed and communicated as a retention bonus, with the company's share price as performance criterion. By describing this incentive in a language that local employees could understand, it would have much more value in their minds.

Employees in different countries and at different times value different things. An effective approach of providing total employment value is to consider offering what the employees value, which sometimes does not cost a lot of money. The movie *Outsourced* is a story of an American manager (Todd) who went to India to train the employees of a call center. At one point, Todd found out that the local Indian employees actually liked the products they were selling, which he considered "junk." He ordered a batch to use as spot rewards for employees who achieved specific sales targets.

Building Relationships with Local Employees

Why do people leave? Conversely, why do people stay? Many organizations have done studies through employee engagement surveys, exit interviews and conversations with high performers. The reasons people leave or stay can be condensed to whether people feel they are doing work they enjoy with people they enjoy working with and whether they feel their contribution is recognized through monetary and nonmonetary rewards. In a nutshell, it is all about "dollars and sense." Talent retention in the global talent market has the same two factors as in North America.

Since we have already discussed the dollars side and examined the question of how to pay people in international locations, let's discuss the sense part, which is all about building relationships. How does relationship building with your employees in international locations differ from relationship building in North America? Here are a few suggestions.

Adjusting to Local Needs

In collective cultures, the workplace is not just a place to work; it is a community where people find friends and a sense of belonging. The employer's role goes beyond paying for the work done on the company premises or for company business; the employer is almost like a village head, who is respected and looks after everyone in the village. A Canadian organization operating an office in the Caribbean shared with us that when one employee has a wedding or funeral, the office closes because everyone attends. As a result, their time-off policy has to be administered in a flexible way to adjust to the local customs.

When operating in international locations, North American organizations find that interactions with employees that are considered as outside the work sphere in North America are now considered the company's business. For example in China, the work unit (or employer) used to provide apartment units to workers. Now, with the housing reform and private real estate market development, employees can choose to look after their own accommodations, but it is still a common practice to provide dormitory units to workers on production lines or in retail operations. Because most are young migrant workers from the country or smaller cities, providing them a "home away from home" instead of leaving them on the street to find their own shelter differentiates a good employer from a poor one. Here is Caroline's experience:

When I became the manager of human resources of a Sino-Canadian joint venture, I found myself managing not only the usual HR responsibilities, I was also managing a dormitory for single workers and apartments for families, a cafeteria that provided three meals a day and the company's vehicle fleet. With a couple of hundred young people staying on company premises twenty-four hours a day, we want to make sure they do something productive after work and get along well. We allocated funding and bought sports equipment so that they spent their spare time on healthy activities. With the help of the union, the workers organized themselves into a Youth League. They participated in competitions in the local community. They organized events for themselves and put on performances. Chinese youth love singing and performing in public! I attended some events. Some of the shows they put on were really good.

The benefit employees most appreciated was our tuition reimbursement program so that the young workers could attend night schools and study for a diploma of their interest. We ran a regular shuttle bus between the company dormitory and the local college. One of the many success stories out of this program was a young worker who completed a diploma in business and got a sales job in the company selling telecommunications equipment. As a result, we had a good reputation in the community, which helped us attract talent and increase engagement, as the workers felt that the company cared about their future.

Building Personal Relationships

In North America, we try to keep our work relationships with colleagues, managers, customers and suppliers professional. This is not the case in collective cultures. People do not separate their professional and personal lives nearly to the same extent as people do in North America. There are many informal lunches and dinners among colleagues. In China, annual outings and New Year parties usually include family members, and the top management of the company toasts the spouses of salespeople to thank them for being supportive of their spouses, who are away from home so often.

All these interactions contribute to building a trusting relationship, which becomes helpful during difficult times. Caroline managed a restructuring that required retaining the employees for three to six months so they could teach subcontractors how to do their jobs. The team achieved outstanding business results and developed personal bonds during this difficult process. They continued their friendship after the restructuring, regardless of where they worked.

Section 7.3: Talent Development

Building local capability is a key mandate for many North American organizations in their first few years of operation in an international location. The next three case studies discuss the following situations in talent development:

- Aligning organization design to local culture
- Adapting learning and development programs to meet the local employees' learning needs
- Teaching local managers decision-making approaches consistent with the company's culture

Case Study #3: Cultural Clash

A North American mining company operates a mine in Brazil. There were two large divisions in this company, Exploration and Operations. The management team had a matrix reporting structure. Each local functional manager reported to either the local head of Exploration or the local head of Operations and to one of the vice presidents in the corporate office. This structure caused quite a bit of confusion and conflict within the local team.

For example, the manager in charge of Community Relationships, who reported to the head of Operations in Brazil and to the vice president of Community Relationships in the corporate office, was responsible for community relationship programs for both Exploration and Operations. This reporting structure created a major challenge for her. First, she was given different directions by her two managers. Second, the head of Operations, who was a Brazilian national, and the head of Exploration, who was an expatriate from France, did not have a good working relationship and openly disagreed on many occasions. As a result, every major decision was escalated to the corporate office and juried by the three vice presidents in charge of Exploration, Operations and Community Relationships, respectively.

Over a short period of time, everyone involved became entrenched into a conflict situation. The three vice presidents frequently flew to the mine site to try and resolve these conflicts. At one of the meetings, several people were standing and shouting at each other, and the Brazilian Community Relationships manager resigned on the spot.

There are two cultural factors in this situation. The first is the difference in people's sense of hierarchy. The double reporting model is very challenging for people from hierarchical cultures, who have a strong need to know who their boss is so they know exactly what they are expected to do. They follow their manager's directions, even if they do not fully agree with their manager. Matrix organizations, which result in people having two or three managers potentially pointing employees in different directions, pose a major challenge for hierarchical employees.

The second cultural factor has to do with the nonverbal cues people use in cross-cultural communication. How much emotions people express in the workplace is cultural. Figure 7.1 shows the different range of positive and negative emotions displayed by people from various parts of the world. While East Asians express much less emotion than Canadians and Americans, people from Latin America or the Middle East express a lot more emotion than Canadians and Americans.

In the previous example, the head office vice presidents felt extremely uncomfortable because of the large amount of negative emotions expressed during meetings on site and concluded that since the relationships were damaged to such an extent, the only solution was to remove some members from the team. In countries where people are used to expressing strong emotions, an employee can say he or she will resign many times without actually leaving the organization. Talking about resignation is a way to express how strongly the employee feels about an issue. The manager, or human resources, will find a way to mediate the conflict so that people will move on and continue to work together.

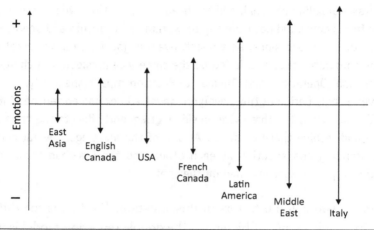

Figure 7.1 Differences in the Range of Emotions

Bridging the Organization Design Gap

The solution to this problem involves taking most of the steps in the PSE solutions framework. The most important is the **organization design**. In order to operate effectively in Brazil, the company created a country general manager position; the local heads of both Exploration and Operations reported to this person, who was ultimately responsible for all business activities in the country and all local employees. This organization structure enabled local employees to operate as one team and to resolve conflict locally. The country manager was carefully selected as a Brazilian immigrant who had worked in high-level positions in the mining industry in North America—he understood how to manage conflict and interpersonal situations in both Brazil and North America. The company also implemented the following steps to bridge the cultural gap:

Build Cultural Awareness and Skills

- The company provided a cross-cultural communication workshop to give everyone a chance to put all the issues on the table and discuss cultural differences in a constructive manner. Once people understood that the conflict among them was a result of cultural differences, they made an effort not to take it personally and started to collaborate by looking for common ground.

- The workshop emphasized the importance of soft skills within the organization. Since most employees in the Brazilian operations came from cultures that place greater importance on technical skills, many realized their need for and the benefits of improving their communication and conflict resolution skills. As a result, local employees asked for further soft skills training sessions.

Reinforce the Desired Behavior through Work Systems

- **Performance management:** The company incorporated soft skills development in the performance goals for its key players and implemented 360-degree feedback in the review process. When people understood that they were held accountable for building good working relationships with their peers and reports, they were more motivated to improve their soft skills.
- **Rewards system:** The company set collective goals for the local management team, which was to obtain the operation permit from the local government by a certain date. When people saw that they were better off working together than working against each other, they tried hard to overcome the difficult hurdles and learn to work together to achieve their common goal.
- **Processes:** The local management agreed on a practical communication and decision-making process that all parties could live with. While there were setbacks along the way, a clear process and people's commitment to the process brought them back to the conversation, and they found a way to move forward that worked for everyone.

The situation in Brazil improved significantly for this mining company. The level of collaboration between departments has increased to the point that the organization plans to implement the same approach in its other mine in Mexico.

Case Study #4: Leadership Development Program

The learning and development (L&D) department of a US multinational pharmaceutical company piloted a leadership development program (LDP) in the US, where it was quite successful. They were considering rolling it out to their international subsidiaries and training local facilitators to deliver the program. Upon review, we found that the program may not be received the same way it was in the US for several reasons:

- The program is rooted in the American definition and concept of leadership. Most of the examples come from the US (Jonas Salk, Mary Kay, presidents Washington, Lincoln and Kennedy, etc.); the remainder come from the UK (Winston Churchill, Shackleton's Arctic Expedition). Each country has heroes and leaders specific to their culture and context; this program could make a number of participants feel like all leaders are either Americans or British.
- The program had loose definitions of terms. For example, it referred to "managers" using several different words: *supervisor, manager, leader, facilitator* and *coach*. In hierarchical cultures, titles are very important, and each term implies a specific level of authority and responsibility attached to it. Some of these terms may not have equivalents in many languages. When translated, some may have a very different connotation than the English word. While the word *coach* implies a more equal relationship with the employee than the word *manager* in North America, it translates into a *trainer* or *teacher* in Spanish, Japanese and Chinese, implying a more hierarchical relationship.
- The program included many open-ended exercises (e.g., blank pages with titles such as "self-reflection," "ideas that I have modeled, discovered and invented" and "group discussion notes"). In particular, one exercise was called "Philosopher's Walk"; it asked participants to walk around the room looking at the concepts and models presented and reflecting on their own. These learning activities would be very confusing to hierarchical learners, who are used to being taught the materials rather than having to learn them by themselves.
- Some exercises were based on the North American culture. For example, one of the exercises designed to emphasize the importance of customer service involved two teams selling and buying hamburgers. The buying team was instructed to give detailed demands such as three pieces of tomato, six pieces of pickle and half a teaspoon of mustard. This activity would be very challenging for many people in international locations because hamburgers are clearly a North American food item. The idea of building your own burger to this kind of detail is based on an individualistic culture where resources are readily available in large quantities. Many countries do not have all the ingredients, and the corresponding

words are foreign to the participants. In many developing countries, one is happy to have food. People would not understand all the fuss of having the exact number of pieces of tomato on the bun.

- The structure of the program material was very loose; the links between the participant workbook and the facilitator's guide were not easily understood, and neither contained clear instructions. This would create a major challenge for facilitators in hierarchical countries, who need structure and clear instructions to understand what they are expected to do. They would not know what to do in some segments of the program.

Bridging the Learning-Needs Gap

In order to increase the global effectiveness and appeal of the LDP, the L&D team made a number of modifications to both the program design and the approach.

- **Involve the local HR team.** Rather than asking local subsidiary trainers to translate the materials, they involved the local HR people in the redesign of the LDP and combined elements of the original program with local content. In particular, the examples used in the localized versions of the course were drawn from examples of past local leaders—as opposed to examples of past American or British leaders.
- **Standardize the language and terms used in the program.** Instead of using five or six words for *manager*, they decided on the term *people leader* and provided a definition up front. They focused on conveying the message of leadership and promoting a sense of egalitarianism among all learners that is consistent with the organization's culture.
- **Increase the percentage of lectures,** especially in the first sections of the program. They then gradually introduced more self-reflection, group discussions and presentations by participants. They modified the exercises and provided a few more choices so that local trainers could choose one that is closer to their cultural context.
- **Tighten the structure and the flow of the program.** They also provided clear instructions on what to do in each section of the program.

- **Train North American trainers on cultural awareness and cross-cultural communication** so that those who provide training in international locations can adapt their teaching style to the needs of local learners.

Revamping the LDP took close to twelve months. Initially, the delay created significant tension and frustration within the US L&D department—several US senior HR leaders wanted to prioritize staying on schedule over program effectiveness. With the help of an external consultant, they realized that revamping the program with local LDP facilitators meant everyone had a much higher degree of commitment to the course content and effectiveness. People involved in the LDP redesign concluded that they significantly deepened their understanding of what leadership is through extensive discussions with colleagues from different cultures. They also learned extensively about cultural differences and their impact on L&D in the process; this knowledge was then applied to other corporate training courses (e.g., communication, presentation).

Case Study #5: Benefit Policy

Sarah assumed a newly created role of director for global HR policies and programs. One of the requests she received in her information gathering from international locations was "We need clear benefit policies in Taiwan." She asked what benefits needed clear policies. The situation was that when an employee experienced a family death, the local custom was to give the employee a small amount of cash in an envelope as a way to show sympathy. The local finance manager wanted a clear policy so he could disburse the exact amount of cash based on the employee's level and the employee's relationship with the deceased family member.

Sarah was surprised by this kind of request. Here in North America, when an employee has a family death or is hospitalized, the department administrative assistant sends flowers to the employee. The administrative assistants use their discretion to decide the amount to spend. They check with their manager when in doubt and speak to each other to keep some consistency. The question rarely comes to HR. Sarah thought to herself, "Don't they have any management discretion?"

One typical response from someone in Sarah's position is, "This is a situation where the local management should use their discretion." However, Sarah should be aware of several consequences of this response:

- The lack of an HR response could be interpreted as the corporate office does not know how to provide directions.
- Local management may start to apply discretion on things that are not consistent with the organization's business or people strategy. Down the road, the corporate office may realize the inconsistency and start to question these decisions or practices. Local people then feel very confused. In their minds, you said, "We don't want to dictate how the local operations run and we want to adapt to the local needs"; now you are saying, "This must be done this way because we are a global company and we must follow the global process." This makes corporate people seem inconsistent.

The gap is clearly a result of the different senses of hierarchy. In equalitarian societies such as Canada and the US, many decisions are made at lower levels of the organization because the egalitarian work culture encourages employees to take initiative and make decisions on how to do their job. In hierarchical societies, the same decisions are made at higher levels because if the employee is criticized once for making the wrong decision, he or she asks the manager for decisions all the time. The manager or the person in an authoritative position should always have an answer. The typical North American answer of "I don't know, you figure it out because it's your job" is often interpreted as lack of leadership.

Bridging the Decision-Making Gap

Teaching a new competence or skill is not easy. Following our PSE framework, the solution to this problem is to first build **awareness** so all people involved realize they are not on the same page as to who should make what decisions because of their different sense of hierarchy. This removes or reduces the chances of people taking it personally or blaming each other and encourages more open communication.

The key solution to this situation is to create a **process** to determine decisions made:

1. **By corporate and executed locally:** These decisions should involve the total rewards including benefits strategy. The local office needs to understand whether the company's overall policy is to remain comparable with peer companies in benefits offerings or to use benefits as a competitive differentiator for recruiting and retention.
2. **By corporate with local input:** Corporate with local input should design the principle of the benefit plan and its main components such as time off, extended health, retirement, life and accident insurance.
3. **Jointly:** Joint decisions should involve adjustments to local legislative requirements and market conditions. Some benefits may make sense in North America (e.g., time off for jury duty) and be irrelevant in some international locations. Certain jurisdictions mandate benefits that are unheard of in North America; for example, in Korea, employers are required to give female employees one day off every month.
4. **Locally and then check with corporate:** These decisions should involve interpretation of the policies and handling exceptions. Once a benefit policy and plan is implemented, local HR and management should be able to answer most questions from employees. Occasionally, an out-of-the-ordinary situation may require that local HR or management decide on a certain course of action and check with the corporate office to ensure consistency.
5. **Locally:** Administration of the plan should be done locally. Gifts or flowers for employees on special occasions can be part of the benefit policy where a spending range can be set and local management discretion applied, based on the circumstances.

The company in Case Study #4 essentially went through the action steps and implemented a new total rewards plan, including a benefit policy that, once set up, enabled local management to be self-sufficient in addressing day-to-day employee situations and questions.

Introducing a new culture and behavior is an ongoing process, which requires continuous recalibration. It can be frustrating, as the pendulum sometimes may go too far on either side. People in the corporate office at times may feel the local people are doing some wild things and that they only find out after the fact. People in the local office may stop asking corporate for any guidance or ask corporate to make all decisions for them. The key is to bring people back to the awareness of cultural differences and commitment to the process so all people involved continuously work on alignment with the corporate strategy and building flexibility to address local needs.

Section 7.4: Regulatory Compliance and Relationship with the Government

Case Study #6: Overtime Policy

When I started working for the Chinese subsidiary of an American company, I needed to finalize the company's overtime pay policy in order to offer the total rewards package to new employees. The Labor Law had very prescriptive standards on how overtime work should be paid, but no provision on who was eligible. In theory, all senior managers were eligible to overtime pay since they were by definition employees. The general manager did not want professional and management staff to clock in and out and preferred to pay a higher salary to compensate for any overtime work these professional and management staff might perform. The regional human resources director, who was based in Singapore, was very concerned that we were not legally compliant.

I visited the local labor department to look for guidance with my Singaporean colleague, who was sent to help me with the start-up. The government staff would not say affirmatively whether the company could or could not define the eligibility in its policy. His advice was that they operate on a complaint basis. If there were no complaint, they would not make an issue (they actually do check on less reputable employers). If there were complaints, they would evaluate each separately and on its own merit.

(Caroline)

This example leads to the discussion on regulatory compliance and relationship with the government. Government plays a very small role in day-to-day business operations in North America because on a world scale, the US and Canada are relatively less hierarchical. In North America, legal compliance and enforcement are achieved through contracts and the legal system. In hierarchical countries, the government gets involved in many aspects of a business' operations. Compliance and enforcement are through government administration and inspection. In China, the government requires all employers to purchase standard employment contracts from the labor department, who then inspects the contracts signed by the employer and the employees at their discretion.

Many hierarchical countries are also relatively more collective than North America, which again emphasizes relationship building with the government, the same as with the employees. This is especially important because in many hierarchical countries there are so many rules that some may contradict each other, and it is important to have a good relationship with the people who interpret the rules.

In the case of China, the growth of new businesses has outpaced the government's ability to regulate them. The government is gradually introducing new laws and regulations to create a regulatory environment that keeps pace with the rapid economic development. The national Labor Act, which was enacted in 1995, sets very general guidelines on employment standards. Special economic zones and major urban centers such as Beijing and Shanghai had created and subsequently updated their local regulations under the principle set by the Labor Law. A new Labor Contract Act came into effect in 2008. The Social Insurance Act was enacted in 2011. In practice, there is a lot of confusion about following and enforcing the law as the law may differ from location to location and from time to time. The process of progress is not linear—it often feels like three steps forward, one step to the side and one step back.

As a result, it is very difficult to follow the law to the letter. What is important is to establish your company as a good corporate citizen in the eyes of the government. After putting a lot of money into developing the infrastructure of business parks or development zones, Chinese government at all levels wants to attract good businesses to operate there and employ local people. So the relationship between the government and foreign investment enterprises can be a mutually beneficial business relationship. Here is how Caroline and her company worked with the local government.

Through visits to various government offices and discussions with other HR professionals in my network, I found a solution to solve our overtime policy dilemma. Since the standard contract purchased from the government had a clause allowing the employer to specify what was not covered by the standard clauses, I wrote up an amendment stating the eligibility of the overtime pay and had the labor department approve the amendment as part of our company's standard contract.[4]

Ongoing communication and a humble learning attitude are key to building a good working relationship with the government. When my Singaporean colleague and I visited the local government for policy guidance, it was clear we wanted to learn and follow the rules. The local government also needed us to showcase a good foreign business when they had other prospective foreign investors visiting the city. So from time to time we hosted such visits and gave the visitors a tour of our facility, which made the government staff very proud of their city's investment environment.

At one time, the company went through a restructuring, which affected a number of employees. I arranged a visit by the Greater China general manager to the mayor. During the visit, the general manager explained the company's long-term growth strategy and its commitment to doing business in China. Then I met the labor department and briefed them on our restructuring plan and the transition support the company was providing to the affected employees. The labor department chief expressed full support for the decisions. She told me that if any of the affected workers had complaints, I could send them to her and she would talk to them and help connect them with other employers.

* * *

The global talent market presents a very complex problem for HR professionals and managers as each country is on its own unique path to development and prosperity, which results in environments very different from the organization's home environment. In our experience, there are many enthusiastic, competent and hardworking people who want to be part of a successful North American organization. HR professionals and managers play an important role in developing the local talent that will take their organization's success into new territories. The key is to have a long-term talent strategy that guides the organization's talent acquisition, retention and development practices in such a way that is sensitive to, reflects and incorporates cultural differences as a key factor in competing in the global talent market.

Notes

1. For simplicity, we refer to all organizations expanding overseas as MNCs, regardless of their size and the numbers of countries they are in.
2. Retrieved from the Ministry of Education's Web (http://www.moe.edu.cn/publicfiles/business/htmlfiles/moe/s7567/list.html) site on May 7, 2013; in 1997 (the earliest year this data is available), there were about 1,000 universities and colleges, with 380,000 bachelor's degree graduates and 447,000 college graduates.
3. Retrieved from China Association of Actuaries' Web site on May 7, 2013. (http://www.e-caa.org.cn/html/brief.jsp)
4. As of the time of this book, companies (including state owned enterprises) are still getting around the problem of lacking eligibility rules for overtime pay in the Labor Law by inserting a clause "salary is inclusive of overtime pay" for management staff.

8

Conclusion

Section 8.1: Are We Converging?

One question we often get asked is, "Are we converging toward a common culture?" It is worded in many different ways, such as "Since most people around the world are learning English, won't we reach the point where there is one universal way of doing business?" or "Since kids today are playing video games (sometimes, the same ones) all around the world, will their common experiences overcome cultural differences?"

We asked the question to a group of Chinese university professors. The vice president of the university, who has studied in and traveled to many countries, answered, "I think we are converging. The question is, what are we converging toward?" What a great answer! While her Chinese modesty prevented her from saying that others are converging to the Chinese way, that was what she had in mind. The word *China* means the "Central Empire"; therefore, it is natural that others want to converge toward the Central Empire. At the same time, it is clear that when our North American audience or clients ask the question, they think the rest of the world is converging toward the North American way. We think we are the center of the universe and consider China as the Far East. Just about everyone has a good reason to think their way of living should be the universal one. Mr. Portokalos, Toula's father in the movie *My Big Fat Greek Wedding*, has a famous line: "Toula, there are two kinds of people—Greeks, and everyone else who wish they were Greek"; and he can show that every English word has a Greek root to prove it!

We hope our readers will agree that the very fact we are all expecting others to converge toward us means we are not converging any time soon. Even though much of Geert Hofstede's research is based on multinational corporations that have strong corporate cultures, he wrote, "Research about the development of cultural values has shown repeatedly that there is very little evidence of international convergence over time. For the next few hundred years, countries will remain culturally very diverse." Michael Adams discussed in his book *Fire and Ice: The United States, Canada and the Myth of Converging Values* that his research of the social values of Canada and the US in 1992, 1996 and 2000 shows that Canada and US are actually moving in opposite directions. If Canada and the US are diverging, what are the chances of global convergence?

We encourage anyone who was born in North America, speaks English and thinks the world is converging to take a trip to China or a French-speaking African country and stay in a hotel that is not part of a Western chain. Without some help from an interpreter, simple tasks like ordering food, buying shampoo or printing a file immediately become a major challenge. At that moment, it usually becomes clear that convergence will not take place in our lifetime.

Section 8.2: Cultural Diversity and Inclusion Is a Business Imperative

So we are not converging, and our workplace is becoming more and more diverse. Over the last two decades, we have seen surges of cultural diversity in many industries driven by different events:

- In June 2005, crude oil prices broke the psychological barrier of $60 per barrel and rose to $145 per barrel before the crash in July 2008. The oil and gas industry in Alberta went through a major round of expansion because it made the extraction of oil from oil sands economically viable on a large scale. Several megaprojects (each worth several billions of dollars and requiring millions of person-hours of work) were initiated between 2005 and 2008, and the demand for skilled workers significantly outstripped supply in Alberta. As a result, both oil and gas companies and their service providers hired scores of immigrants and brought in people from overseas, leading to a significant surge of cultural diversity in their ranks.

- A similar surge in cultural diversity happened in the IT industry in the late 1990s as a result of the combination of Y2K and the dot-com bubble. Many IT professionals who arrived in North America in the late 1990s were able to find employment in their field very quickly, even if their soft skills were low, because IT organizations were desperately looking for people who could program in languages such as C++ or Java. At that point, Chinese programmers who could not speak much English found jobs—their employers paired them up with other Chinese programmers who spoke Chinese and English and essentially acted as both mentors and translators.

- Public accounting firms experienced a very similar challenge in the mid-2000s as a result of Sarbanes–Oxley. This act was passed by the US Congress in 2002 to prevent repeats of Enron-style frauds by setting or enhancing accounting standards for all corporations publicly traded in the US. Because organizations had to be compliant by a given date, this created millions of billable hours for public accounting firms who were asked to help their clients implement the provisions of this act. This created a shortage of auditors in North America, and public accounting firms brought in many experienced senior associates and managers from their overseas offices.

In each of these situations, bringing in immigrants or foreign workers was simply a necessity for many organizations to run their business and grow. Integrating culturally diverse employees and serving culturally diverse customers became a business imperative. There was no alternative.

Section 8.3: Cultural Diversity and Inclusion as a Competitive Advantage

Since cultural diversity is going to remain a source of both dangers and opportunities for the foreseeable future, how does it become a competitive advantage? While there are many research studies funded by various governments and NGOs on the business success brought by cultural diversity, we want to focus on an invisible advantage. Cultural diversity fosters innovation and spawns creativity in several ways:

- It helps people look at the same problem from different angles, thereby increasing their creativity.
- It brings together people who have very different sets of "adjacent possible" (explained in detail later), thereby enabling them to come up with solutions nobody could have come up with independently.
- It creates connections between separate "idea-spaces," thereby increasing the speed of diffusion of new ideas.

Looking at the Problem from a Different Angle

Cultural diversity helps people see the problem from a different angle. The impact of having someone look at a problem from a different angle is best demonstrated by the experiments conducted by Charlan Nemeth at Berkeley.[1] She showed people a series of slides, each dominated by a single color, and asked her test subjects to free-associate that color. While most people tend to view free association as a creative activity in itself, it turns out that most of us come up with the very same free associations—about 80 percent of all people immediately think of *sky* when seeing the color blue, another color or the word *color*.

The less common free associations are considered by psychologists as the creative ones. For example, in the case of the color blue, coming up with words such as *sad*, *lonely* or *jeans* is considered more creative than coming up with *sky*, the word *color* or another color. Through repeated experiments like these, psychologists have created tables that show the probability of people coming up with certain words when asked to free-associate with given words; they then use this tool to measure creativity and look for environments that foster it. If you can find an environment where people come up with *lonely* more frequently than with *sky* when asked to free-associate with a blue slide, you have found a source of creativity.

Through one of her experiments, Nemeth demonstrated the impact of having someone see the situation from a different angle. She asked groups of people to free-associate colored slides; however, she planted in each group one person who was instructed to describe the slide in a different way (this person would describe a yellow slide as blue, for example). She found that, when the test group was asked to free-associate, they now came up with the more creative words more frequently than the average groups.

Since having one person in a team who sees things from a different angle nudges the whole team toward creativity, having culturally different members in a team leads the whole team to be more creative. Because of their background or way of communicating, they are likely to see and describe the problems the team is facing in a different way. This, in turn, helps everyone tackle the problem in a more creative way. Here is a situation where a fresh perspective made a major difference to the team:

I hired a technician—Mohammed, a chemist from Somalia—to run experiments for me. I showed him how to run these experiments and then asked him to run one in front of me. The last step of any chemical experiment is to wash all the glassware. Mohammed washed each beaker by pouring a small amount of water in it, carefully rinsing the inside of the beaker to ensure the water covered the entire surface of the beaker. I asked him why he was doing it this way. He told me that distilled water was very scarce in Somalia, so every Somali chemist learns to use it very carefully.

A year later, our research team had come up with a new formulation for one of our main products, and we were ready to commercialize it. In order to anticipate the problems we might run into as we scaled up, we conducted a project review meeting. We had people from different departments of the company (research, engineering, product marketing and manufacturing) meet together to discuss the scale-up and commercialization plan. Halfway through the afternoon, one of the production engineers raised a point: We had not considered the amount of water that was required to wash the product at the end of the process. After some calculations, we realized that the amount of distilled water that would be required when we reached full-scale production was simply orders of magnitude greater than what was available in any of our production plants; we had to go back to the drawing board and find a way to use a lot less distilled water.

We spent the next year researching a solution. Mohammed's knowledge became invaluable to us at this point. He taught us how to use less water at every step of the process. More important, he helped us think of water in a different way—as a precious resource, rather than an inexhaustible commodity.

(Canadian chemical engineer)

Finding More Creative Solutions

The term *adjacent possible*, first coined by the scientist Stuart Kauffman,[2] was made popular by Steven Johnson through the extensive use of this phrase in his book *Where Good Ideas Come From: The Natural History of Innovation*. This term refers to the set of new concepts, ideas, tools, machines, devices and so on that can be created by recombining all the known concepts, ideas, tools, machines, devices and so on that are currently available at a given time and place. As this phrase implies, most innovative breakthroughs involve recombining existing "parts" into a new whole, rather than making a leapfrog jump involving the creation of several completely new parts. As Steven Johnson explains, "This term captures both the limits and the creative potential of change and innovation"—innovation brings new possibility by creating more combinations, but not all combinations are possible at a given point in time. We cannot jump from stone tools to cars in one innovation (except in cartoons such as *The Flintstones*).

It is possible for people to come up with visionary ideas that are "ahead of their time"—these ideas truly transcend the adjacent possible. While this has happened on many occasions throughout history, these leapfrog jumps into the future did not lead anywhere in the sense that the new concepts they created were not incorporated into any other design and they ended up being reinvented separately many years later, when they finally became part of the adjacent possible. Here are a few examples:

• In his book, Steven Johnson describes several examples of ideas that were so far ahead of their times that they died along the way and were reinvented in other forms later. One such example is the Analytical Engine, a machine designed by the nineteenth-century inventor Charles Babbage; this machine was the ancestor of programmable computers and predated them by more than 100 years. It never went much beyond the blueprint stage; while truly visionary, nothing ever came out of it because it was too far out of the adjacent possible of its time. Building and running such a machine using the power sources and technology available at the time (coal, steam and steam engines) was a dead end—computers needed electricity, vacuum tubes and integrated circuits in order to be effective and useful.

• In his book *Guns, Germs and Steel: The Fates of Human Societies,* Jared Diamond describes the invention of precursors to movable type in Crete more than 1,000 years before the invention of movable type by Bi Sheng, in China, in AD 1040, or the invention of printing by Gutenberg, around AD 1450. As with Babbage's invention, this invention did not lead to anything because the technologies needed to build upon the concept of using the same blocks repeatedly to "write" did not exist at the time. In particular, there was no medium on which to store the writing other than on clay plates—this inventor did not have paper as one of the "parts" readily available.

In other words, the vast majority of the new ideas people end up putting into practice are based on a recombination of existing parts in a new way or the addition of one new element to an existing base. This is one of the reasons cultural diversity is so powerful in spawning creativity—people who are culturally different from us have different sets of adjacent possible. By putting together the adjacent possible of American engineers with the adjacent possible of their Russian or Japanese counterparts, we can create ideas or devices that neither could have come up with independently at the time because they were outside their adjacent possible when taken separately, but within the combined adjacent possible when put together.

In his book *Smart World: Breakthrough Creativity and the New Science of Ideas,* Richard Ogle introduces the concept of idea-spaces— a combination of all the tools, concepts, knowledge and objects of study.—and shows that many creative people made breakthroughs when they accessed new idea-spaces through their networks. Steven

Johnson builds on this idea in Chapter 6 ("Exaptation") of his book and demonstrates that creative people have broad social networks that enable them to come in contact with ideas that are shared or known to people from their networks but not readily known to themselves or the people they typically work with. By bringing ideas from one idea-space to another, they can come up with solutions their peers are not able to see.

Culturally different people are well suited to become "idea-space bridges." This connection may take the simple form of being able to read books or articles published in another language and applying the learning in their work or sharing the content with their colleagues. This is particularly visible in the fields of science, engineering and marketing. Having someone who can summarize for the whole team the content of a new patent, a new research article or a new type of mortgage can help increase the speed of diffusion of new ideas from one idea-space to another, from one culture to another.

Culturally different employees also bring ideas, concepts or knowledge of technologies from their home countries to their organizations. For example, one oil and gas company nicknamed one of its Russian engineers the "nine-million-dollar man" after he adapted technology developed for the Russian space program to their gas metering system, thereby saving nine million dollars for the company. On a much larger scale, the American *Apollo* program made extensive use of the rocket technology developed by Wernher von Braun and his German colleagues in Peenemunde. Lionel experienced the adjacent possible and connecting idea-spaces when working at a multinational imaging products company.

I was assigned to study one set of four distillation columns that were not operating the way they were expected to. In parallel, an American engineer, Jim, was also assigned to study the same problem by another department. Our different engineering training led us down different paths:

- I tackled the problem from a theoretical perspective, as I was trained to do in France. I started by writing the differential equations that represented all columns of this type. When I realized I could not solve them analytically, I tried to find a numerical solution and found out that the company had developed its own software to simulate distillation columns.

- Jim used a typical American approach—he decided to do something practical and see what happened. He spiked the feed of one of the four columns and took many samples at various points of that column over a period of time to see how the column responded to this disturbance.

When Jim and I met by chance in the lab, we realized we were tackling the same problem in different ways. At first, both reacted by dismissing the other's approach. Jim's reaction to my approach was along the lines of, "It will take you forever to reach any meaningful result." My reaction to Jim's approach can be summarized as, "Even if you happen to stumble upon a solution for one column, you will not be able to reapply it to the other three columns."

After some back and forth where each were trying to convince the other of the superiority of his own approach, we realized we could join forces by studying all four columns (but not the general case) and use the results of Jim's experiments to help my modeling. Over the course of the next three months, we came up with a solution that was eventually implemented. This solution was, in turn, one of the key concepts that drove my further research at Caltech. Down the road, this concept led to my Ph.D. thesis and extensive research by other researchers.

This small success illustrates the value of combining the adjacent possible and connecting idea-spaces by having culturally different people work together. Together, they can come up with solutions that neither could have invented on their own.

Section 8.4: The Inclusion Journey

As we conclude this book, we want to reflect on its key messages as described in Chapter 1:

- Give people the benefit of the doubt.
- Make it safe to discuss cultural differences in a constructive way.
- Focus on what we can each do to bridge the gap.
- HR professionals and managers need to lead change at the organization level.

Implementing these suggestions means we all need to change behavior, both at the individual level and at the organization level. Changing behavior is not easy. Anybody who has tried to learn a new skill or behavior knows it takes time and continuous effort.

Becoming a Richer Human Being

As part of my New Year resolutions, I decided I needed to exercise more. I signed up for a Zumba class at the community center because the time in the week suited me. I had been to cardio or aerobic classes before but had no idea what Zumba was. The first couple of classes came as a shock. The music was very loud. The dance movements were complex, and many involved moving certain body parts I did not know could move on their own, in order to look "hot and sexy." I was struggling to follow the steps. Just when I got the hang of a step pattern, the instructor moved on to a new one. I had no bandwidth to look hot or sexy, as following the steps was enough of a challenge. At the end of the second class, I was tempted to withdraw, but I thought I should just stick it out for the term.

As time went by, I started to recognize familiar tunes and patterns in the movements. Zumba is a fun dance. The instructor was always smiling while dancing and showed tremendous energy and enthusiasm. I guess it was hard to dance to this kind of music with a serious face. Depending on the day, the class had about three white women, four Chinese women and five South Asian (India, Pakistan and Sri Lanka) women, very typical of any of the Greater Toronto Area municipalities. Some of them had been to Zumba classes before and had a much better grasp of the dance than I did. Even when their movements did not look like those of the instructor, they were clearly enjoying it. (Caroline)

I think this is exactly what happens to all of us when we work with people from diverse cultures. The Conscious Competence Learning Matrix, developed by Noel Burch of Gordon Training International, indicates that we all go through four stages as we learn a new skill or behavior (see Figure 8.1).

Stage 1: We don't know that we don't know, as when I signed up for the Zumba class. We are not aware of cultural differences and what it takes to work with people who are culturally different from us.

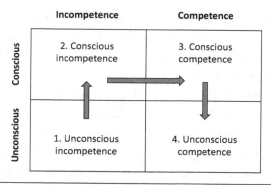

Figure 8.1 Conscious Competence Learning Matrix

Stage 2: We realize that we don't know, as when I attended my first class. We are uncomfortable in the presence of people who are culturally different from us and realize that working with them requires skills that are out of the range of our past experience. Many of us do try, but it is hard. We may even consider quitting or deciding we will stick with people with whom we feel comfortable.

Stage 3: We have gained appreciation of the benefits of building cultural competence and some proficiency, but we still need to make a conscious effort, like the other women in the Zumba class did.

Stage 4: We enjoy working with people from all over the world so much that it becomes natural. I have heard people who grew up in Toronto or New York City say they find it strange when they go to a community without much diversity to the point of feeling uncomfortable. I found out that the Zumba instructor is actually of Armenian heritage; she grew up in Toronto and has never been to Latin America. Yet she learned Zumba to the point that it has become part of her.

Being aware of the stages we go through in order to develop cultural competence helps us be patient with ourselves and others. We still feel frustrated, inadequate and awkward at times and wonder why we got ourselves into this. We make mistakes along the way, and so do people we work with. It is important to remember that building cultural competence is a journey and to have confidence that we will eventually become proficient if we keep trying. Over time, we become more successful professionally because we develop skills to handle a wider variety of assignments that involve a wider range of people from diverse backgrounds. We also become richer human beings, with increased knowledge of and experience with our fellow human beings, no matter where they grew up.

Caroline worked with a technology company where recent immigrants accounted for half of the workforce. As one time, she worked with a manager to manage a very difficult employee relations case involving a recent immigrant employee. Despite the difficulties experienced with this employee, the next person this manager (a white Anglo-Saxon) hired was an immigrant from the same country. This example shows that the manager and the company have accumulated enough experience of working with employees from diverse cultures that hiring the best person for the job has become a habit. They have the confidence that they can manage cultural diversity and turn it into a competitive advantage for their organization.

Leading Change and Fostering an Inclusive Culture

In order to effectively lead change and foster an inclusive culture at their organizations, HR professionals and managers need to keep in mind that people from different parts of the world want change to happen differently. Here are two examples where this difference came into play:

The manager of the regulatory affairs department of an American medical device manufacturing company expressed significant frustration with the speed at which Health Canada was approving changes relative to its American counterpart, the Federal Drug Administration (FDA). She characterized the situation as "Canadians are afraid of change."

A senior manager in a professional service firm was transferred to Canada in order to introduce a new line of services the firm had previously developed in the UK. While their market study indicated there were significant opportunities in Canada, his business development efforts were initially quite unsuccessful. He was able to meet with prospective clients and generate enough interest to be asked to submit proposals, but things seem to stall at that point—his prospects were sitting on his proposals for months, discussing them extensively without making any decisions. After six months of frustrating efforts, less than 20 percent of his prospects had agreed to try his services, whereas his success rate in the UK was much higher.

What was really going on in these situations? Change happens in different ways in different parts of the world, and this is rooted in their political history. Let us just compare the US and Canada, which were both British colonies at one point, and the way they broke off from the UK:

- The US became independent over a relatively short period of time that involved significant armed struggle: The US went from the Boston Tea Party (in 1773) to the Declaration of Independence (in 1776) to the Treaty of Paris (in 1783). In less than ten years, the US went from being a British colony to being completely independent, and the celebrations on July 4 commemorate this rapid coming of age.
- By contrast, Canada became independent gradually, over a period of 150 years. The entire change took place with very few casualties and extensive negotiations. While the first rebellions took place in 1837 and the Dominion of Canada was created in 1867, Canada initially lacked many of the attributes of an independent country; they were put in place gradually, one by one:
  - The first Canadian army was created in 1915. Canadian soldiers were part of the British army prior to that.
  - The Canadian Central Bank was created in 1934. There was no independent Canadian monetary policy before that.
  - Canadian citizenship was created, and the first Canadian passports were issued in 1947. Until then, Canadians were British citizens who happened to live in Canada.
  - The Canadian flag was created in 1965. The Canadian flag before that was the Red Ensign.
  - In 1982, Canada patriated its constitution. Concretely, this means that Canadians can now change their constitution without asking the UK for approval.
  - Canada still has the British Queen as head of state.

What does this mean? While people in the US are used to change taking place quickly, Canadians have a strong preference for incremental change. We have found that the fastest way to get our ideas rejected in Canada is to tell Canadians, "I have a great idea. We are going to change everything, and we will improve productivity by 50 percent." Invariably, Canadians react by saying, "It will never work." And they are right—it will never work, in Canada. It works in the US or some other countries, but not in Canada.

So what is the solution? When trying to introduce change in Canada, we have learned to approach the problem in one of two ways, which can be described as either the "sliced bread" approach or the "pilot" approach:

- The sliced bread approach involves dividing the change you want to introduce into as many small components as possible. This approach works well when you can go from beginning to end by changing things a little bit at a time. In this case, we found that the best approach is to state the general direction in relatively broad terms and give specifics only related to the first, small step. When this step is almost completed, you then describe the next little step. Many Canadian companies will introduce a new version, which is a slight modification of the existing product, and gradually evolve it into the new product.
- The pilot approach is the preferred approach for any change that involves discontinuity—for example, implementing a new policy that supersedes an existing one or installing a new IT system that is not compatible with the existing one. In this case, both Americans and Canadians run pilot projects, but they pilot them differently. If the change to be made is of size 100, Americans typically do one pilot at size 25, learn from it and then roll it out. Canadians start with a pilot at size 1 or 2, and then do another pilot at size 30, then a third pilot at size 60. They make sure all stakeholders are represented; in particular, in the case of a change that spans the whole country, they ensure that people from each region of the country (British Columbia, Prairies, Ontario, Quebec and the Atlantic provinces) are involved in the pilot project and have a chance to provide feedback.

Here is how these approaches are put in practice in the two opening examples:

The American medical device manufacturing company decided to use the sliced bread approach. Instead of emphasizing how many additional benefits the product change would bring and how big the changes were, the regulatory affairs department decided to showcase future changes as small and incremental in order to speed up approval in Canada. The manager of regulatory affairs found that understanding why Canadians react differently from Americans, and identifying an alternate approach, significantly decreased the frustration experienced by her team.

The senior manager from the UK realized the key challenge was the size of the initial projects he was proposing. He had structured his proposals the way he would have structured them in the UK (i.e., with an initial investment of $500,000, at least). When he understood the cultural preference Canadians have for incremental change, he decided to decrease the size of the initial investment his clients had to make from $500,000 to $20,000. By presenting the initial project as a pilot that was designed, if successful, to lead to much bigger projects, he was able to increase his success rate from less than 20 percent to more than 80 percent and decrease the response time of his clients from several months to a few weeks.

By contrast, Americans want change to be revolutionary. In the US, new initiatives are presented like revolutions, and their launches involve many balloons and much fanfare (if you look at them from a Canadian perspective). We have observed that, to be implemented effectively, the same change needs to be presented as "big and revolutionary" in the US, whereas it needs to be introduced as "small and incremental" in Canada. Neither approach is right or wrong in absolute terms, but using the Canadian approach in the US usually gets you nowhere— and vice versa. If the difference between the US and Canada has such a profound impact in business practices, we can appreciate that people from countries that are much farther away approach change very differently from what we are used to.

One of our clients, a vice president of human resources in a professional service firm, introduced a diversity and inclusion strategy and program in her organization. She said that leading change means understanding where people are initially and how they want change to take place and supporting them along the way. Here are the highlights of their program:

Business case: The leaders of this firm recognized that as their business grows, their client base is becoming more and more culturally diverse. They conducted market research to understand future business opportunities and identified diversity and inclusion as one of the main business drivers for the next decade.

Leadership championship: The CEO of the company and his leadership team started the journey by attending training to develop their own cultural competence. They then selected high performing and high potential business leaders to become designated Inclusion Champions. Because of the high profile of this initiative, the Inclusion Champions truly see the value it brings to their business and are fully committed to leading the change in their organization, as opposed to treating it like another HR program. The CEO remains the driver of this initiative. He or a member of the executive team kicks off every training session for managers, thereby sending a clear message.

Continuous learning: Cultural competence training is incorporated into leadership training and strategic planning processes. All managers attend a cultural competence module as part of the leadership program, and a time slot is allocated to discussions on cultural diversity and inclusion at the semiannual business review conference to either provide additional training or a forum for managers to share their successes or challenges.

Business practices: Diversity and inclusion are embedded in the firm's business practice, such as project team selection, performance management and promotion process. The Inclusion Champions have regular conversations with managers to help them resolve issues related to serving clients or developing employees who are culturally different. They also play an important role during the annual review of partner promotions and make inclusive behavior one of the qualification criteria.

The results speak for themselves. In a survey conducted by the Great Place to Work Institute Canada, the company has been recognized as one of the Best Workplaces in Canada for the sixth consecutive year; this is based on a survey of over 57,000 employees with over 300 nominations. This organization was also recognized by the trade journal in its sector as having achieved stronger growth than the other large global firms operating in the same sector in Canada through its "Top 30" ranking.

* * *

Turning cultural diversity into a competitive advantage is a journey. As the old Chinese saying goes, "A journey of a thousand miles starts with the first step." Wherever you and your organizations are on this journey, let us embark on and continue this journey. Remember, danger can be turned into an opportunity.

Notes

1. Charlan J. Nemeth is a professor in the Department of Psychology, University of California, Berkeley. She conducted research on group decision making with a particular emphasis on the value of properly managed dissent for stimulating thought and creativity.
2. Stuart A. Kauffman is an American theoretical biologist and complex systems researcher who studies the origin of life on Earth.

Suggested Readings

Adams, Michael: *Fire and Ice: The United States, Canada and the Myth of Converging Values*. Toronto: Penguin Canada, 2003.

Asselin, G. and Mastron R. *Au Contraire: Figuring Out the French* Boston, MA Nicholas Brealy Publishing, 2010.

Condon, J. C. *Good Neighbors: Communicating with the Mexicans* Boston, MA Nicholas Brealy Publishing, 1997.

Condon, J. C. and Masumoto, T. *With Respect to the Japanese: Going to Work in Japan* Boston, MA Nicholas Brealy Publishing, 2010

Couto, Vinay, et al.: *Offshoring 2.0: Contracting Knowledge and Innovation to Expand Global Capabilities*. Durham, NC Center for International Business Education and Research, Duke University, 2007.

Diamond, Jared: *Guns, Germs, and Steel: The Fates of Human Societies*. New York: W.W. Norton, 1997.

Fail-Safe. 1964. Columbia Pictures, California. Director: Sidney Lumet.

Gilmore, Jason: *The 2008 Canadian Immigrant Labour Market: Analysis of Quality of Employment*. Labour Statistics Division; Statistics Canada; Catalogue no. 71–606-X, no. 5.

Gladwell, Malcolm: *Outliers: The Story of Success*. New York: Little, Brown, 2008.

Grove, C. N., Wenzhong, Hu, Enping, Zhuang *Encountering the Chinese: A Modern Country, An Ancient Culture* Boston, MA Nicholas Brealy Publishing, 2010.

Hersey, Paul, and Ken H. Blanchard: *Management of Organizational Behavior: Utilizing Human Resources*, 3rd ed. Englewood, New Jersey: Prentice Hall, 1977.

Hofstede, Geert: *Culture's Consequences: Comparing Values, Behaviors, Institutions, and Organizations across Nations*, 2nd ed. Newbury Park, CA: Sage Publications, 2003.

Hofstede, Geert: *Cultures and Organizations: Software of the Mind*, 2nd ed. New York: McGraw-Hill, 1997 pp. 238.

Jacka, Mike, and Paulette Keller: *Business Process Mapping: Improving Customer Satisfaction*. New Jersey: John Wiley and Sons, 2009.

Johansson Robinowitz, C. and Werner Carr, L. *Modern Day Vikings: A Practical Guide to Interacting with Swedes* Boston, MA Nicholas Brealy Publishing, 2001.

Johnson, Steven: *Where Good Ideas Come From: The Natural History of Innovation*. New York: Penguin Group, 2010 p. 31.

Laroche, Lionel: *Managing Cultural Diversity in Technical Professions*. Boston: Elsevier Butterworth-Heinemann, 2003.

Laroche, Lionel, and Don Rutherford: *Recruiting, Retaining, and Promoting Culturally Different Employee*. Boston: Elsevier Butterworth-Heinemann, 2007.

Nemeth, C.J. "Dissent as Driving Cognition, Attitudes, and Judgments." *Social Cognition* 13, no. 3 (1995): pp. 273–91.

Peterson, Erik et al.: *Offshoring Opportunities amid Economic Turbulence—The A. T. Kearney Global Services Location Index 2011*. Chicago, IL: A. T. Kearney, 2011.

Storti, Craig: *Speaking of India*. Boston: Intercultural Press, 2007.

Tuckman, Bruce: "Developmental Sequence in Small Groups." *Psychological Bulletin* 63, no. 6 (1965): 384–99.

Yang, Caroline: "Global Alignment and Local Flexibility." *HR Professional*, May/June 2011: 39–41.

Yang, Caroline: "Maximize Employee Retention through Total Rewards Programs." *Workspan*, June 2011: 25–28

Wattley-Ames, H. *Spain is Different* Boston, MA Nicholas Brealy Publishing, 1999.

Index

accommodation 58
accountability 132, 228
action items 39, 89, 148, 153, 182, 207, 215
action plan 20, 42, 142–3
action steps 17, 38, 50, 77, 89, 122, 147, 171, 246
Adams, M. 252
adaptability 228
adjacent possible 254, 256–9
affinity groups 24
Alley, R. 118
Americans 3, 10–11, 13, 15, 30–2, 40, 45–6, 62, 65, 67, 80, 116, 118, 149, 175, 190, 192, 202–3, 205–6, 208, 212, 221, 239, 242, 264–5
analysis paralysis 110, 111, 195
Asia 63, 90, 108, 160, 222, 224, 226
Asians 2, 11, 46, 49, 63, 83, 239
Australia 69, 134, 175
awareness 18–19, 22, 38–40, 44, 52, 69, 80–1, 100–1, 150, 186, 224, 244, 245, 247

behavioral interview 127, 129, 131, 228
benefit of the doubt 2, 3, 11, 128, 214, 259
best practices 127, 132, 228, 230
body language 45, 55, 57, 171
Brazil 238, 240–1
business case 8, 25, 266
business contexts *see* business situations
business model 24, 91, 179, 186, 222, 231
business situations 19, 28, 74, 119
business strategy 18, 228, 233

Canada 2–3, 10, 15–16, 24–5, 30–3, 48, 55, 61, 74–5, 92–3, 108, 116–18, 124–6, 132, 134, 136–7, 147, 150, 152–3, 163, 165, 169, 186, 190–1, 199, 207, 210, 227, 245, 248, 252, 262–7
Canadians 3, 10, 11, 13, 15, 31–2, 40, 45–6, 62, 65, 67, 80, 116–18, 147, 149, 175, 202, 205, 207–8, 220, 239, 262–5
career management 43, 156
career path 41, 231–2
Chinese 1, 10, 13, 33–4, 37, 49, 53, 63, 66, 94–5, 97, 118, 202, 212–13, 224–6, 229–35, 237, 242, 247–8, 251, 267
chit-chat 108, 172, 211
choice of words 65, 67
coaching 12, 19, 39–41, 44–5, 56, 69, 88, 92, 100, 119, 138–9, 141–6, 151, 157, 169, 215
collaboration 23, 24, 58, 63, 106, 241
colleague 13, 39, 63, 76, 102, 112–13, 133, 141, 186, 227, 247, 249
collective *see* individualism
commitment 59, 64, 94, 97, 113, 146, 186, 217, 233–4, 241, 244, 247, 249
common goal 23, 97, 209, 216–7, 241
communication protocols 51, 58, 174, 202
communication style 12, 45, 71, 127, 209
compensation 26, 90, 106, 112, 114, 180–1, 223, 229–30
competitive advantage 8, 18, 23, 25, 117, 254, 262, 267